The Music of the Future

Critical Conjunctures in
Music & Sound

Series Editors Jairo Moreno and Gavin Steingo

Composing the World: Harmony in the Medieval Platonic Cosmos, Andrew Hicks

Music Theory, Embodiment, and the Phenomenology of Reading, Maryam Moshaver

Music and Belonging Between Revolution and Restoration, Naomi Waltham-Smith

The Musical Gift: Sonic Generosity in Post-War Sri Lanka, Jim Sykes

Audible Infrastructures: Music, Sound, Media, edited by Kyle Devine and Alexandrine Boudreault-Fournier

Wild Sound: Maryanne Amacher and the Tenses of Audible Life, Amy Cimini

The Music of the Future

Sound and Vision in the Caribbean

Martin Munro

OXFORD
UNIVERSITY PRESS

Oxford University Press is a department of the University of Oxford. It furthers
the University's objective of excellence in research, scholarship, and education
by publishing worldwide. Oxford is a registered trade mark of Oxford University
Press in the UK and certain other countries.

Published in the United States of America by Oxford University Press
198 Madison Avenue, New York, NY 10016, United States of America.

© Oxford University Press 2024

All rights reserved. No part of this publication may be reproduced, stored in
a retrieval system, or transmitted, in any form or by any means, without the
prior permission in writing of Oxford University Press, or as expressly permitted
by law, by license, or under terms agreed with the appropriate reproduction
rights organization. Inquiries concerning reproduction outside the scope of the
above should be sent to the Rights Department, Oxford University Press, at the
address above.

You must not circulate this work in any other form
and you must impose this same condition on any acquirer.

Library of Congress Cataloging-in-Publication Data
Names: Munro, Martin, author.
Title: The music of the future : sound and vision in the Caribbean / Martin Munro.
Description: New York : Oxford University Press, 2024. |
Series: Critical conjunctures in music and sound |
Includes bibliographical references and index.
Identifiers: LCCN 2023057102 (print) | LCCN 2023057103 (ebook) |
ISBN 9780197759790 (hardback) | ISBN 9780197759813 (epub)
Subjects: LCSH: Black people—Music—Caribbean Area—History and criticism. |
Popular music—Caribbean Area—History and criticism. | Music—Social
aspects—Caribbean Area. | Colonies—Caribbean Area. | Senses and sensation.
Classification: LCC ML3486.A1 M86 2024 (print) | LCC ML3486.A1 (ebook) |
DDC 781.63097293—dc23/eng/20240131
LC record available at https://lccn.loc.gov/2023057102
LC ebook record available at https://lccn.loc.gov/2023057103

DOI: 10.1093/oso/9780197759790.001.0001

Printed by Integrated Books International, United States of America

Contents

Series Editors' Foreword   vii
Acknowledgments   ix

Introduction: Sound Clashes   1

1. Sounding Francophone Caribbean Poetics   20

2. Time Out in Trinidad: White "Expatriates" in the Late Colonial Period   69

3. Sound Touristics   112

4. Who Stole the Soul? Rhythm and Race in the Digital Age   144

Coda: The Music of the Future   173
Bibliography   189
Index   199

Series Editors' Foreword

Critical Conjunctures in Music and Sound offers a space from which to engage urgent questions currently animating the humanities from the perspectives of music, sound, and listening. Tied together by a common epistemological attitude, the books in this series reconstitute the place of scholarship in response to a world rapidly transforming under economic and technological integration, on the one hand, and political and social disintegration, on the other. Authors articulate new musical and sonic relations to the composition of the political, the social, and the economic, while developing new ways to analyze music's ever-shifting associations with aurality, human/non-human divides, materiality, nature, and ontology. These relations and associations in turn provoke new questions about the past, and a reassessment of our historical and ethnographic priorities—both empirical and speculative. The series urges philosophical and theoretical critique to mediate and question the relationship of music studies to other forms of knowledge production. What it proposes, therefore, is, a form of conjunctural analysis that does not foreclose in advance how sound, music, and other forces are or have been articulated together. "Conjuncture" captures the immediate and mobile sets of circumstances determining the present, which authors engage by challenging theoretical categories and forms from a variety of disciplinary, historical, or geographical homes.

Acknowledgments

Part of the work for this book was supported by a National Humanities Center Fellowship (2020-21), and I hereby record my gratitude to the N.H.C.

Introduction

Sound Clashes

> For the rastaman—it is true—dismisses
> Too easily the cartographic view;
> Believes himself slighted
> By its imperial gaze.
>
> (Miller, 21)

A European mapmaker, voiceless, soundless, ventures into Jamaica, intent on rendering the island according to his silent art of lines, contours, limits, and borders: an art of the eyes. A Jamaican rastaman, voluble, articulate, engages with the European, and questions the outsider's art, resisting it with his own: an art of the mouth, the ears, the hands, the whole sonorous, vibrating, living body. Such is the premise of Kei Miller's 2014 poem *The Cartographer Tries to Map a Way to Zion*, which sets up a largely indirect encounter between a visually oriented cartographer and a Rastafarian who critiques the practice and methods of mapmaking, and as such challenges the power of the white, European eye, to the point that this power is eventually undercut and gradually superseded by the voice, and by the sounds of the Jamaican and his island. As such, Miller reenacts one of the Caribbean's longest standing cultural clashes, between the visualism—the belief in and reliance on the eye as the primary bodily source of knowledge and power—of the colonizers and their successors, and the more sound-centered existence of the African and Creole people, a way of being and knowing that is partly the legacy of African heritage and partly the result of the plantation and its aftermaths, the myriad ways in which sounds were and are used and adapted as markers of identity and resistance.[1]

The conflict in the poem is about seeing and hearing, mapping and sounding, ways of knowing space and consequently people—for Miller's speaker, words and verse are themselves means of mapmaking, creating

---

[1] See, for example, my previous work in *Different Drummers*, and *Listening to the Caribbean*.

irregular forms, shapes, and sounds on the page and in the mind, while for the cartographer, the map is silent, definitive, and made by "universal men who look nothing and sound nothing" like the speaker (12). Before the arrival of the Europeans, the island, "unflattened and unsugared," was sonorous, even in its flora: hibiscuses "throw raucous / syllables at crows" in a place that is no paradise, and is still "unwritten, unsettled, unmapped" (14). The landscape is not something that can be flattened or rendered immobile in the way the mapmaker intends: history and the land "fidget," are restless and will "slip out from your grip" (15). For all that the cartographer seeks to delineate and contain by visual means and claims to "show the full of a place in just a glance" (18), the speaker insists he is not all-seeing, and also makes things "invisible," specifically the everyday places and objects around which people's lives are formed and which do not feature on maps (17). The rastaman proposes that the cartographer draw a map of what he sees and then, he says, "I will draw a map of what you never see," which will, he suggests, "tell [a] larger truth" (19) than can ever be apprehended by the "imperial gaze" of the "cartographic view" (21). The island resists and indeed returns this gaze, as the speaker advises the white man to "know that this ground, these bushes, these trees observe you with suspicion many centuries deep" (26).

A major reason for the island's unmappability relates to the sounds of the place, a literal soundscape where roads give out "hems and haws" (28) that suggest the ways in which the past maps out the present in sounds and echoes that the mapmaker in turn seeks to silence as part of "history's disgrace" (29). Indeed, the roads sing their history, "dirging [. . .] and every mile, another song" (31). Sounds cannot be distorted in the ways that sights can, and seeing is fundamentally unreliable and subjective: the sea is to the white man a "glittering parabola," while to the rastaman it is many things, including "an upturned dutch pot [and] a silver tale of greed in the midst of famine" (33). Where the whites' eyes "smoothly scan the green canefields," the same sight makes the rastaman "uneasy" and he sees there only the "brutal architecture of history" (33) and hears always the "loud" sounds of the island and its history (36). Chief among these sounds are those of the people, the musicians, deejays, and soundmen—"Bob Marley, Luciano, Junior Gong, Wingless Angels, Delroy Morgan, Buju Banton"—the cacophony of which leads the rastaman to ask whether the white man will "ever understand / why such songs spring from this strange land?" (39). Equally, the rhythmic qualities of these songs are mysterious, unheard, or misunderstood by the mapmaker—the rastaman plays a "nyabinghi beat [. . .] a heartbeat riddim," that is unfamiliar to the white man, as "there ain't nutt'n iambic bout dis," says the drummer, who hears and feels in the beat "the outlawed measure [. . .] the riddim of cutlass and cane [. . .] the terrible metre of hurricanes" (40). Sounds never die; they return in this way, as historical echoes with corrective and reparative functions, for as the rastaman says, "when victims live long enough they get their say in history" (41). Slavery is remembered as a cry, that of a Mandingo man "bawling out a bruck-spirit sound" that is audible even to those who never heard it, as a sound-memory (65). Thus, sounds and people are never truly silenced, any victory for the visualism of the mapmaker is temporary, and the people will always at some point "get their say" (65).

It is the sounds of the island and its history, along with the drummer's rhythms that unsettle the mapmaker, as he is gradually attuned to the real measure of the people and the place, and starts to "finally find [...] his feet" (40) and "lose[s] himself" and "smok[es] a chillum," which gives him a new "vantage point to see the island by," one that includes sounds, the way the birds at sunset "sing the sky to black" (43). The cartographer also gets lost in language, the "rastaman's talk," which he comes to recognize as "a partial map of this world," and sees and hears as a means to "navigate ourselves / away from dark corners" so that through speaking, through sound, "we become, / each one of us, cartographers" (45). The mapmaker begins to question his profession and asks, "how does one map a place that is not quite a place? How does one draw towards the heart?" (50). Part of the answer to these questions lies in sound, in realizing that "them roads was mapped out by song," in forms of music that do not however "sound no harmony" that the mapmaker would know (54). The European eyes are yet always potentially like weapons, "cannonballs," means of silencing the people and "cut[ting] the tongue out of natty, / out of all Zion's children / telling dem how dem words / was rough and uncomely— / how dem language / was nothing more than a tegareg sound" (57).

In ways that echo the primary concerns of this book, Miller's poetry situates itself at points of relation, connection, and conflict between the Caribbean and its visitors, and between sound and vision, an already age-old site to which these encounters seem inevitably drawn. At such a point of sound-and-vision relation one senses most keenly the ways in which the past continues to inhabit the present—the people's collective memory in the poem of the Mandingo man's crying, the sounds of the environment, the ways in which the white man's eye has never ceased to be a means of coercion and control. In large degree, the relationship between visuality and sound in the poem and in the history it seeks to understand is also that between the white outsider and the Caribbean, the place and its people: one cannot understand anything about the Caribbean, the poem implies, unless one recognizes the primacy of the sound–vision relation and its multiple resonances and implications. Again, such an awareness of this relation is also vital to understanding notions of time—the mapmaker implicitly thinks of his work as timeless and universal, a means of capturing and no doubt trapping a place in a certain time, while the rastaman refuses such a closed notion of time, place, and being; and it is sound and noise that disrupt the European's intentions. Sound-making is therefore also about creating and marking out place, about being; it is also fundamentally about time-making.

In effect, Miller's critique of mapmaking can be related to Nicholas Mirzoeff's notion of "oversight," an aspect of "modern visual culture," which Mirzoeff says resulted from a new formation of the senses that began in seventeenth-century Europe, whereby, "there was a gap between things and words, a gap that could be crossed by seeing, a form of seeing that would dictate what it was possible to say. [There was] a new set of priorities attached to sensory perception. Taste and smell became less important, now being understood as imprecise, hearsay was simply excluded, while touch was limited to a series of binary distinctions" (49). The term "oversight" is used by Mirzoeff to describe the visually based system of control in the plantations: "It created a regime of taxonomy, observation, and enforcement that came to be known as 'economy.' It maintained a delineated space in which all life and labor were directed from its central viewpoint because the production of colonial cash crops, especially sugar, required a precise discipline, centered on surveillance, while being dependent on spectacular and excessive physical punishment" (50). Oversight was not however a completely successful enterprise, largely because of the resistance of the enslaved, and their creation of what Mirzoeff calls a "counter-theater" to the system of surveillance and discipline. This "counter-theater" as Mirzoeff puts it was, by contrast to the visually-controlled world of oversight, full of noise—the voices and sounds that were never silenced and that ever challenged the regime of the eye. Miller's poem and the relation it sets up between the visually directed European and the rastaman, forever attuned to sound and the other senses, is in effect a contemporary staging of this counter-theater, a knowing, seeing, and hearing riposte to the mapmaker's intention to flatten and mute the island and its people in soundless lines, names, and figures.

* * *

Kingston, Jamaica, November 1977, Miller's imagined encounter brought to life in another, different but related, version of the meeting between the Caribbean place, time, and people and the European, colonially tinged eye: two young Englishmen step out from the Pegasus Hotel into the hot tropical day. Disoriented, not sure where to go, they wander the streets of the

Jamaican capital, as if they were walking in their native London. They are not dressed for the weather: in "full punk regalia" they attract a lot of attention, especially when they reach the harbor area, where few tourists would knowingly venture. Later, and throughout their ten-day trip, they variously score drugs and go to the cinema, where instead of feeling more at home they are further disoriented, as they later recount:

> It was like *The Harder They Come* not on the screen but in the audience. I don't know how we weren't filleted and served up on a bed of chips. [We] wandered around the harbor; I think they mistook us for sailors, merchant seamen [. . .] they must have just let us pass because they probably thought we were madmen or something. But [we] didn't have a clue what we were doing there. We didn't know anybody—we were just wandering around in Kingston like lunatics. (Salewicz 197)

The two Englishmen were Joe Strummer and Mick Jones, members of The Clash, sent to Jamaica by their manager to write songs for their second album. Their first album, released the previous year, had featured a cover version of Junior Murvin's "Police and Thieves," a song about gang war and police brutality on the streets of Kingston. Strummer and fellow Clash member Paul Simonon had heard it at the 1976 Notting Hill Carnival, which itself ended in confrontations between police and carnival goers, including both Strummer and Simonon. The song seemed to transpose itself easily from Kingston to London, from reggae to punk. Strummer and Jones were apparently expecting the same for their visit to Jamaica—that they could shift easily from one country to the other and translate themselves in a sense into everyday Kingston. Their experience in Jamaica was a rude awakening for them: there could be no easy transposition for the white English punk rockers onto the physical, social, cultural, and musical landscape of Kingston. Holed up in their hotel rooms, they did find inspiration in Jamaica for one of their finest songs, but not in the ways they might have expected. "Safe European Home" features on the 1978 album *Give 'em Enough Rope*, and bears the distinct traces of the two men's discomforting trip to Jamaica. Strummer's original lyrics for the song were some fifty lines long, which gives a sense of the emotion he felt in writing it. The final version has a mere sixteen lines and does not offer a particularly coherent account of the trip, though that in itself could suggest their confusion and mixed emotions about the Caribbean visit.

The initial emotion in the song is of relief at a safe return: "Well I just got back and I wish I never leave now." By saying that he wished he never went, Strummer suggests the rawness of the experience. After every line, Jones sings, "Where'd ya go?," which gives the song a call-and-response structure. "Who that Martian arrival at the airport, yeah?" Strummer asks, suggesting that to arrive in Jamaica was like landing on another planet. Their misadventures with drug dealers are alluded to in the lines, "How many local dollars for a local anesthetic / The Johnny on the corner wasn't very sympathetic." The first verse expresses most directly how their whiteness made them feel vulnerable, and their determination never to return: "I went to the place where every white face / Is an invitation to robbery / An' sitting here in my safe European home / Don't wanna go back there again." In returning to England, they therefore feel a sense of relief at having survived their ordeal, which, though they do not acknowledge it, was created by their own behavior. "They got the sun and they got the palm trees," the second verse goes, "They got the weed and they got the taxis [. . .] Whoa, *The Harder They Come* and the home of ol' Bluebeat / I'd stay and be a tourist but I can't take the gun play." Jamaica does not conform to his idea of a tourist paradise, and even back in his safe European home, Strummer is clearly still shaken; indeed, on his return to London, he stated he would never go back to Jamaica.

What was it that so shook up the two men, and Strummer in particular? No doubt their reckless misadventures around Kingston trying to score drugs did not go to plan, and the two realize that politically tense Kingston is a different proposition to London. What did they expect? There is a fascinating possible response to these questions in a comment Jones makes later about the trip:

> When we were walking through the streets to the movies, Joe told me Jamaica was just like the places he lived when he was young. "This is just like it was when I was a kid," he said. In those days you could still really feel the colonial presence. (Salewicz 197)

This is remarkable in that it suggests that Strummer has a kind of flashback in Kingston to his own childhood, which colors his view of Jamaica and its people. Born in Ankara, Turkey, and christened John Graham Mellor, Strummer was the son of a career diplomat, and had also lived in Cairo and Mexico City before going to private school in England around the age of ten. His statement that Jamaica reminded him of the places of his youth is related to colonialism, an indistinct but nonetheless strong and persistent feeling, an instinct almost, that Jamaica's colonial past lived still in the way it determined race, and indeed mapped out the very space of the city—the ways in which the presence of white people in certain parts of town would be seen as a form of trespass, disrespect even, an infringement of the colonial code that Strummer seems to be alive to. Perhaps part of his initial swagger in Kingston is down to the familiarity he thinks he feels in the place, even if he has never visited there before: in this colonial place, the white man can go where he wishes, in safety. As part of a diplomatic family, he would have enjoyed those privileges and that security wherever he went, but now in 1970s Kingston the colonial imprint may still be there but the white foreigner is no longer all-powerful, and Strummer feels that loss of power acutely. His indignation is that of one whose privileges have been stripped, who realizes suddenly the world has changed and that his place in it is uncertain. This colonial background could also explain the ways in which he often retreats into racial binaries when he writes about the meetings of cultures: in "Safe European Home," he seeks safety behind an us-and-them idea of race, and offers caricatures of "Rudie" the Jamaican rude boy; in "White Riot," he wants white people to have their own violent demonstrations; and in "White Man in Hammersmith Palais," he again writes of feeling exposed racially in a crowd of black people. Notably, when The Clash did play a show in Jamaica in 1982, they played none of these three songs. Strummer seems to seek out these situations only to retreat from them, and to search for safety in ways that do appear related to his own childhood experiences of being foreign and alone in distinctly colonial contexts—Jones by contrast expresses no such colonial anxieties—only now his whiteness is no longer a passport that guarantees free and unfettered movement: "white pigs," the two are called as they walk the streets of Kingston.[2]

Strummer finds no respite in the cinema, to which one imagines the two men went to be less visible and to find the peace and quiet they seem to want. However, in sharp contrast to British cinemagoers, Caribbean film audiences are at times noisy: as Strummer says, "It was like *The Harder They Come* not on the screen but in the audience" (Salewicz 197). That two punk rockers should feel unsettled in a rowdy atmosphere suggests again the unease of Strummer, in particular, in situations that remind him of his quasi-colonial childhood, but without the privileges and security of whiteness that he and his family had previously enjoyed. In ways that echo Miller's mapmaker with his "imperial eye," the problem for Strummer and Jones is that they are too visual; that is, they dress deliberately in their punk rock clothes which, along with their white skin mark them out as radically different—this is whiteness stripped of its visual power, the imperial eye turned back on the white Englishmen,

[2] Lloyd I. Vayo writes of the complex relationship between The Clash and reggae music. "At first glance, reggae and The Clash make for an unlikely combination, and lead singer Joe Strummer, the son of a British diplomat, an unlikely mouthpiece for tales of downpression and sufferation." However, he argues, the connection is valid, in that "As reggae arises from a turning away from imposed culture in favour of a localized, spiritual understanding of the world [...], so too does punk arise from a sense of disenfranchisement with a culture created by and for others [...]. Both the Jamaican artists at the heart of reggae and The Clash and like-minded punks are the victims and detritus of British colonialism" ("Turning Rebellion into Money: The Roots of the Clash" 66). Clearly, however, Strummer's relationship with British colonialism is itself more complex, as is suggested in his experience in Jamaica.

and it is this that Strummer feels, and that unsettles him so that he retreats into a black-white binary that clashes with the other prevalent legacy of his childhood wanderings: his worldliness, his openness to other people and other sounds that were already part of his music and which would become ever more important as his life and career developed, for instance in the global music he played on his BBC World Service show "London Calling," which ran from 1999 to 2001.[3]

In remarkable ways, the case of Joe Strummer in Kingston—colonial, expatriate, tourist—relates to the situation of the mapmaker in Miller's poem. Both white men are initially confident in themselves and their relationship to the island, which they think they can know and delineate. Strummer as much as the cartographer sets out to map the place, to put his mark on it and get to know it in ways that echo his own previous experiences in quasi-colonial places. Both men's intentions are abruptly upended, as they realize that the island is not as they would have liked it to be. The island as both men come to realize is noisy, full of sounds that dredge up colonial pasts in ways that unsettle the Europeans, unexpectedly.

The cases of Miller's mapmaker and Strummer, both in Jamaica, reflect in fact many much earlier cases of European colonial encounters with the Caribbean, which I have previously analyzed.[4] For example, the French Jesuit priest Father Fauque writes in Cayenne in 1751 of the problem of runaway slaves, the maroons who flee the plantations to live free in the vast forests of the Guyanese hinterland. In order to bring the maroons back to the plantations, the French governor sends a detachment of troops and militia into the forests and, believing it to be in accordance with his ministry, Fauque decides to accompany the soldiers. He soon finds himself disoriented in the forest, and that sense of disorientation strikes him in primarily auditory terms: his blasts on a conch shell and his shouted pleas to the maroons are met with no response, and he is left powerless in the unsettling silence of the woods. When, however, he gives up his vocal supplications to the maroons and introduces a visual symbol—before he leaves, he erects "a Cross of a kind of hard wood"—the effect is immediate: "as soon as the negro maroons saw it, they came there to say their prayers; it being their custom, notwithstanding their reckless wickedness [. . .] to pray to God morning and evening" (55). As Fauque realizes, it is the visual symbol of the cross that "was the means of rendering my enterprise successful" (55). He learns later that as soon as the maroons saw "the sign of our redemption set up on their ground, they were at length convinced that

---

[3] See the playlists here: https://exchange.prx.org/playlists/32765 (accessed October 6, 2020).
[4] See Munro, *Listening to the Caribbean*.

the time had come to obtain pardon, both for their souls and their bodies" (56). The visually based power of the French is further suggested in Fauque's account of the maroon children who, having been born in the forests, have never seen "any white person, or the house of a Frenchman, [and] were never tired of observing them, while, according to their fashion, they manifested their admiration" (56). Thus, the effect of seeing the cross is compounded by the sight of the white people and their homes in a kind of visual trinity of French colonialism: the Church, the white race, and the material wealth of the French are all-too-visible signs of power to which even the maroons surrender, and which form the basis of colonial authority.

Separated by more than two centuries, the sound-and-vision experiences of Fauque, Strummer, and Miller's cartographer nevertheless chime with each other. The Europeans trade on their visual power—Fauque finally brings in the maroons thanks to the cross he takes with him into the forests; Strummer's strikingly visual appearance on the streets of downtown Kingston in punk-rock clothing and white skin is less successful, indeed it is his undoing, no longer is whiteness or its visualism a passport or a kind of protective armor; the mapmaker is presented as an inheritor of the imperial eye. In different ways, the white men deal with a spirit of black revolt and are in a sense lost in sound—Fauque in the silent forest, Strummer in the raucous cinema, the mapmaker in the sounds of language, music, and landscape. While the cartographer does gradually embrace to some degree the sounds of the place and the people, both Fauque and Strummer seek sanctuary, the priest in the colonial town, the musician in his hotel in the postcolonial capital. In these latter cases however the sense of disorientation remains and stays with them as a memory of the limits of their power and of how in the realm of black sound they, like so many other visually directed white Europeans in the Caribbean, are radically, helplessly disorientated, powerless, marooned.

If, as these three examples, and particularly Miller's, suggest, to understand and begin to transform the past, present, and future of Caribbean relations with its invaders, oppressors, visitors, and tourists, one must do so at the node of sound and vision, then it follows that Caribbean studies of all kinds—literary, historical, ethnographic, philosophical—should also pay fuller attention to the ways in which sound and vision are fundamental elements in Caribbean histories, societies, and cultures. To achieve this realignment of Caribbean studies, there is a particular need to pay attention to sound, as most scholarship to date has tended not to explore fully the sonic dimensions of Caribbean art, literature, travel writing, history, and society.

For all that non-Caribbean people tend to know the Caribbean first and principally through sounds, primarily of music, and that sound is a dynamic, ever-present force in shaping Caribbean history and cultures, it is surprising that relatively few scholars have undertaken a "sound-studies" approach to the region. Certainly, there is a long and distinguished history of Caribbean musicology, produced by scholars such as Gage Averill, Michael Largey, Jocelyne Guilbault, Dudley Shannon, Gordon Rohlehr, Brenda Berrian, Timothy Rommen, Timothy Reiss, Ken Bilby, Matthew J. Smith, and Norman Stolzoff. However, few of these scholars have gone beyond music to consider the broader sonic environments of slavery, colonialism, and postcolonialism in the Caribbean. More recently, however, pioneering works by, for example, Alejandra Bronfman, have begun to shift attention to sound as a dynamic means of connecting Caribbean people to each other and to the broader world, and onto the "longer story of the entangled relationships linking communications technologies, nature, empire, and the poetics of listening" (*Isles of Noise* 4). In particular, Bronfman examines how the rapid spread of radio technologies in the early twentieth-century Caribbean both "propelled and enabled" the growing and "voluble" presence of the United States across the region (5). Perceptively arguing that the mapping of wires and sound waves during this period contributed in turn to the ongoing and shifting mapping of the Caribbean itself, her interests parallel to some degree those of Miller's poetry. Moreover, Bronfman insists that listening is always an active rather than passive activity, in which engagement with sound and its technologies contributes to the ongoing evolution of notions of culture, place, race, and being. In different, though complementary ways, Edwin C. Hill Jr.'s *Black Soundscapes, White Stages*, further extends the scholarly study of the broader auditory cultural history of the Caribbean in new and promising ways, arguing, for example, that representations of sounds found in colonial travel chronicles, ethnographies, and other narratives produce the sense of an "imperial ear" that echoes Miller again and that is analogous to the "imperial gaze" that Mary Louise Pratt writes about.[5] Hill's book stands as an example of the ways in which scholars can tease out representations of sounds and noise in classic colonial works by, for example, Du Tertre and Labat, to show that the Caribbean soundscape often escaped classification and control.[6]

While one might lament the apparent lack of sound-studies work in and on the Caribbean, the reasons for this critical absence are more complex than a

---

[5] See Pratt, *Imperial Eyes: Travel Writing and Transculturation*.
[6] For similar recent work in a related context, see Dylon Lamar Robbins, *Audible Geographies*. See also, for example, Glyne A. Griffith, *The BBC and the Development of Anglophone Caribbean Literature*; Njelle W. Hamilton, *Phonographic Memories: Popular Music and the Contemporary Caribbean Novel*; Jocelyne Guilbault and Timothy Rommen (eds.), *Sounds of Vacation*; Tom McEnaney, *Acoustic Properties: Radio, Narrative, and the New Neighborhood of the Americas*; yasser elhariry (ed.), *Sounds Senses*.

simple reluctance or delay on behalf of researchers. Perhaps it is that a strict application of sound-studies principles would not work in the Caribbean. Indeed, and having advocated for the importance of sound and sound studies in the Caribbean, the more I personally have pursued that approach the more I find that one cannot isolate sound completely and indefinitely from vision, as these two elements are still as closely connected as they have ever been, to the point where they almost fuse into another, hybrid sense in which might be found the knotty truths and realities of the region, its people, and its relations with others.

Nevertheless, while it does largely situate itself at the node of sound and vision, this book proposes that far closer attention to sound be paid in the field of Caribbean studies, which to date has tended to replicate blindly the ocularcentric perspectives and biases of colonial discourse. That is, Caribbean studies has largely taken its conceptual and critical cues from all manner of European texts, from travel narratives to natural histories, novels to chronicles, ethnographies to photography, in considering the region, its cultures, history, and people in primarily visual terms—the all-seeing imperial eye has in effect been translated into the disciplines that purport to challenge the legacies of colonialism. If the Caribbean decolonial project remains incomplete, this is in no small part due to its inattention to its own visual biases, and its particular reluctance to open its ears, and *listen* to history, to tune in to the great clamor of the past and the ways it resonates into the present. Eschewing the primarily visual orientation of Caribbean studies as much as the colonial discourses that preceded it, this book proposes a true, radical, decolonial Caribbean studies, and argues that to achieve this, we must thoroughly interrogate the visualism that has shaped the discipline to date. There is a need to decolonize the eye and the ear, and to listen to the myriad ways in which sounds have long been the unheard harbingers of true, radical, noisy liberation. What would a renewed and revitalized Caribbean studies *sound* like?

The book seeks to continue to effect a shift in Caribbean studies away from the predominantly visual methodologies of most scholarly works and toward a fuller understanding of Caribbean societies through listening in to the past as much as to the present and thinking critically of how the auditory and the visual meet, relate, and interact. Paying close attention to auditory elements in a diverse range of sources allows us to unlock the sounds that are registered and recorded there, so that one gains a more sensorially full understanding of the society; and the voices and subjectivities of Caribbean people are brought out of the silence to which they have been largely consigned. The book is in fact a continuation of my own previous work on rhythm and sound studies, which analyzed, for example, Caribbean legal texts, travel writing, natural histories, chronicles, ethnographies, and other works, in order to illustrate how sound is a constant yet evolving and dynamic phenomenon across different times and places, from slavery to the end of the nineteenth century. In *Listening to the Caribbean: Sounds of Slavery, Revolt, and Race*, I proposed and explored the notion of an Atlantic "culture of the ear," which has to do with sound, but also with the ear as a site of punishment and control, adornment, and expression. I considered what it meant for the maroons of Guiana and other French colonies to have their ears cropped for running away in the manner stipulated by the Code Noir of 1685, why the French chose this particular punishment, and how was it applied across the Caribbean and Louisiana. This inquiry formed part of a broader consideration of the importance of hearing and the ear more generally to the African people of the Americas. Importantly, the work explored how West African people understood the senses, and how that understanding related to that of the Europeans. Can the Western taxonomy of the senses be applied to people of African descent?

An answer to that question is proposed in the work of the American anthropologist, Kathryn Linn Guerts, who undertook a series of field trips in Anloland, in southeastern Ghana in the early 1990s. Her aim was to investigate how the Anlo-Ewe people of that region understood the human senses, and to compare that understanding to the accepted categorization of the senses in the West where, she says, "we often treat the domain of sensation and perception as definitively precultural and eminently natural, one of the most basic of the human psychobiological systems [and assume] that all humans possess identical sensory capabilities and that any cultural differences we might find would be inconsequential" (*Culture and the Senses* 3). The goal of her work is to present a non-Western society where there is a quite different experience of the senses, and thereby to show that the Western understanding is "only a folk model" (3).[7] *Sensing*, as she puts it, is a matter of "bodily ways of gathering information," and is profoundly entangled with "a society's epistemology, the

---

[7] As Guerts writes in a footnote, there are relatively few studies that question the Western taxonomy of the senses:

> Within the discipline of anthropology, an exception to this is Howes's dissertation (1992) comparing sensory orders in the West to those in Melanesia, as well as my own dissertation (Geurts 1998) describing an Anlo-Ewe sensorium in West Africa. There is a growing literature on the anthropology of the senses (described later), but few scholars have actually excavated the indigenous sensorium of other cultural groups (linguistically, historically, ethnographically). This means that systematic ethnographic accounts of alternate epistemologies of sensory experience are difficult to find in the literature, despite the fact that descriptions of subjective and sensory experiences of and with the Other have increased in ethnographic accounts over the past twenty-five years. Within psychology, Wober developed what he referred to as a "sensotype" hypothesis (1966) proposing that cultural groups would vary in terms of the typical sensory orientation most individuals would hold, but little research was subsequently carried out to test this hypothesis. (*Culture and the Senses* p. 3, note 3)

development of its cultural identity, and its forms of being-in-the-world" (3). Guerts finds that, in contrast to the Western categorization of the five senses, the people of West Africa "were not aware of any clearly delineated taxonomy or system for the senses" (4). One of Guerts's most significant findings emerged when she asked the West African people which sense they would least like to lose. The answer was unequivocal: hearing. Loss of hearing, she writes, "was the most grave impairment of sense perception, not only because deafness cuts you off from people, but because with this loss would come a disruption to your sense of balance" ("Consciousness" 169). Guerts's work is vital to understanding the ways in which West African people conceive of and experience the senses. Although she writes of West Africa, it seems reasonable to extend her argument that people from that part of the world understand the senses quite differently from Westerners to the African diaspora, and specifically to the Caribbean. In particular, for studies of auditory culture, her finding that of the senses hearing is the most important to West African people is crucial, as it adds weight to the general arguments of my work on the sensorial primacy of hearing for people of African descent in the Caribbean. Also, in the case of the ear-cropping punishment prescribed by the Code Noir, Guerts's work allows us to judge just how acutely the loss of the ears would have been felt by the victims. Further, in addition to the full or partial loss of hearing, the victim's sense of balance would be affected, and in the case of, for example, the maroons, such a loss would lead to a literal feeling of disorientation, of loss of equilibrium and in turn a disruption of the sensory self that was grounded largely in hearing.

The importance of hearing to the enslaved was borne out in my readings of historical archives and critical studies, which compare and contrast the soundscapes of enslavement and freedom in the Caribbean with special emphasis on Guadeloupe, Haiti, and Jamaica. Close readings of primary and secondary sources—principally by Labat, Moreau de Saint-Méry, Descourtilz, Henry Bleby, and an anonymous Scottish-Caribbean novel—enabled me to listen in to the auditory dimensions of enslaved experience, and to show how certain sounds—of music, ritual (chiefly religious worship), and work—survived the Middle Passage, while others—mainly of African languages—largely perished or were creolized in the new place.

Sounds were key elements in slave resistance and revolts—they were used deliberately and knowingly in battles and skirmishes, particularly by maroons and enslaved people, who demonstrated their acute sensitivity to their sonic environment, in general contrast to the whites, who appear lost in the same environment, and to be constantly on the back foot when their visual power is diminished. Everyday resistance included the use of silence, indirect language, mockery, and composing songs, while the sounds of slave revolts often destabilized the visually centered control of the whites. The sounds of black revolt—the cries, the chants, the beating of drums, the overall clamor—struck fear into the whites, creating panic and disorder that the enslaved armies would exploit, sometimes with striking results.

For example, if, as Zoellner argues, the Sam Sharpe Rebellion of 1831 "proved to be the spark that ignited the movement to end British slavery less than two and a half years later" (5), then the sound culture of the people played a vital part in that process, and the poor listening skills of the British led to their own downfall, remarkably so. In short, the insurrection began with the widespread burning of plantations, and it was a distinctly noisy scene, one that recalled in the minds of the whites, just as in countless other Caribbean slave revolts, "those terrible scenes of cruelty and massacre which had taken place in St. Domingo a few years before" (Bleby 8). The prerevolt silence is shattered by the attacking insurgents, who approach in two groups, "raising a loud discordant noise with shells, horns, &c." It is the sound, which is "discordant" to the ears of the whites, that unnerves the militiamen: unlike the melodious, rhythmic sounds of work or festivity, these are deliberately jarring sounds that call to mind the conditions of the enslaved, in that shells, horns, and other objects were used on the plantations to call them to work and to mark out time, but in this instance they sound together in ways that represent in sonic terms the overturning of the dominant order. The sounds have the desired impact: the noise has "a wonderful effect on the nerves of the gallant Col. Grignon and his men, wholly incapacitating them for making any effectual resistance" (Bleby 9). Apparently stunned by the noise, the colonel and his men "remained inactive, drawn up in a hollow square; or acted only on the defensive" (Bleby 10). Perhaps significantly, a company of free coloreds is less affected by the noise of the insurgents and while the white soldiers freeze, unable to move, the colored company resists the attack. No doubt the sounds of the enslaved would have been more familiar and less threatening to the free colored soldiers, and yet the reaction of the whites remains a startling example of the power of sound and noise to unnerve and spread fear among that minority population.

The white regiment's oral accounts of the attack served only to perpetuate the round of gossip and hearsay that was a fundamental part of the conflict: retreating to Montego Bay, they "gave the most exaggerated statements [...] exciting needless alarm among the pacific portion of the inhabitants," by, for example, claiming that there were 10,000 insurgents, when in fact as the chronicler Henry Bleby later learns from his own conversations with some of the leaders, they numbered between 400 and 500. The white army's retreat inspired the insurgents, who were ready to give up the fight before they realized that they had severely frightened the whites. The insurgents also took control of vast parts of the interior, which cut communications between the principal towns on the island, and further obscured the truth of the scale of the insurgency. Also, many more of the enslaved were encouraged to join the insurrection as a result of the whites' retreat (12–13). All these gains, remarkably, were occasioned by sound, the noise of the approaching few hundred, poorly armed enslaved group, which struck such fear into the whites that they first froze then retreated, inventing fanciful stories of a great army of blacks that was in fact only a few hundred strong, disorganized and unsure of itself.

My previous work on sound also considers some of the ways in which, following abolition, notions of race continued to be figured around the senses, and particularly hearing, as certain anthropologists sought means of measuring hearing acuity, within the context of a discipline that was generally concerned with asserting the superiority of the white race, intellectually, morally, and in relation to sensorial capacity. Extending the focus beyond the Caribbean, to the Torres Straits expedition and the St. Louis Exposition of 1904 allowed for contextualization of the earlier material, and served as a coda to the long period of Atlantic slavery, just as the twentieth century begins, bringing with it advances in sound and visual technology that would continue to be crucial in shaping ideas of race and culture in ways that echo the past but also suggest something of the new struggles and triumphs that the century would bring.

This is where the new book begins: post-slavery, and largely in the twentieth century, where sound continues to be a dynamic force in shaping history, politics, and culture in the Caribbean. As in my previous work, however, and to reiterate points made above, even if the primary objective is to shift attention to sound, there is no intent to deny the enduring importance of the visual to notions of race, culture, and society in the Caribbean. As such, I echo Sterne's insistence on not overstating the visual and textual bias over sound. "As there was an Enlightenment, so too was there an 'Ensoniment,'" he writes, "Between about 1750 and 1925, sound itself became an object and a domain of thought and practice" (*The Audible Past* 40). There has always been, he says, in terms that could be applied to Miller's poetry, "a heady audacity to the claim that vision is the social chart of modernity. While I do not claim that listening is the social chart of modernity, it certainly charts a significant field of modern practice. There is always more than one map for a territory, and sound provides a particular path through history" (41). Similarly, the remapping that this book carries out does not—cannot—erase centuries of visually led writing on the Caribbean. It is not so much a rewriting of the past that is proposed than an opening up of the auditory elements that have long lain dormant in virtually any text about the Caribbean, and that opening up in itself will constitute a quite radical and revealing shift in the study of the region, its history, and cultures.

As such, we continue to build, still incompletely and provisionally, something of the soundscape of the Caribbean, in ways that reflect Kay and Noudelmann's conviction that the concept of the soundscape offers new ways of listening, and of thinking about listening:

> In the first place, it integrates the fields of aesthetic, ethical and political culture through the medium of listening, by bending our ears towards sounds that are usually excluded from attention, all at once making them worthy of interest. Second, it trains our attention on this environment so that we listen to it with the same care and discrimination we would devote to a work of music, discerning and comprehending its components and their articulation. ("Introduction" 5)

Sounds of Caribbean writing, everyday experience, tourism, and visual art are indeed usually excluded from attention, even by most Caribbeanist scholars. A further ramification of exploring the soundscapes of the past and present is the "radical rethinking of our whole concept of the historical archive, which needs to be extended far beyond the traditionally recognized archival category of the 'document'" (Kay and Noudelmann 7). Or else, as the following chapters show, archival objects of many kinds, including poems, amateur films, records, and paintings, can be read in ways that bring out the sounds that have always been recorded there, in various ways. Thus sounds, far from being dead or lost forever, can travel through time: "echoes may be picked up, faintly perhaps, but still discernibly, in texts, images, sculptures or other artefacts in which those noises were recorded" (Kay and Noudelmann 8). As such, in the rest of the book, we pay attention to the "acousmatic" dimension of texts, listening to them even if, as is no doubt true of many of the works considered, they were not intended to be listened to, and remain mindful of their role in "thickening and complicating the textual environment" (Kay and Noudelmann 9).

* * *

The primary materials under consideration are certainly varied—poems, novels, travel writing, amateur films, tourist movies, music—and what unites them is the presence to differing degrees and in diverse forms of the European-Caribbean, sound-vision dynamic that shapes Miller's poem and so many other accounts of cultural encounter in the region. The intention is to trace this dynamic across the various materials to give some sense of how it reappears across different times and places to become a defining element of European–Caribbean cultural and social relations and of how and why sound in its myriad manifestations becomes such a prevalent marker of Caribbean being, culture, and society.

Following a short discussion of writing slavery in the twenty-first century, with reference to Fabienne Kanor's *Humus* (2006), Chapter 1, "Sounding Francophone Caribbean Poetics," argues that poetry is a particularly rich source in which to explore some of the ways in which sound is a key marker of identity, resistance, and history-making in the region. I pay particular attention to how the poetic works of Aimé Césaire, Léon Gontran Damas, and Edouard Glissant evoke sounds as means of remaining opaque and unknowable, and of resisting incorporation into broader systems of visually centered knowing. Importantly, the analyses also highlight the sound textures, the musicality of poems written for example by Damas, who was also a jazz musician. The poetry begins, however, in the early nineteenth century, specifically the works anthologized in the 2015 collection edited by Doris Kadish and Deborah Jenson, *Poetry of Haitian Independence*, a bilingual volume that gathers many forgotten and neglected poems written between 1804 and the late 1840s. In engaging directly with these early poems, the chapter explores the various ways in which sounds are used by the poets as the new nation sought to assert itself on its own terms and create a sense of unity and common purpose in a land torn apart by a long period of war, and by the legacies of colonialism and slavery. By reading and listening to the poems in this way, the reader gains a sense of the importance of sounds to the written form, and by extension to the broader culture, in ways that confirm that sound was a vital element in forming early Caribbean subjectivities. More broadly, the chapter serves to underscore the argument that in contrast to the visually determined culture of colonialism and racism—critiqued by Glissant, for example—the cultures and subjectivities of slavery and post-slavery societies in the Caribbean were formed around strong vocal and aural elements. In short, sounds were of primary importance to the cultures of the enslaved and have remained important in postcolonial societies. The chapter asserts that one of the future thrusts of Caribbean criticism should involve *listening* more attentively to the history and literature of the region, and demonstrates that by paying close attention to the representations and uses of sounds of various kind in written texts, sound is rescued in a sense from the historical oblivion more conventionally assigned to it. The chapter further argues that, because the written text in the Caribbean has never been a "silent medium" but has always had strong sonic elements, the sounds of literature convey across time a strong sense of the ways in which ideas of culture and being have evolved, and of how these sounds drew on the past but were also always inventive, forward-looking, means of sounding out times to come.

Chapters 2 and 3 shift from principally written materials produced by Caribbean authors to visual forms—amateur movies made by white "expatriates" and tourists—to explore further the node of sound and vision, and demonstrate how silent, visual media may be read in ways that consider the auditory elements that are key parts of the representations of people and places and yet remain unheard due to the technical limitations of the media. Chapter 2, "Time Out in Trinidad: White 'Expatriates' in the Late Colonial Period," engages with a series of amateur movies made in the late 1950s by a white British family, which details their experiences in south Trinidad, working in the country's burgeoning oil and gas industries. The silence of the films is read and heard as a means of reflecting on the family's individual and collective experiences, as the close analyses reveal the privileges of this particular group of travelers at a crucial time in Trinidadian history. Beginning with analysis of a nineteenth-century Scotswoman's narrative of travel to the Caribbean, Chapter 3, "Sound Touristics," proceeds to draw on the extensive, previously neglected resource of home movies (mostly available online) made about Haiti, which are analyzed here as key pieces of evidence in the early, "golden age" of Caribbean tourism in the 1940s and 1950s. In this period, music became an important part of how Caribbean tourism was marketed, and a means of intra-Caribbean exchange and encounter. The experiences represented in the films are interpreted as instances of what Michael Largey calls "sonic tourism" in the Caribbean, according to which the sounds of the place are as important as the visual experience. Drawing on the work of Michael Gaudio and David Toop, and reflecting again the interests of Miller's poetry, the two chapters seek to carry out readings that rely less on a binary notion of sound and vision, and move toward the kind of blended, visual-auditory understanding that Glissant gestures toward in *Poetic Intention*. Can we begin to see through the ears and hear through the eyes?

Chapter 4, "Who Stole the Soul? Rhythm and Race in the Digital Age," builds on previous work on rhythm and race, and asks the following basic questions: What happens to the relationship between rhythm and race in the digital age? What happens when mastery of rhythm is no longer necessarily tied to ritual, to manual drumming, and to the physical, bodily re-creation of rhythm? When electronic and digital media allow virtually anyone the ability to "drum" and to create rhythmic music, what happens to the long-standing association between blackness and rhythm, perhaps one of the most enduring tropes of Caribbean sound cultures? Referring to David Scott's arguments on a stalled, tragic time in the Caribbean in particular, and paying close attention to the role of technology in the evolution of Jamaican music, the chapter draws connections between the apparent redundancy of revolutionary, anticolonial thinking in the present and the perhaps less apparent decoupling of rhythm and race in contemporary musical styles. If, as Scott says, the teleologies of anticolonial politics no longer hold true, has rhythm as a marker of time, and an integral element in the poetics of resistance, lost its association with radical blackness, and become a deracialized, dehistoricized commodity?

The book ends with a coda, "The Music of the Future," in which I analyze the 2016 collaboration between Derek Walcott and Peter Doig, *Morning, Paramin*. This work in effect, much like Miller's poetry, turns around the binaries that shape this whole book—Caribbean/European, sonic/visual, art/poetry, noise/silence—and underlines the idea that these are long-standing, ever crucial nodes of Caribbean being and culture. It is Trinidad that connects the two men, the island where both lived for considerable parts of their lives and that continually draws them back. It was apparently Doig who instigated the collaboration, who asked Walcott to participate in this experimental meeting of the visual and the verbal, the European and the Caribbean, poetry and painting. For his part, Walcott wonders how the verbal may be transformed, translated, or otherwise represented in painting: will Doig's work take on an accent, the "singsong" tones of Trinidadian language and thereby "infect" the "melody" of the art? In Walcott's words, the visual, in the form of the mask, is a means of concealment, a way of hiding from the "bullshit" in the society. The visual is therefore unreliable in this sense, the society an ongoing play of masks. It is by contrast in sound that the "endeavor" of the country may be heard, in its multiplicity of song and languages, and which ultimately brings the two men together: "this craziness is just where we belong," Walcott writes, the "great noise" in and from which the society is composed, and which he feels will inevitably find its way into Doig's work. To what extent, the book finally asks, echoing the questions raised in Miller's poetry and the account of Joe Strummer's visit to Kingston, can or should Doig, or any other European, become part of the "great noise" that for Walcott characterizes Trinidad, and that, the chapters of this book suggest, also characterizes much of the history of the postslavery Caribbean, the "music of the future," as Doig puts it in the title of one of his paintings.

1
Sounding Francophone Caribbean Poetics

This chapter engages principally with the postslavery period in Haiti and the Francophone Caribbean, and in order to demonstrate how slavery still echoes in the present. It begins with a brief consideration of Fabienne Kanor's 2006 work *Humus*, a striking example of writing slavery in the twenty-first century remarkable for its use of sound in evoking that experience and its contemporary resonances. How, then, to know, speak, or write of slavery in the twenty-first century? Should one even try? What are the stakes? How can one write of the Caribbean without addressing slavery? In many regards, authors cannot write about slavery in any satisfactory way, and yet it is a theme that returns, or never departs, echoing from the past to the present and into the future.

In her novel *Humus*, Fabienne Kanor attempts this impossible, inevitable undertaking, and in ways that recall contemporary accounts of slavery, her narrative evokes sounds as markers of memory and being for the enslaved populations and for their ancestors. As the narrator writes, the project begins in a 1774 document discovered in the archives of the city of Nantes, which she reads as a matter of sonic transformation:

> On the 23rd of March last, fourteen black women apparently leaped overboard, from the poop deck into the sea, all together and in one movement.... Despite all possible diligence, with the sea extremely choppy and the wind blowing a gale, sharks had already eaten several of them before any could be hauled back on board, yet seven were saved, one of whom died that evening at seven o'clock, being in very bad shape when rescued, so in the end, eight were lost in this incident.
> —Excerpt from the logbook of Louis Mosnier, captain of the slave ship *Le Soleil*

After reading the account, the narrator feels compelled to "swap" the "technical discourse" of the captain for the "spoken word. The cant of the seaman for the scream of the captives" (9). This is her immediate response to the question that prompts the writing of the novel: "How to tell, how to retell this story told by men? Without fuss or artifice. Otherwise. Upend the reader's expectations" (9). Cautioning the reader to "abandon all hope" of a novel of adventure, full of action, tragedy, and heroism, she further advises that she will not provide "Vivid description to move you, make you see it, as if I'd been there" (9). Instead of evoking a visual memory of slavery, she will take make the reader "captive. Chained to the words against your will. Locked up in this story that repeats itself like a chant" (9). Tellingly, she insists the novel is not a story, but a poem, therefore closer to the oral, the spoken, the auditory. In this way, it is related to the poetry that will be studied later in the chapter. There can be no full and satisfying visual memory, as the narrative will be told from the "darkness of a bottomless blue-black sea," a space in which there are no longer witnesses to speak, and where has occurred the "death of the spoken word" (9). The reader will not be able to see the story, nor to move, but will have to "listen with no other distraction to this chorus of women. At the risk of losing your bearings, hear once more these hearts beating" (9). Already, then, the visual is more or less cast aside, and any truth will be revealed through sounds, through listening to the silenced yet clamorous voices of the women.

Accordingly, the first chapter is titled "The Mute Woman," a woman who "saw everything," she says, but it seems like that visual memory is erased with her death, and that even her language is lost so she would have to invent "Words for laughing, words for forgetting words, words for acting as if" (13). The visual descriptions she does offer—"The sea is blue. A ship sits upon it"—are deliberately bland and meaningless, while the auditory memories she retains are meaningful: she writes of a woman who rocked her in her arms, of whom "Only the husky voice has stayed, the voice of a crazy sky" (13). Also, in Africa, which she refers to as "the country," she remembers the sound of the river, the work songs of the women, which last all day and into the night, so that it is "Always the same story playing on their lips" (13). When she was stolen from her home, "the words fell away" so that she is left without language, in silence (14). Words and language are replaced by the cries in the ship's hold, and the laughter as the women jump overboard (15). And yet, dragged back from the sea and into the hold, a form of language returns, or is born there in the darkness. "A song rises," she says, "Song of a thousand tongues, all saying the same, accompanying the rising of friends' souls" (16). A single word also returns, which weighs her down and which she cannot speak: it is her name that she has lost and that she cannot say (17). She imagines all the other lost words and that saying them aloud "would make the world exist and once again be as it was before" (17). The arrival on the island of Saint Domingue is marked by silence—the women's throats tighten so that this new form of soundlessness accompanies the end of the journey and the first moments on the other side. Quite tellingly, it is only when she stumbles on her reflection that her name comes back to her—seeing herself is vital to knowing herself and the brutal processes of uprooting and transportation take away the ability to see oneself in ways other than those dictated by the whites (18). Almost by default, therefore, and with the more or less complete control of the visual domain by the whites, knowing oneself becomes a matter of the other senses, principally hearing and sound. The new class of people she encounters—the "Negroes—are distinguished by sounds, the "booming, explosive laughter" she hears around the houses, and indeed the lack of sounds—she writes of those with cut tongues, a sign of the masters' need to control the sounds of the enslaved (18).

The second narrator, "the old woman," thinks in sounds, or at least her memory of the slave ship comes back, she says, "like a laugh in your throat. You have to spit it out fast if you don't want it to choke you" (23). Just as the memory lives in a sense, so do customs such as cooking: "You can't kill life," she says. Her memory of leaving the ship is olfactory, the "stench" of the hold, which distracted them from the sights of the corpses they left behind, for "Smelling meant not seeing" (24). Her most vivid remembrances of capture in Africa relate to sounds, the "noise" of the town where she was sold, the "strange words" of the people she encountered there, the "cries of pain" of the women, and the pounding sounds that they would hear at night, which made them think their graves were being dug (25–26). Together, the women pay more attention to sounds than sights, and with time they dare not meet each other's gaze, afraid of seeing reflected their "own decay, the shame of still being here" (26). In contrast, they talk as a means of sharing their experiences or else they hold their silences, those that "don't trust memory" (26). The old woman needs to speak, to tell her story, which makes another woman weep, as she has forgotten her own story, her head full of her recent suffering. Tellingly, when the guard pounds on the door, they "fall silent," so that sound and language become intimate, guarded affairs for survival and for "scheming" in ways that anticipate the uses of sounds that they will encounter and adopt on the plantations. In effect, capture, captivity, and subsequent transportation establish the dominant and polarized sonic modes of plantation existence: intense volubility and noisemaking countered and complemented by deep, impenetrable silences.

On the plantation, a woman ordered to whip her own son, determined not to show emotion returns to the field "with a light step" and "whistling" (31), while the rest of the people, "haunted" by the memory of the punishment are "Seized with a desire to sing. A melody unlike anything here. Put dark thoughts in your head" (32). Resistance comes first through sounds: the old woman is unable to keep her "mouth shut"; or indeed silences, as she creeps to the master's house "Silently," and when she loses the desire to kill the master's family, she says "The song is gone now" from her head (32). Likewise, it is the words of the white woman that hurt her and make her want to exact revenge. To quell her anger, she says, "I act as if I hear nothing" (34). Similarly, the men laboring in the fields mark each gesture with a "grunt. A collective, muted *unh hunh*," which she says was not the result of work, but "voiced all the power contained in these men" and their potential for revolt (35). The whites, by contrast, use sounds to order time and work—following a storm, the return to the fields is marked by the ringing of church bells, and each day the people are "called by the bell" to start work (34–35), while on the slave ship the "bells clang" to announce the time for gruel to be served (67). In a striking phrase, the woman underscores the importance of sounds and language to the people: "Man is word," she says, "his silence cannot endure" (35).

In ways that echo the work of Julius Scott in *The Common Wind*, the ideas and acts of revolt are founded on rumors, that spread first from France to the island then across to other islands.[1] The rumors as such "took on a life on their own" (35). Significantly, too, it is amid the fevered swirl of noise and rumors that one of the women confronts the white mistress and "shot her a look—a look that would blow up their steeples," an act that radically undercuts the power of the white women's gaze and is fueled by the atmosphere of rumor and revolt (36). The white woman is further shaken by the sound of the *assoto* drum at night, and by that of the young woman Nulpar singing, which precedes the death of one of the white children. The song rings across the courtyard as the child is discovered, and stays with the old woman, who, months later and after the young woman has disappeared, finds herself "humming her song," and this humming is shared with the other women, who lower their voices when they hear the sound of the grasses rustling, which signals the arrival of the master (37). In these ways, sounds are modified and moderated according to circumstance, and the sonic world of the enslaved in large part excludes the whites, who are known by their own sounds, in this case the rustling grasses that alert the women to the white's presence. It is at night and in darkness, when the visual power of the whites is most diminished, that the people gather, "guided by the echo of drums" (37) fomenting the revolt that will conclude in 1804 with the Independence of Haiti.

It is striking that, while the various narratives speak both of life in Africa before being stolen away and of existence in the Caribbean following transportation, the description of sounds is far more prominent in the evocation

---

[1] Scott's work will be discussed more fully below.

of the plantation. Sounds do feature in the descriptions of Africa, but they are generally environmental and unthreatening—the "song of the wind" that the narrator named "the slave" recalls, for example (45). When the narratives switch to the Caribbean, however, the sounds tend to be human-made—the bells that order time and work, the sounds of whips, the groans and cries of the suffering people, or else the noise and clamor of the people in revolt: the drums, the shouts, the songs that accompany acts of resistance. Also, silences are virtually absent in the narratives of Africa, while they are far more present in descriptions of the plantation. Similarly, there is more of a sense of being seen, surveilled, and controlled by and from the eyes in the Caribbean—freedom of movement and expression is constantly curtailed on the plantation under the eyes of the whites, which almost unconsciously leads the enslaved to create sonic realms of liberty and resistance that, again, do not seem to exist to the same degree in Africa. On the other hand, control of both the visual and sonic domains is vital to the policing of the enslaved people, and to the functioning of the plantation. Something of the visual power of the whites is suggested in the description of Sister Martha, who teaches catechism to the enslaved on the island. Her blue eyes enchant the slave woman: "when she is one with her gaze [. . .] I dive into it as into a river. For those eyes, it's tempting to believe her" (55). The whites more broadly are condemned as irreligious; if one goes to church, she says, "you can believe he closes his ears to the commandments of God," which again underscores, in another way, the importance of appearances to the whites, and the need to silence words and sounds that would in any way delegitimize the very existence of the plantation. The woman's own Muslim faith is practiced in secret, "hidden from all eyes," and the Word has a force that "rises and bursts through the roof. Cradles us, brings us a sweet shiver" (56). Crucially, her faith protects her from the controlling sounds of the plantation, as she says of her fellow Muslims "It is not their bells that wake us at dawn. Nor their dogs, nor their whips, no!" Instead, it is the sound of prayer, and the "memory of the first muezzin" that wakes and comforts them, an aural memory that persists still on the island (56).

Far from the din of the plantation, in the mountains there "reigned a silence broken only by the wind," according to "the amazon," who immediately on her arrival escapes to the hills and encounters the famous maroon Makandal (68). The two cannot communicate other than by hand signals, and in a quite fascinating sign of the sensory battles that form part of island life, he refers to the whites by pinching his ear (68). This gesture may be a reference to the mocking nickname given to whites, which is described by Edouard Glissant as follows: "*Zoreill* or *zoreye* or *zorey*. This is how whites are called in Martinique.

Perhaps because they have red ears from the effect of the sun? The term spread to the extent that it no longer has a pejorative connotation" (*Caribbean Discourse* 270). That whites are known in Creole languages by the word for ears indicates something of the importance of the ear in relation to identity and difference in the Caribbean. The name no doubt does derive from the physical appearance of the white's ear, reddened by the sun. The name could also be related to listening—the historical importance of the auditory in controlling the people, the ears of the whites ever attuned to the conversations of the enslaved, which suggests the importance of language, and of coded ways of speaking and communicating that would escape the comprehension of the whites. The name could also refer indirectly to the Code Noir, to the ear cropping that was used to punish maroons such as Makandal, and to limit their ability to hear, and thereby to know places, people, animals, and the sounds they make. If there is irony and mockery in the term *zorey* then it is grounded in history, and in the ways in which the ear was and is a site of control and resistance, of identity and power.[2] Indeed, in Kanor's novel, slavery is described as "this strange war in which your body is not yours for fighting, your feet for running, your eyes for scanning the horizon," which suggests the whites' control of the visual domain, and that the ear and the auditory realm are relatively less easy to control, and thus again almost by default become a form of sensory home for captives and maroons alike (70). Notably in this regard, the whites are unsettled by the noise of the captives, especially that of the drums, and one calls for the "bamboulas" to be banned, while the growing spirit of revolt is described as "the same solemn song [. . .] the lament of the shoeless" (150–51). More generally, too, the novel reinforces the importance of the oral culture of the people. It is finally this quality of the text that Francis evokes in her description of the ways in which "testimonies, dances, chants, storytelling, [and] Creole proverbs," are sonic registers in the historical archive that continue to denote rebellion and noncompliance, and that echo and resonate endlessly so that they cannot ever be unheard or erased ("Afterword" 196). As Kanor's text unequivocally shows, to evoke slavery in the twenty-first century one must listen attentively to the sounds of the captive people, and sound out the ways in which the auditory became, partly by necessity and partly by retaining and adapting West African cultural forms, a fundamental element of Caribbean being.

* * *

---

[2] See Munro, *Listening to the Caribbean*.

Indeed, as Kanor's novel amply shows, slave revolts across the Caribbean, from Trinidad and Dominica, to Jamaica and Haiti, began with noise—of shells, bells, drums, voices—and were spread in large part by the sounds of rumors, songs, half-truths, exaggerations, and language in general. In various Caribbean sites, sounds were and are to a large extent the revolution, and the revolution was and is sound. This is one of the implications of Julius Scott's work which, in Marcus Rediker's words, shows how those who "inhaled the history of Toussaint and the revolution and who whispered it all out again as subversive stories [made it] circulate with velocity and force around the Atlantic ("Foreword" ix). That Rediker's commentary and the title of Scott's book (*The Common Wind*) refer to a poem—Wordsworth's famous 1802 sonnet to Toussaint Louverture—suggests that poetry was one of the most potent means of communicating meaning around the Atlantic, and indeed in the Caribbean itself. There was poetry in song, in the simple chants made to sing about Haiti across the Caribbean, in the expressive culture of the enslaved in general, in their knowing use of language and detour and mimicry, their proverbs taken from Africa and translated into Creole, and the slogans that echoed across the Atlantic and that resonate still today. Is there any more poetic statement of surrender than that attributed to Louverture in 1802: "By overthrowing me, they have only brought down the trunk of the tree of liberty in Saint-Domingue; it will grow back as its roots are deep and many"? Indeed, poetry played a part in the betrayal of Toussaint, as his son Isaac, duped by Napoleon into thinking the French would leave his father unharmed, "was so flattered that he composed a poem in the first consul's honor. It showcased a mastery of the French language that would have made his father proud, but a political naivete that would have horrified him. 'Young and valiant hero,' Isaac intoned in Napoleon's honor, 'your grandeur / Of the shining day, increase the splendor'" (Girard, *Toussaint Louverture* 232–33). When Haitian independence was declared in 1804, it was with great poetic flourishes: "I have avenged America," Dessalines announced. Great authors and thinkers, not just Wordsworth, but also Lamartine, Glissant, Walcott, James, and many others, have been drawn to the story of the revolution, its poetry. The revolution is sound; it is also poetry.

It is no coincidence that it is Louverture and Haiti that inspired Glissant in his 1961 play *Monsieur Toussaint* to propose a "prophetic vision of the past," and to insist that in the Caribbean the work of the historian must be complemented and indeed completed by the work of the poet, "in order to fill the considerable gaps specific to Caribbean history—the slave trade, Middle Passage, plantation slavery, anticolonial rebellion, and so on" (Douglas, *Making "The Black Jacobins"* 23). Glissant's famous essay, "The

Quarrel with History," explains how the poetic and the literary are essential in understanding Caribbean history. Referring to a conference paper presented by Edward Baugh, Glissant questions initially the idea of Caribbean nonhistory, before insisting on the disjuncture between a group's "relation with its surroundings (what we would call its nature)" and its "accumulation of experiences (what we would call its culture)" (*Caribbean Discourse* 61). In such a context, he says, history as a discipline that seeks to record the lived reality of a people "will suffer a serious epistemological deficiency: it will not know how to make the link." As such, a "creative approach" is required to understanding history in the Caribbean, which is the "site of a history characterized by ruptures and that began with a brutal dislocation, the slave trade" (61). Faced with the "erasure of the collective memory" (62), the Caribbean writer is charged with inscribing memory, and "history as a consciousness at work and history as lived experience are therefore not the business of historians exclusively" (65):

A reality that was long concealed from itself and that took shape in some way along with the consciousness that the people had of it, has as much to do with the problematics of investigation as with a historical organization of things. It is this "literary" implication that orients the thrust of historical thought, from which none of us can claim to be exempt (65).

Thus, the literary and the poetic are part of the means of understanding and knowing history: the form of the investigation is as important as its content. Poetics is conversely more than an issue of style and form, and poets are almost obliged to engage with history so that poetry becomes history to some extent and vice versa. It is not that poetry reveals history in any direct, visible way; rather, as Glissant says: "Little more than an indiscernible revelation, poetry is not formal knowledge" (*Poetic Intention* 54). The kind of knowledge he reaches for is not poetic thought, but what he calls a *"poetics of thought"* (57, emphasis in original).

Described as a "Land of Poets," with more poets per square mile than anywhere else in the world, the recording of national history in Haiti begins in the poetry of the Declaration of Haitian independence, the grand rhetorical statements and lofty ideals that announced the arrival of the new nation (Hoffmann, "The Climate of Haitian Poetry" 62). And as Hoffmann suggests, even if poetry has been the "exclusive apanage of the elite," the Haitian oral traditions contain the three major literary forms: "The novel becomes the Creole folk tale, poetry is found in the lyrics of popular *méringues* and the embryo of a theater is found in pantomime and dance" (63). Haiti did not invent Caribbean poetry: it was already there in the uses of language described by European chroniclers such as Fauque, Labat, and countless others, in the wordplay, the knowing uses of language, allegory, indirection, imagery, and of course, sound.

This chapter further argues that by *listening* to the history and literature of the region, and by paying close attention to the representations and uses of sounds of various kinds of poetry in this case, sound is rescued in a sense from the historical oblivion more conventionally assigned to it—the idea that because sound is "intangible" and "transitory" it is necessarily "a haunting, a ghost" that "vanishes into air and past time" (Toop, *Sinister Resonance* xv). Through readings of early Haitian poetry and later works by Césaire, Damas, and Glissant, the chapter instead argues that, because the written text in the Caribbean has never been a "silent medium" but has always had strong sonic elements, sound in literature has a presence and indeed permanence that requires the reader only to listen in to the sonorous qualities that echo across time and register ideas of culture and being that drew on the past but which were also future oriented, vital means of sounding out times and situations to come. As Charles Bernstein writes, to be heard, indeed to be understood, "poetry needs to be sounded," whether by listening to the poet in performance, or through a "process of active, or interactive reading of a work."[3] It is this type of reading that the chapter undertakes.

Poetry of Haitian Independence

Haiti's independence was announced, again, in sounds and words, in the 1804 Declaration of Independence, which was, as Edwidge Danticat says, "itself a poetic text, filled with poignant and elaborate imagery and passionate language" ("Foreword," xii). Early poetry in Haiti was similarly charged with declarative functions and forms; made to be heard, it was as the historian Émile Nau put it, "the song of the multitude, a general outpouring, an epic" (qtd. in Kadish and Jenson "Introduction," xxi). To have an impact, to be heard, such a song for the people drew on the "oral, rhythmic traditions" of popular culture, the sounds that had survived slavery and served as markers of identity and solidarity during the long war of independence (xxi). To read this early poetry is, as Jenson puts it, to go "beyond the slave narrative," the dominant genre of early Afro-diasporic literature in the Anglophone world. As Jenson writes, in the early literature of independent Haiti, the attention is less on slavery than on the means through which individuals and communities

---

[3] Charles Bernstein, "Introduction." *Close Listening: Poetry and the Performed Word* (Oxford University Press, 1998), 3–26, p. 7.

"revolutionized the discursive sphere as well as the political sphere of Atlantic modernity" (*Beyond the Slave Narrative* 1). When taken as the "gold standard" of literary testimony from the enslaved and their descendants, the slave narrative "obscures the existence of genres [. . .] that *were* produced [and] disrupts our view of a longer continuum of multilingual New World African diasporan expression and discourages comparative study of the African diaspora across language traditions" (3). As Jenson perceptively argues, while slave narratives relate the experience of becoming enslaved, work such as the body of poetry in her volume (and indeed the twentieth-century poetry discussed later in the chapter), relates the process of "*un-becoming* the legal property of another human being" (3). Jenson tellingly contends, in a way that supports some of the major premises of this chapter, that the writings of political figures such as Toussaint Louverture and Jean-Jacques Dessalines "are literary in the degree to which they harnessed poetics to persuade large audiences, represent the stakes of freedom and domination, and engage in political construction of themselves and their constituencies" (9).

That writing is a crucial part of what Jenson calls "un-becoming" a slave, and that even today it can have similar effects is suggested in a remarkable passage from the Haitian intellectual Jean Casimir's *The Haitians: A Decolonial History* (2020), in which the author reflects on how the act of writing has transformed his understanding of history, and of the Haitian people:

> If readers ask what I have learned from writing this book that I now offer to them, my answer is that above all, in how I live my personal life, I no longer see my ancestors as former slaves. I don't even think of them as a dominated class. Their misery is only the most superficial aspect of their reality. It is the reality that colonialists prefer to emphasize, along with those among them who oppose the cruelty of some colonists but don't ultimately reject colonization itself. Having finished the book, I have come to realize that my ancestors, as individuals and as a group, never stopped resisting slavery and domination. I am the child of a collective of fighters, not of the vanquished. I have chosen to venerate them, to honor these captives reduced to slavery, and those emancipated in thanks for their military service to colonialism. I do so despite their errors and their occasional failures. (3)

Casimir emphasizes the ways in which his writing has transformed his perspective on the past, which of course also changes his own sense of himself in the present. Just as Jenson recognizes the poetics at play in the writings of Louverture and Dessalines, so there is in Casimir's declaration a profound poetry, and it is the poetry of un-becoming, or even of *re*-becoming a subject not defined by the past, by imposed notions of race—it is noticeable that he makes no mention of race or color in claiming his sense of himself and his people. Vitally, too, in his preface to the book, Casimir insists on the importance of listening as the primary means of knowing Haitian people and their history:

> This study is destined for those who wish to listen to the Haitian people in order to understand what they are saying. Their speech is barely audible, because the modern world imprisons it within the dominant culture and its writing of the past, trying to make us believe it doesn't even exist. (xvii)

The Haitian people, he asserts, "are not voiceless," even if the West has "plug[ed] its ears" to those people it wishes to keep as "prisoners to the past" (xvii). Across different times and places, the poets studied in this chapter are united in this desire to un-silence, un-become, and to re-become by means of poetry, that which Casimir insists they truly are: unvanquished, free, never silenced.[4]

The early nineteenth century was a time of transition and change, politically, but also culturally, and there is in the early postindependence poetry of Haiti a sense of a culture shifting "between the diverse arts and cultures brought from Africa and the poetry later in Haitian history that would represent the black republic in Creole" (Kadish and Jenson "Introduction," xxiv). As Casimir points out, resistance to the French imperial project was rooted in speech, in the language that was created by the captives, "who appropriated the popular forms of speech, transforming them into a tool of expression that completely escaped the comprehension of a supposedly all-powerful political power" (*The Haitians* 251). The fact that French language could not establish itself in the daily lives of the people represents to Casimir "a gradual reversal in the class relationships" of the evolving society, and the "universal implantation of a language of contestation consecrated an epistemological rupture whose significance has not been fully explored. It shattered the colonial matrix of power" (251). Such a linguistic splintering of colonial power is one of the foundations of Casimir's claim that Haitians were never truly dominated and, citing Thomas Madiou's question—"'For his part, did the African—even though enslaved—ever completely cease to be free?'"—Casimir poses his own question: "was he even colonized?" (252).

---

[4] As Walter D. Mignolo comments on Casimir's book: "A human being named *slave* vanishes as a human being, absorbed by the meaning of the world. To delink from that illusion is one of the tasks of decolonial reading, of exposing the ontological fiction of Western modernity's vocabulary in all its modern vernacular languages. That is why Casimir insists on distinguishing *captive* from *slave*" ("Foreword: Thinking Decoloniality" xiv).

The triumph of the revolution in large part dictated the ways in which the country's social structure took form in the nineteenth century. In short, the war was predicated on "deep social and class conflicts and competing interests in colonial St Domingue, and these were transmuted and remade in the independence era" (Yelvington et al., "Caribbean Social Structure in the Nineteenth Century" 289). The generals and other senior black military officers joined emancipated blacks of all classes in challenging the presumed ascendancy of the former *affranchi* class, the free coloreds who had been property owners, and slaveowners, "perhaps the most powerful such group in the Caribbean" (290). Faced with the need to maintain a strong army, Toussaint and other leaders that followed, including Dessalines himself, believed they needed to continue large-scale export agriculture, which meant forcing free workers and their managers to remain on the plantations. When Dessalines was assassinated in 1806, Haiti split into a northern kingdom, led by King Henry I, and a republic in the west and south led by the mulatto Alexandre Pétion (291). The Haitian army created the State, and "the ideology of militarism [...] came to play a defining role in Haitian state formation," and played a "repressive" role throughout the nineteenth century (292). In the course of the century, twenty-six heads of state ruled Haiti, and twenty-five of those leaders were generals. While the State was concerned above all with the defense of independence, the vast majority of the formerly enslaved and their descendants "began to settle the territory as peasants" (293). The *lakou* system of interrelated conjugal families sharing a common yard and forming a pool of cooperative labor, replaced the plantation as a site of home and work. It was here, too, that the Vodou religion was seated, alongside a family cemetery. As Dubois writes, the rural population of Haiti "effectively undid the plantation model" (*Haiti: The Aftershocks* 13). At the same time, however, the country was in effect split between the ruling class and the broader population, as Dubois explains:

Over time—often convinced that the masses were simply not ready to participate in political life—the Haitian governing elites crafted state institutions that excluded most Haitians from formal political involvement. [...] For almost all of Haiti's history, most of its population has literally been unable to read the laws under which they have been governed (*Haiti: The Aftershocks* 14).

Haiti's internal conflicts were exacerbated by external issues, notably the increasing interference of foreign governments in the country's economy and politics. Notoriously, France demanded an indemnity of 150 million francs (roughly $3 billion in today's currency) to compensate the slaveholders for their losses. To pay the indemnity, the Haitian government took out loans from French banks. Though the amount of the indemnity was later reduced to 60 million francs by France, the cycle of debt had been established and, by 1898, "fully half of Haiti's government budget went to paying France and the French banks. By 1914, that proportion had climbed to 80 percent" (Dubois, *Haiti: The Aftershocks* 15).

The poetry that we read in this section is therefore far from being the unfiltered "voice of the people": the poetry of the people existed in their religion, their music, their proverbs, and in the rich culture that sustained them even as they were ignored and neglected by the state. Poetry was nevertheless an important means of exploring social and political issues, and indeed was something of a weapon during the civil war period, as Chelsea Stieber has shown in her work on Hérard Dumesle's writings, which are forms of travel writing, but which include poetry in their hybrid forms. Stieber terms this work a kind of "romantic ruin poetry," which stands in sharp contrast "to the ceremonial pomp of commemorative verse produced in the northern monarchy" (*Haiti's Paper War* 138). In this section, I draw on some of the earliest Haitian poetry to show the ways in which sounds were important means of asserting the new nation's sense of itself, or at least the elite's version of itself, communicating its understanding of its place in the world, and imagining history and memory in a time marked by upheavals and uncertainty, and the persistent reminders of the legacies of the colonial past.[5]

Poetry inevitably involves the "structuring of sound," and yet arguably "no other poetic feature is currently as neglected" (Perloff and Dworkin, "Introduction: The Sound of Poetry" 10). In Jacques Roubaud's discussion of the evolution of the lyric and music, he points out "The breaking of the bond between word and sound, which occurred during the fourteenth century, brought about a new *double form* called *poetry*. This form would combine the words of language in writing and in speech such that they would be indissociable. That other form which brings word and sound together has by no means disappeared; we call it *song*. A song is not a poem and a poem is not a song" (qtd. in Perloff and Dworkin 5). Poetic language is made in large part through sound; it is sound, a "language made strange, made somehow extraordinary by the use of verbal and sound repetition, visual configuration, and syntactic deformation." Sound is also poetic meaning, or at least "the semantics of a given poem can no longer be separated from its sound" (Perloff and Dworkin 7). Poetry is in effect intimately connected to the idea of the "auditory imagination" as it is conceived by T.S. Eliot. The auditory imagination, Eliot says, is the "feeling for syllable and rhythm, penetrating far below the conscious levels

---

[5] For a broader discussion of nineteenth-century literary depictions of the Haitian Revolution in particular, see Marlene L. Daut, *Tropics of Haiti*.

of thought and feeling, invigorating every word; sinking to the most primitive and forgotten, returning to the origin and bringing something back, seeking the beginning and the end" (*The Use of Poetry* 11). The poet is in this sense primarily a listener, feeling, sounding the imagination that is itself made of sounds.

In the corpus of nineteenth-century Haitian poetry to be read and listened to in this section,[6] the interest lies less in the sonic qualities of specific words or phrases, and more in the way that sounds are used, represented, and talked about. Sounds proliferate throughout these poems and may be broken down into the following categories: sound as voice and freedom; sound as veneration of male leaders, panegyric; sound as gender (the female voice); sound as nation-building; sound as a conventional trope of epic; and sound as a marker of slave time. In many cases, sound in the poems is closely associated with voice, with speakers vocalizing ideas of time, history, society, and culture in ways that insert sounds and voices into the discourse of history which, the poems suggest, would not be a simple matter of recording dates and events, but of registering and listening to voices and sounds as crucial parts of the construction of history.

Quite significantly, the earliest poems of Haitian independence invoke sounds as markers of freedom. Set to the tune of the *Marseillaise*, the very title of the anonymously written poem "What? Native Race! Would You Remain Silent?" asserts in 1804 the importance of breaking the silence that was an inherent part of colonial experience: "What? Native race! Would you remain / Silent, unmoved when Hero's hand / Avenges you, breaks slavery's chain" (3). The hero in question is Dessalines, and in this charged, muscular poem, the speaker calls for the people to "sing with one manly voice" the praises of the leader, who "reigns wisely over us" (3). Quite tellingly, the call for the people to raise their voices is at once a call to sing their freedom, but also to express their deference to the new leader, the "Good father," in whom the poem urges the people to invest their faith and hope, and to whom give away their liberty, at least in part. When memory is evoked, it is also through sounds—the "anguished cries" of the "victims" of the crimes of slavery, who also "cry from the dark eternal night: / 'Good Father, he, who thus / Reigns wisely over us" (5). The cries and songs of the dead further confirm the status of Dessalines as the rightful protector of the new nation, and in invoking the memory of the dead, the poem suggests that not to follow Dessalines would be to betray that memory. Singing as one creates a kind of unity, but also encourages an

---

[6] Doris Y. Kadish and Deborah Jenson, eds., *Poetry of Haitian Independence* (New Haven, CT: Yale University Press, 2015).

unquestioning spirit that serves to reinforce the power of the male leader. As the poem projects into the future, evoking the newborn citizens, who may all "Stammer his name in babblings dim" it is again through sounds and voice that Dessalines's name will be transmitted, and along with it, a certain vision of muscular government that would prove to have an enduring presence in Haitian political history (7).

Similar sentiments are expressed in C. César Télémaque's "Let Us Now Sing Our Glory!," which calls for the friends of Haiti to "sing our glory" and to be "eternally / Thankful" to the emperor Dessalines (9). He is the father of the nation; the people are his "children" who, again, must sing his praises in order to create the postrevolution sense of nation and togetherness (9). One can perhaps sense some of the paradoxes and contradictions of independence in the poem's unquestioning veneration of a strongman leader, while they also call for freedom, as in the refrain of the work "Nature, in wisdom infinite": "Sing we, sing we stoutheartedly: / Equality forevermore! / Banished, banished be cruel slavery: Equality forevermore!" (13). Thus, the poems vaunt the qualities of a self-appointed emperor, while singing for everlasting equality in ways that pose already the question of how any form of equality can exist while there exists a desire (and perhaps need) for an authoritarian form of leadership. These paradoxes are in fact part of the great cacophony that greets the early independence period, the "hurly-burly sound" as an 1805 poem by Justin Chanlatte puts it, referring to the noise of the crowd, "As the throngs the throne surround / In ecstasy" (19). Together, the crowd sing "with passion's voice, in manly wise: / We who accept the rule of Jacques Premier, / Fete our own feast on our king's holy day" (19). Dessalines's voice echoes through history, as in the later poem "There Did He Fall (The Pont-Rouge)" (1835), which remembers the leader through his words, and the cry, the "lion's cry," the "sublime cry," that turns slaves into warriors and which reinforces the connection between manly revolt and the cry, the scream of rebellion that characterizes the popular memory of Dessalines (180). Similarly, Ignace Nau's "Dessalines! ... At That Name, Doff Hats, My Friends!" (1839) remembers the leader "to the sound of the fanfare and the artillery," sounds of war that are intimately related to "the single cry," the noise that marked the people's unity, and a paradoxical sense of harmony and oneness that seems unattainable in the time of putative peace that has followed the revolution (184). Indeed, in this poem "the sound of battle" precedes and announces a prophesied future of harmony, where "the bird will sing to us once more its songs of love / The voice of the forests will resonate again." The sounds of peace thus seem intimately related to those of war, which suggests more broadly the difficulty in imagining peace without a preceding, clamorous war: conflict is a part of historical memory and is reassuring in the sense that history's most cherished moments are closely related to and indeed dependent on it. Already, in these works, Dessalines is an almost religious figure, a man, but also invested with superhuman qualities that implicitly call into question the particular notion of equality that is being promoted, its limits and contradictions.

The veneration of the male leader figure continues in the poems dedicated to Henri Christophe, notably the poem that was sung at his coronation in 1814, "What sweet chants, these, that strike, entrance my ear" (23). The title is interesting in that it emphasizes the sounds, the sweetness of the chants and their entrancing effect, which could suggest the songs have an almost mystifying intent, charming the listener into believing that the sweetness of the sounds is reflected in the spirit of the leader. Listening is the key to believing in the glory of the leader (and of the country): "Lo! Hear the blaring brasses joyously / Temper and blend their brash cacophony / With fanfares' trumpets, horns, resounding!" (23). The subtle sense of uncertainty and dreaminess is emphasized in the chorus, which asks, "Are we awake? Or are sleep's smiling, / Lying dreams, with fictions beguiling, / Lulling, plying our spirit and sense?," which may be read as a statement of awareness that the sounds of the song may dull the senses, quite deliberately, and render "spirit and sense" suspect, and liable to being charmed or fooled (23). Sounds are also the means of recording history and transmitting memory, as the poem suggests: "Clio, fair Muse of History, / Shall sing his exploits, first to last, / And, hundred-voiced, cause them to shine, / In Glory's light forever cast, / Engraved in memory's hallowed shrine" (23). The leader's voice communicates his "brilliance" and has a dramatic effect: "Henry speaks. All at once, the waters / Bow to new masters" (27). The voice thus is the means through which power is manifested and deference and order maintained.

It seems every leader must have their poem, their song, and the work "Haitians All, Come and Rally Round" praises Alexandre Pétion: "'Long live PÉTION,' sings everyone! / Long live the FATHERLAND! All hail!" (43). The French version closely allies Pétion and the "patrie," so that between these poems one hears a growing number of voices clamoring to be heard, and each one is a father figure, the embodiment of the masculine nation. The poems stress harmony and unity, while in truth the nation was divided between the north, controlled by Henri Christophe, and the south, controlled by Pétion, a division that also had color and class connotations—Pétion was a French-educated mulatto, while Christophe was a worker, freed from slavery at a young age, and darker skinned.

The call for unity is apparent in the anonymous poem "Join Now Our Voices," which asks "Let the echoes ring / In accents of hearts' joy and love"

(47), and which again equates Pétion with the fatherland. There is also an interesting historical debate that is hinted at in these early poems, and which will mark a lot of subsequent intellectual reflection on the revolution. Namely, the question of who were the real liberators of Haiti, the black or mulatto leaders.[7] In this poem, it is the mulatto who saves the "weak, mortal men" from slavery, and who is presented as a wise hero figure and who is "Throughout the isle adored, revered" for delivering the slaves into their "blessed refuge" (47). The role, or duty, of the liberated is now to praise the glorious leader with their "flattering tongues," which through repetition reinforces the one-sided view of history. Even a poem such as Jules Solime Milscent's "To Smite the Tyrant's Shackle-Curse," which calls for a unified Haitian republic, does so by asking the south to cede to the north and to join together as "Liberty's children" (51).

It is further striking that in a poem by Juste Chanlatte that marks the reunification of Haiti following the suicide of Henri Christophe in October 1820, the voice of reconciliation is that of a female "august patroness," who descends from on high and bestows the boons of peace and justice (59). The figure brings new life to a "newborn" people (63), and offers maternal support in a voice that contrasts with that of the male leaders:

> Her voice, imperious,
> Makes speak the gods; her shield,
> Hovering, covers us;
> Her glittering lance, revealed,
> Glimmers, dazzles our glance,
> As Nature, suddenly,
> In rich exuberance
> Unbound, luxuriantly
> Spreads around her greenery. (61)

The female voice is a form of intermediary, between the two factions, and between the time of war and the reinstatement of the male power, this time in the form of Jean-Pierre Boyer, president of Haiti from 1820 to 1843. It is the intervention of the female figure that brings the new life and allows the people to be "newborn," but following that her voice disappears and it is the male father figure that dominates once more as the poem calls to Boyer: "Our judge and our protector be! And yes, / Father, no less!" and to sow "fertility's / Seeds" to ensure the continued vitality of the nation (63). Whereas some of

---

[7] For a comprehensive discussion of issues of race, color, and the historiography of the revolution, see Daut's introduction to *Tropics of Haiti*.

the other poems lay bare the race and class issues with which the new nation struggled, in this poem the issue of gender is subtly but quite tellingly invoked in ways that suggest the ambiguous situation of women, as peacemakers and life givers, intermediaries and conciliators, brought to the fore to resolve the male-dominated conflict, but then silenced again as the primary role of the male leader is reasserted and a national discourse of manliness and virility gradually but quite decisively comes to prominence.

Independence is thus, as in an 1821 poem by Juste Chanlatte, "fair fruit of manly pride," to be sung and praised in an act of memory, "recalling thus / Our solemn righting of that wrong" (65). The same poem features a succession of voices proclaiming the virtues of Boyer, and virtually all of these voices are male: a trumpeter; a piper; lieutenants; and captains. The two female voices that are included serve to bolster the theme of manly militarism. The first, of a "Young Female Warrior," calls out to "Haitian lads," to clean "our long-wrought wounds," for "Such is the surest path to ply / If you would reach our hearts" (77). For their part, the young women will succumb to the virile male warrior: "Can a lover's zeal deny / When he avenges nature's woe?" (77). The second female voice is of a "Woman warrior pointing out to her child the column erected to Independence" (77), which is a metonym for the nation, clearly phallic in connotation, and designed to impress by its "soaring eminence," and also to strike fear into the child, for as the woman says, if the child should ever betray the nation, she will be eaten by a caiman (77). The message is then that the sexualized male metonym of the nation should be looked at in wonder, without questioning, and if such wonder and respect should fail, there will be violent consequences. Behind the chorus and praise, communicated at the end through sounds—"What sounds! What notes enchant the air!"—lies therefore a discernible note of menace, directed especially to women, and those who stray from their prescribed roles as willing lovers and virtuous mothers.

It is important to realize in reading these poems that the idea of the new nation is being created, and that works such as these form part of that effort. What was the significance of Haiti's independence? What kind of nation was it going to be? How would relations be between all of the nation's people? What could be done with the legacies of colonialism and slavery that are still so fresh in the memory? How could the complex events of the long war of independence be synthesized into a coherent national narrative? The very term "the Haitian Revolution" was coined a full twenty years after independence, possibly by Hérard Dumesle in his travel account, *Voyage dans le nord d'Haïti* (1824). It is also in this volume that appears the earliest-known transcription of the "Oath of the Cayman Woods," which took place on August 14,

1791, at a Vodou ceremony that marked the beginning of the revolt. The oath appears in a poem composed by Dumesle and reproduced in *Poetry of Haitian Independence*, which frames the events with references to classical figures and symbols, such as Virgil, Aeolus, and Spartacus. The oath itself is important as it represents dramatically the power of the spoken word, and demonstrates how important the heard history of Haiti and the broader Caribbean is: with little or no popular written culture, the participants in the ceremony are electrified by the sounds of the words, which propel them into their long and deadly war of independence.

It is significant that as Dumesle sets the scene for the ceremony, the enslaved participants, the "poor oppressed" stand "in silence," voiceless against the "dread cacophony" of history, characterized in the image and sound of "gale winds howling" (93). The only sounds emitted by the people are "dour laments" that move "nature," a harmonizing force whose laws are held "in suspense" by the "foul crimes" of the colonists (93–94). The slaves' desire for vengeance is what motivates the uprising and animates the ceremony, which begins with an animal sacrifice (95). The animal is killed by "an orator," who following the deed pronounces his prophetic words: "'Now you the noble purpose see / Whence heroes rise to immortality!'" (97). The words are all the more potent and effective in that they are spoken in Creole, "that tongue that our forebears used, / So simple that it seemed to have suffused / Their very breath; tongue natural, naïve" (97). The language is closely related to their being; it is "the portrait of their soul" and it "electrified their hearts" (97). The speech itself talks of the "white man's sins against your land, your race," and draws a distinction between the whites' religion, which leads to crime," and Vodou, which "leads to grace / And goodliness" (97). The oracle's words lead the fire to swirl "in an all-devouring hunger," a clear metaphor for the enflamed spirits of the participants (97). When the fire finally burns out, the slaves "consecrate this wood" with "prayer-chants and many a sacred vow," spoken acts that contrast with their initial silence, and which again show the importance of the oral elements, of finding a voice, and in this case, of expressing themselves in their native tongue, all acts that mark their desire to take back the land and repossess their very selves (99).

Songs and speeches continued to mark important occasions, such as the poem "The World Has Hailed Your Sons" by Jean-Baptiste Romane that was sung at the festivities to mark France's recognition of Haitian independence in 1825. Romane's poem was sung to the dignitaries present, including a representative of France, and speaks of the celebration spreading across the land, in sounds and chants—the waters of the "Majestic Artibonite" river "murmur" and ring with the cry "Vive Haïti! Vive la France!," while Boyer's pronouncement of the same phrase was "spoken to end our ills" (108–110). The song is finally addressed to God, who is called on to "accept our songs" and to bless Boyer and Charles X, and to hear them both call out to the glory of the two countries (111). In contrast to Dumesle's poem about Bois Cayman, this work tends to look forward temporally, to a time that would never arrive of Haiti's settled and peaceable external relations leading to national prosperity. Indeed, the poem is remarkable in that it does not mention Haiti's indemnity to France of 150 m gold francs, which was ten times the nation's annual revenues in 1825, and which threw it into a spiral of debt that it arguably has never recovered from. The chants celebrating the glory of the countries and the "clemency" of Charles in particular seem empty and to ignore the punitive aspects of the agreement, the effects of which would last far longer than the cries for peace and prosperity that ring throughout the poem, and which show the ways in which song and sound can capture a certain fleeting national feeling, which is subsequently forgotten and silenced as the realities of debt and economic hardship become clearer.

Even as Haiti's economic independence and future prosperity were compromised by France's indemnity, the idea of a muscular, robust, male state persisted, and continued to be celebrated in poems such as *The Haïtiade*, the "only formal epic of the Haitian revolution" (xxviii).[8] The first canto of the poem insists on the newness of what is to follow:

> O Muse, now to new songs I tune my lyre:
> Come, flame my heart with your mad passion-fire;
> Let my voice, proud, with manly accents, ring;
> Come, Muse, let us now Haiti's freedom sing. (121)

One senses still the freshness of the memory of the revolution, but also a concurrent feeling that the passage of time is eroding the memory, or at least that it needs to be set to words and music in order to preserve it. Again, manliness is seen as a virtue, and not a fundamental flaw in the political culture of the new nation. The song itself must by then have been somewhat familiar, and not altogether new; the tale of the slaves' overcoming and of how they transformed slavery into liberation and "beat to avenging blades their chains of old" (121). There is also a degree of revisionism in the way the poem states there was an easy transition from slavery to nominally free field labor, that the hoe, previously "a burden so heavy when it fed / The cruel, slave-driving

---

[8] For a discussion of the "French and Haitian literary collaboration involved in the creation and publication of this poem," see Jenson and Kadish, "Introduction," pp. xxviii–xxix.

master" now "weighed ever so lightly in the withered hand / Of soldier citizen who saved his land" (123). In truth, attempts to force the freed people back onto the land were hugely unpopular and controversial.[9]

The glossing over of the issue of forced labor deliberately precedes the first mention of Toussaint Louverture, who is presented as a godly figure, "Heaven-endowed with power supreme" and one of those powers lies in his voice, as it was he "whose tongue decreed the Haitians' laws" (123). Having suffered "labors of the vilest kind," he rose up, and again this is presented in vocal terms: "his valor rang with cries of war" (125). Another noisy marker of revolt, the "conch shell's blaring sound," gathers the soldiers around Toussaint, though this sound is soon replaced by those that accompany the pious Toussaint's prayers: "Voices rise up, the Heavens' height inspires / Hymns intoned by celestial angel choirs" (127). Articulacy is a potent and necessary complement to the physical acts of revolt; much like Toussaint, the revolutionary general Télémaque is praised for "his eloquence," which "framed the laws / Adopted in the councils" (133); while Pétion's silence "binds all hearts," and his speech "conquers all" (139). Of all the heroes lauded in the poem, however, it is only Toussaint whose voice is communicated in direct speech, and who by implication becomes the voice of the revolution, which is ultimately a univocal phenomenon: the memory will be channeled through the voice of this single, paternalistic figure, who "will govern like a father" (144). Similarly, Toussaint's singular voice is received by the crowd as it vows to "keep the law [. . .] all in one voice" (147). The memorial intentions of the speaker are subsequently reaffirmed in the call to "let our minds now stand free / Of deathly scorn's vile, hateful memory" (147), which suggests that Toussaint's voice can silence the memory of all that preceded him, and is also a kind of prophecy in that it projects forward into a future in which it is the manly, heroic voice that controls history, and leaves in silence aspects of that history that would call into question the value of promoting a univocal male version of history, and of maintaining a people in thrall to that voice.

It is perhaps one of the signs of the early confusion over national identity—the unprecedented condition of being a "black nation" and modern at the same time[10]—that there are very few mentions of popular culture in the

---

[9] See, for example, Laurent Dubois's argument that "Louverture never really considered breaking up the plantations, however. He saw the continuation of the plantation system as the only viable choice for his people. How else, after all, could the economy of an export-oriented colony function? During his time as leader of Saint-Domingue, Louverture steadfastly defended the plantation system, telling the ex-slaves that they had to prove to the world that it was possible to produce sugar and coffee without slavery. He argued fervently that in order to preserve their hard-won freedom, the ex-slaves of Saint-Domingue had to accept the restrictions that would keep the plantations going" (*Haiti: The Aftershocks of History* 31).

[10] See, for example, Eugene Genovese's argument that under Toussaint, the revolution "did not aspire to restore some lost African world or build an isolated African-American enclave that could have played no autonomous role in world affairs [. . .]. Toussaint, and after his death, Dessalines and Henri Christophe,

poetry of the first three decades of independence. The derivative French style, language, and form in many of these works is reinforced by the classical themes and references. Even *The Haïtiade* is quite conventional in its attempt to present the events of the revolution in an epic form that seems to preclude any references to the culture of the newly freed people. This tension would endure for much of the rest of the century, and indeed into the indigenist period that began during the American occupation of 1915–34. Coriolan Ardouin's 1835 poem "The Bechouans" prefigures the indigenists to some degree in its references to drum and dancing, even if the poem is largely situated in Africa, which is rather exoticized, not to say feminized and sexualized. The poem presents "Bechouan belles" who "dance through the night, casting the spells / That grace and fascinate the eye" (151). The ear is also attuned to the spectacle, and to the sounds of a drum that "echo deep into the forest" (150). The poet's awareness of Haitian popular culture is shown in the way the Bechouan maid dances rhythmically to the drum, "gliding above the *sotor*'s sound," in the reference to the assotor drum, which is a Haitian instrument, used in Vodou ceremonies and to send coded messages during the revolution (153). The sounds and sights are in harmony, in rhythm and time with each other, and with the natural environment, in that the "sweet music of the dance / carries through to the heart of the forest" (152). The dance is moreover "poetic," and the speaker encourages the young women to dance on, as they sing in one voice (152).

The subsequent scene of the maidens bathing peacefully in the river is interrupted by "a distant sound" that rises and dies so that they are not sure if it is real or "a dream" (156). The women flee as they realize the sound is that of the Bushmen, who are presented as barbaric hunters whose "terrible sounds" mix with the cries of a victim (157, 158). The captured women are bound for the slave ship, and say farewell to the place and sounds of their homeland, notably the "sound of the drum," which echoes across the seas, in much the same way that the image of the idealized African woman is carried across the ocean, so that the exiled woman becomes an imagined figure, a fantasy, as the speaker puts it, "That angel who comes to us in our nightly dreams" (158, 160).

Ardouin's 1835 poem "Oh! I Recall That Day (Mila)" in a sense picks up where "The Bechouans" ends, in its romantic presentation of a beautiful "Daughter of Angola" and her doomed love affair with her "Creole beau," Osala. Mila marks out the plantation through sound, her songs that echo across the "attentive valley," and the echoes of which betray her presence to the white master, Ebreuil (168). Her "simple song" charms him, though she

---

tried to forge a modern black state." *From Rebellion to Revolution: Afro-American Slave Revolts in the Making of the Modern World*, 88.

sings of Osala, and this moves him to approach her, first in the "language [...] of a white," and then "changing tone," he flatters her, saying "her voice is that of the dove" (170). When she rejects him, he walks away, falling into silence, and plotting to get rid of Osala (170).

Sounds mark out the slaves' time, and their relationship with space, as in a scene where "It is the silver bell / that sounds rest time," and during that time is heard the song of a nightingale (170–72). The speaker implores the slaves to come and hear the bird's song, as "this beloved cantor of the skies will be no less sweet / If it is a slave who hears her voice" (172). This is important, as it suggests something of the ways in which sounds escape the control of the planters, and remain accessible and enlivening to the enslaved people: the ear retains its freedom, and such sounds are there for all. It is also significant that the young Creole beau, Osala, appears whistling, a sound that connects him to the bird, and thus to nature; not only are sounds accessible to the enslaved, they are also able to make their own sounds that humanize them in a sense, and also are small acts of resistance that contrast with the gloomy silence of the master and the industrial clanging of the silver bell (172).

Osala's connection to natural things is reinforced in the presents he brings to Mila—fruits and flowers; and he says his "suffering" is over "For I see you, and hear your voice," the two senses being markers of their intimacy and their freedom to communicate and be together (172). Her wish is that he "will sing / some of his airs on his mandolin" for her, while she will tell him a "story from the native land," which signals her love for Africa, and the ways in which songs and storytelling express that love and to some extent ease the suffering of their exile (174). Time is important in this, too, for the plans they make are for the night, when "They will be able to cradle each other in their sweet words" (174), and in the day, time is marked by the bell: when "Two o'clock tolls" she must run back to her work, and await the freedom that the night and its sounds bring. When their plans are foiled by the white planter, who sends Osala to work in chains "on another plain," his new exile is marked by sounds, or rather their absence—the realization that "never will he hear / The gardens echo with the name of his Mila!" (178). Strikingly, too, Mila's pain is manifested in broken, interrupted sounds: she wanders "a dreamy and sad madwoman" who "Ceaselessly begins a Creole song / That she never completes!" and when she dies she is taken away "without a sound, without a flower" (178). The broken, unfinished song is also a sign of the ruptures of history and being that are the legacies of the colonial era, and which in this poem echo into the present via the contrasting sounds of the poem: the bird and human song, related to love and nature; the broody, ominous silence of the master; the sounds of work and time; and finally, the broken songs and broken lives that emerge from it all.

It is finally telling that it is in the poems that present "popular" or peasant characters that notions of memory and history are the most fragmented and troubling—although they are far from being realistic attempts to communicate trauma, there is a sense that the people's memory of the revolution is marked by ruptures and discontinuities, and that these broken memories are more important to them than the official, collective memory of glorious revolution, which is communicated, for example, at the end of the anonymous poem, "Father, Dear, How I Love to Cast My Glance over These Hills and Fields" (1839). The sounds used here are quite different to the tears and broken songs of the popular poems. On the anniversary of independence, church bells ring out, priests chant their litanies of thanks, cannons "thunder long and loud," mixed with "the song of the horn," and the echoing sound of the cannons, which carry the memory of war and victory: "So that your sounds, carried from mountain to mountain, / Remind today every last person / That he had sworn to live independent!" (208). The sounds here are clamorous and loud, sounds of bells and cannons that may in other contexts be heard as contradictory—religious devotion mixed with a glorified memory of war—but which here indicate again the paradoxes of national memory: how memories of war announce feelings of peace; and how the booming sounds of war form the most coherent auditory memory of the revolution, where again notions of peace and togetherness are closely associated with conflict and suffering.[11]

Césaire's Sounds of Silence

In many ways, the early poems of Haitian independence are atypical in the broader spectrum of Francophone Caribbean poetry. It is rare, for instance, to find in subsequent Caribbean writing a similar tendency to glorify the past, and to use the past as a means of sounding out the future. Also, poetry would seldom again have such a public, communal function, made to be spoken or sung out loud. There is an assuredness about history and memory in much of the early poetry that stands in stark contrast to some of the works produced by the great poets of the mid-twentieth century, whose works will be discussed in the rest of the chapter. These later works bear closer comparison to the Haitian poetry that presents popular or peasant characters, in that in both cases issues of memory and history are more troubling and fragmented than they are in much of the triumphant poetry of Haitian independence. Also, the celebratory

---

[11] For a fuller study of early Haitian poetry, see Amy Reinsel, "Poetry of Revolution."

poetry tends to be more direct and unambiguous in its style and content: the new nation is largely sure of itself, its history, and its future. The later poetry is by contrast characterized more by uncertainty, opacity, and the indirection that is identified in early accounts of the cultures of the enslaved, by chroniclers such as Fauque, Labat, Moreau, Descourtilz, *Marly*, Bleby, and others.[12]

Many of the auditory tropes identified in those early accounts of enslaved vocal culture reappear in the work of Aimé Césaire. Indirection, opacity, improvisation, tone, silence, and rhythm are some of the markers of Caribbean vocal and auditory experience that shape and to a large extent constitute Césaire's poetics. By listening to these elements of Césaire's work, by mapping out its particular soundscape, we can sound out its deepest resonances, and gain a more sensorially full appreciation of the historical and contemporary experience that Césaire seeks to understand and express. In these ways, reading Caribbean poetry is also a matter of, to use Mary Gallagher's term, "sounding," a particular way of reading and knowing that responds to the "fluid, volatile space/time" of the Caribbean (*Soundings* 3). In addition, the term is used "to register respect for the integrity or resistance of the writing approached here" (3). Importantly, Gallagher evokes Walter Ong's idea that "'hearing can register interiority without violating it. I can rap a box to find whether it is empty or full or a wall to find whether it is hollow or solid inside'" (3).[13] These are helpful metaphors for the work of Caribbean literary criticism: rapping it, striking it to hear its echoes, what it holds inside, its emptiness and plenitude. Indeed, Gallagher's further citation from Ong, "the field of sound is not spread out before me but is all around me," is all the more helpful in that it can be applied directly to the modern poetry to be analyzed in the rest of this chapter. For these poets—Césaire, Damas, Glissant—it is primarily the past that they sense all around them, unfinished, ongoing, unending, and if, as Ong says, sound also has that quality of being past, present, and future, then sound must be one of the primary means of understanding, knowing, sensing this past. Sounding as such, is a question of depths, layers, resonances, and echoes, and should, Gallagher says, "counteract the temptation to remain safely at the surface" (4).

Much like Gallagher, Mireille Rosello is a listener-reader, and in Rosello's case reading is a matter of "listening to noise" in Caribbean writing (*Littérature et identité* 30).[14] The search for such noise imposes itself, Rosello says, "because

---

[12] See Munro, *Listening to the Caribbean*.
[13] See also, Sarah Kay and François Noudelmann's use of the term "sounding," chosen as it "designates both the physical sound in the process of being sounded out, and the fathoming of meaning or opinions." "Introduction: Soundings and Soundscapes," 2.
[14] Rosello's notion of noise or "bruit" draws on Michel Serres's work, *Le Parasite*.

it is neither analysis of a semantic content, nor necessarily analysis of anything other than the semantic content" (30). For Rosello, as for Gallagher, and as we will see, for Césaire, and especially Glissant, paradox is inherent to any such process of listening-reading, for "if the tactical discourse of Antillean discourse manages to make a noise, these noises will often be incomprehensible, undecipherable for those who hear them from inside the canon. These noises might sometimes (and this is not the least of their paradoxes) resemble closely to the utterances enshrined in the canon" (30). Rosello finds "noise," for instance, in the well-known phrase from *Eloge de la créolité*, that "We are still in a state of pre-literature," and in Glissant's similar statement, " 'I do not believe that there exists yet an Antillean literature in the sense that a literature supposes a movement of action and reaction between a public and works produced' " (31). As Rosello observes, such statements employ the very arguments that have often served to "justify the devalorization or the exclusion of certain texts" (31). "Noise" in these statements, and in similar pronouncements of Maryse Condé, is paradoxical: it is, Rosello says, a "signal of silence" (33): "But this noise, this unsettling repetition, this murmur, signals the presence of a silence, and means that the reader must listen in" (34). This is noise less as sound than as disruption and paradox, the discordant elements of a literature that is there but not read, cacophonous but unheard.

Gallagher, drawing on Ong, is moreover sensitive to the ways in which colonization is a distinctly visual operation: "In reality, as Ong reminds us, it is vision, not hearing, and surveys, not soundings, that present surfaces ready to be mapped, 'fixed,' explored, colonized, and ultimately, dominated" (4). Finally, Gallagher writes, pointing to a crucial question in all Caribbean writing, "the notion of 'soundings' registers the transience of the spoken word, whose impact cannot be rendered in graphic patterns. Indeed, the cognitive dissonance in my title between 'soundings' on the one hand and 'writing' on the other, adverts to the crucial tension between orality and writing in Caribbean culture" (4). As such, the work of the literary critic is described by Gallagher in terms of auditory soundings, and she argues that "in registering some of the major vibrations and gravitations of French Caribbean writing, we can move closer to a sense of the Caribbean in general" (6). Such is the work carried out in the rest of the chapter.

Perhaps the most prevalent auditory element of this experience in Césaire's work is not noise or sound, but silence, a state of voicelessness rarely evoked in the early Haitian poetry. From the first issue of the journal *Tropiques* Césaire writes of his (and Martinique's) predicament in terms of silence and voicelessness. His land, as he listens to it, is "mute and sterile," and stands in contrast to the "howling" of steel, tom–toms, and prayers that he says he hears, and which seem to stand for the sounds of the Old World—Europe, Africa, and Asia. In Martinique he hears and is aware of nothing but the "prodigious mutism" of the people, which has been brought about by violence, by the "monstrous atrophy of the voice" ("Présentation" 5).

Césaire had in fact already written of Martinique in terms of mutedness and silence. In *Cahier d'un retour au pays natal* (1939) he evokes Fort-de-France as an inert city, in which a "squalling throng" emits not its "true cry," but only a muted, half-strangled sound that does not communicate the reality of their lived situation, their "hunger [. . .] poverty [. . .] revolt [and] hatred" (*The Complete Poetry* 15). This cry nevertheless exists within and inhabits the crowd; it can be felt, Césaire says, in some internal "deep refuge of shadow" (15). An important part of Césaire's intentions in the poem will be to access this hidden, psychic refuge and to reinstate and make heard what he terms the "true cry" of the people. At this stage, however, he presents an image of his people as one that speaks, but not with its own voice, which is "so strangely chattering and mute," that paradoxically speaks constantly but never says anything (15). This image is reinforced in the very real example of Césaire's father, who is evoked as an unknowable, voiceless figure, "gnawed by one persistent ache" the cause or nature of which Césaire never learns (23). The overall effect is something like a film in which the actions of the people are out of sync with its vocal elements; there is a radical disjuncture between surface appearances and deeper realities, between the sounds the crowd thinks it is making and their meanings as they are received by Césaire the listener. Sounds are also evoked in Césaire's image of an obscure woman who "seems to float belly up on the Capot River," but who appears to merge into the water and be finally nothing but a "bundle of sonorous water" (17). It is as if the water and its sounds contain the ghostly memory of the woman, who is or was a kind of Ophelia figure, a lifeless body who dissipates into nothing, but whose silent death still echoes in the sounds of the water. Thus, the auditory component of racial, political, and cultural alienation is established and emphasized early in the poem. Sounds, or the lack of them, are indicators of Césaire's conception of lives lived out of tune with history and without awareness of the "true" self, the "true cry."

It is significant then that when Césaire presents a more satisfying memory of Caribbean life in the poem, it contains prominent auditory elements. His recollections of Christmas suggest a more felicitously rhythmic passage of time, of the seasons passing in more or less natural cycles. In particular, his memory of Christmas night comes to him first in a series of sounds: the church filled "the laughter, the whispers, the secrets, the love talk, the gossip and the guttural cacophony of a plucky singer and also boisterous pals," while the village is but a "bouquet of singing" (21). The auditory memory in turn leads to further sensory recollections: the spicy, herby tastes of black pudding; the smells of coffee, sweet anise, and rum. It is however the sounds that are the most prominent of the sensory memories. The laughter mixes with the singing, the rhythmic refrains of "*Alleluia/Kyrie eleison . . . leison . . .leison.*" It is not only, Césaire says, the voices that sing, "but the hands, the feet, the buttocks, the genitals, and your entire being that liquefies into sounds, voices and rhythm" (21). Strikingly, then, this (fleeting) sense of liberation, of apparent existential wholeness, and of living fully in the present moment is brought about primarily by sounds, by rhythmic singing, which is not simply a vocal expression, but a bodily phenomenon that engages the whole being. Significantly, too, as with the unnamed woman on the river, the memory, the sounds liquefy, as if the Christmas celebrants like the woman become bundles of "sonorous water."

The liquefying of the people and the memory is related to the transient nature of the moment, and its precariousness. Immediately after reaching the joyful crescendo there is a sharp fall and the general feeling of joy "bursts like a cloud" (21). The songs do not stop immediately, but are now charged with previously obscured anxieties as they roll "anxious and heavy through the valleys of fear, the tunnels of anguish and the fires of hell" (21). In a final, increasingly desperate, attempt to revive the ecstatic moment the people lose themselves in drinking, screaming and singing, and live for a time "as in a dream" (23). Their anxiety is apparently raised by the unconscious realization that Christmas night is passing and the new day is dawning. This realization ruptures the dreamlike state, the singing stops, and the day comes in with its sensory reminders of mundane everyday realities: "liquid manure smell of the cacao trees . . . the obsessive bells, and the rain, / the bells . . . the rain . . . / that tinkle, tinkle tinkle" (23). The "obsession" with, or of, the bells is an obsession with time, with the everyday routines of work that mark out time with their own rhythms. These rhythms contrast sharply with the sounds and rhythms of the night, which bring the people more fully to a state of complete and conscious being. Tellingly, the sounds that mark the end of the festivity are nonhuman, and seem to drown out the human voices, returning them to the alienating state of silence that is their more common condition.

Other nonhuman sounds form part of Césaire's memory of his childhood, in particular of his modest family home. The shack, he says, was blistered and cracked, its thin roof patched up with bits of kerosene cans that leaked rust into the straw roof. When the wind whistled, he says, the disparate parts of the roof "make a noise bizarre, first like the crackling of frying, then like a brand dropped into water the smoke of its twigs flying up" (25). The strange compound noise appears as a sonic marker of poverty, of a singularly desperate situation. The straw of the roof seems to be a traditional (and perhaps African-derived) material, the pastoral effectiveness of which is undermined by the presence of the kerosene tins, whose rusty liquid contaminates the straw, exacerbating the problem of the already faulty traditional roof. The hybrid roof seems to represent the nature of Césaire's family's poverty: the straw indicates a more folksy, peasant poverty that is made worse by the modern, industrial element, the rusty can. Tellingly, the description of the bizarre noise as like that of a brand being plunged into water is an image (and sound) that recalls slavery, and suggests that the shack and the people within have been branded by societal, historical, and economic forces that have changed little from the time of slavery. Again, Césaire's memory of his childhood is contained and expressed in sound, in noises that speak the complex nature of his particular experience of poverty in ways that the human voice apparently cannot.

It is further significant that Césaire's initial conception of what he thought he would achieve on going to Europe is related as a movement out of silence and toward making his voice heard. "And if all I can do is speak, it is for you I shall speak," he says, His return to Martinique will, he foresees, mark the moment of his and his people's final delivery from silence; he will, he says, be their voice, his mouth will be "'the mouth of those calamities that have no mouth'" (27).

The prophesied liberation is enacted toward the end of the poem, as Césaire attains the state of upright union with the land; as he says they stand together "hair in the wind, my hand puny in its enormous fist" (53). Significantly, he says that the force that has brought them together is not something within them but which exists above them in the sound of "voice that drills the night and the hearing like the penetrance of an apocalyptic wasp" (53). This piercing, penetrating voice is the "true cry" that he has been seeking to bring into being, one that transcends personal and collective voices, and stands as a receptacle of the truth that history has silenced. The voice pronounces that Europe has fed black peoples with lies, that it is not true that the work of humankind is finished, but is only beginning and that no single race possesses alone either beauty, intelligence, or strength (55). Césaire subsequently announces the death of "the old negritude," that is, of the old, passive and voiceless conception of black being. This death is greeted with a great cheer by Césaire—"I say hurrah"—and is followed by images of the slave ship cracking, the sounds of which, its "intestinal rumblings," indicate a deeply felt, irresistible collective growl that marks the end of his silence (57). Tellingly, too, as if to underscore the significance of sounds and voices, Césaire presents the captain of the slave ship hanging from the main yard, throwing overboard or feeding to his dogs "the biggest loudmouth" of the captive people (59).

The movement the poem effects from inertia to movement is also a movement from imposed silence to liberated clamor. Sounds are also some of the most important means of accessing memory, notably in the sections that recall Césaire's childhood. Sounds of poverty, of festivity, of work, and of silence seem to echo through the poem, demarcating the extent of Césaire's initial alienation. The control of sounds and indeed of silence is a fundamental part of Césaire's struggle with memory and history. The successful outcome of this struggle in *Cahier d'un retour au pays natal* prepares the way for his subsequent poetry, in which he continues to appropriate language and sounds as primary means of self-affirmation.

It is not that the trope of silenced alienation disappears after *Cahier d'un retour au pays natal*; rather it resurfaces continually in the poetry as an ever-present threat to the precarious appropriation of sounds and language.[15] "I inhabit," the voice says, "a long silence" (653), while Martinique remains largely a "country of silence" (551), and the colonial enterprise is seen in terms of "Crusade of silence" (379), in which "Thinking is too noisy" (467). Nature is often presented as a silent phenomenon; in "La forêt vierge" volcanoes are "silent" (129), while the forest itself grows out of the "silence of the earth" (131).[16] Suffering, too, is a silent state; tears are soundless, unheard, and ignored (121), and history is experienced as "the great silent airing of the wrenching" (677). In the poem "Grand sang sans merci" the motif of an unsettling, sterile silence reappears, and is again connected to troubled, fragmented, half-forgotten history. Césaire writes from this soundless state, "from the depths of a country of silence," where there exist still shreds of history, the charred bones that stand as reminders of slavery (351). Significantly, too, this country is also characterized by repressed voices, by "screams held back and muzzled" (351). This is the site of a historical shipwreck, of a people washed up on a beach with black sand, as if the (volcanic) sand bears the imprint of the Africans cast upon the shore. Tellingly, too, the sand has been "force-fed with a peculiar silence" (551). In resituating the strange silence from the city, as in *Cahier d'un retour au pays natal*, to the beach, Césaire also moves the motif back in time, to the

---

[15] Less commonly, silence is evoked in terms of a defiant muteness. For example, in "Ode à la Guinée" the eponymous African nation is said to be "mute after all from an astral depth of medusas" (451).

[16] At other times, the sounds of nature express the people's sadness and pain, as in the poem "Blues," where the rain downpour, the "Aguacero," is a "beautiful musician" that exists among the "lost harmonies" and the "defeated memories" and which slowly unravels the "leading rein of a sorrow" (339). See also the poem "À l'Afrique," which states that the soil contains "the burden of speech as well as of silence" (411).

point of encounter that it seems marked the beginning of the silence that still haunts him, and which has deposited its meaning and memory into the very sand of the shore, which is itself a kind of threshold between the Old World and the New, and between sound and silence.

The prophetic moment, the sense of future liberation that marks the end of many of Césaire's poems is almost without exception a clamorous event, as in the poem "Millibars de l'orage" with its "noise of tears" (361) and in "Conquête de l'aube," which the dawn announces its ultimate conquest of the "Marvelous death of nothing" in a "glory of scarlet-barked free trumpets" (123). The clamor of the free trumpets is seen as a force of appropriation, which steals from the "great voice"—perhaps official, accepted speech or language—its sharper, more raucous and energetic elements, the incendiary and heady "cavalcade, tumults," a collective noise that proclaims the death of silence and inertia. Ultimately, sounds are for Césaire the means by which the Caribbean will truly (and violently) come into being: "I shall raise a cry so violent," says the speaker in "Corps perdu" "that I shall splatter the entire sky... and "I shall command the islands to exist" (499).

It seems finally difficult for Césaire to visualize history in any clear way. Significantly, colonialism is seen as "the invasion of opacity" (663), and is said to have blinded Africa, and by extension the African diaspora: "your clairvoyance," the poetic voice says, "they've put out its eyes" (629). Typically, visual images of the past remain opaque, obscured, and deformed by the traumas of the past—"I inhabit," the speaker says, "an obscure will" (653)—or else the visual "dissolves" and is supplanted by sounds (393). Sounds, on the other hand, contain memories and are the means by which access to the past is gained, as for instance in "Corps perdu," where the speaker says "I hiss yes I hiss very ancient things / of serpents of cavernous things" (499). Seeing is often associated with racial violence, as in the poem "Lynch," in which the perpetrators of the crime are said to have an "eye without shores without memories," while the victim by contrast exists and persists in the realm of sounds, retaining a "perfidious chant" that lives in "the indestructible ruins of his silence" (375).[17] Césaire's mistrust of the eye, and his association of seeing with the white colonizer, are suggested strongly near the end of the poem "Annonciation," where he writes of a "green eye ringed with yellow oxide loaded with moons noon eye loaded with torches" (133). The color of the eye seems to associate it with the European, while the yellow oxide ring

---

[17] See also the poem "Nous savoir...," in which Césaire evokes the collective "heavy heart," which is a "huge rock tumbled hollowed from within / by some ineffable music held prisoner / of a melody nevertheless to be saved from Disaster" (549).

that surrounds it suggests that there is something deathly about it, that its humanity has been tainted by the chemical, which is related to industrialization, and which in turn is associated with the "torches," the combination of light and fire that can be read as a reference to the effects of colonialism. Significantly, it is the eye that is associated with the European and the destructive effects of colonialism. This is further suggested in the poem "Le temps de la liberté," which celebrates the end of colonialism in Africa and which imagines a newly confident Africa, one that fights as never before and that "looks . . . right into the eyes of the governors of prey / of the perishable bankers" (601). The association of the eye with power is clear here; the ability to look the European in the eye implies equality. More commonly, Césaire writes from a position of imposed inferiority, and is less at ease in the visual realm. By implication, it is in the auditory dimension that Césaire feels most free—he writes for example of the "ultimate power of my mouth" (595)—away from the deadening gaze of the European. However, for all that he has difficulty rendering the past in visual terms, history remains for Césaire a constant, haunting preoccupation. When he visits the past, he is often attuned to its sounds, as if they are more living remnants of the past than the visual images. History in this sense echoes through Césaire's work and into present time. If he is constantly struggling against alienation, and if he vacillates between this state of alienation and the tentative realization of a fuller Antillean being, he seems by contrast more "at home" in the realm of sounds.

In his poetry, Césaire reaffirms the importance of the auditory realm in Caribbean experience. In reading his work (and Caribbean literature more generally) we should pay particular attention to its auditory elements, and to the ways in which sounds interact with subjectivity in history and contemporary reality. By listening to Aimé Césaire, we can hear echoes of the past, its reverberations in the present, and also begin to discern something of the shape of the future.

Listening to Damas

Similar patterns of sound and time may be found in the poetry of Césaire's fellow Negritude poet, Léon Gontran Damas—sounds as means of recording, marking, and breaking with colonial experience. Like any writer or artist of his generation, educated in the French colonial system, Damas would have been exposed to a great cacophony of sounds and rhythms, as Carrie Noland suggests: "different sonic patterns (including those of jazz and African or African-derived forms) might have impressed themselves on

Damas at various points during his lifetime; however, they would have been mingled with, among others, the rhythms of the French spoken at the Lycée Schoelcher and the rhythms of Mallarmé that so moved Damas when he first started writing" (*Voices of Negritude* 148). As such, as Noland states, Damas's poems "contain a rich palimpsest of rhythmic influences" (148). Edwin C. Hill similarly lays the emphasis on rhythm in his discussion of the sonic qualities of Damas's poetry: "His entire oeuvre rhythmically stages the New World black subject's struggle with French imperial culture and history by figuring it as a percussive series of temporal breaks and corporeal seizures" (*Black Soundscapes* 109). Hill further draws comparisons between Damas, Césaire, and Fanon:

> While Césaire creates an apocalyptic *fin du monde* in order to recover a primal *bombement* ("The Thoroughbreds") and Fanon distances himself from this screaming explosion of blackness, Damas skips and stumbles through the beat, for "It's less a matter of starting over / than continuing to be" (31). The black beats of negritude rarely portray a hero who has not faltered, yet Damas tactically follows through on this line of complicity in a distinct way, notably by drawing out the resonance between the musical-corporeal beatings of the past and those of popular culture of the interwar years. (115)

Drawing another, more fundamental distinction with Césaire in particular, Hill says that if Césaire's work "represents the dominant beat of negritude [...] Damas's contributions to black rhythm and time can be considered part of an overlooked genealogy of negritude in the minor." In contrast to what Hill calls the "high modernist tone of Césaire, and to the icy-hot response to the scream and the beat in Fanon," Damas, he says, "engages in an 'aesthetics of misery' [...] largely rejected and effaced in negritude and Fanonist discourse" (122). The idea of "negritude in the minor" is helpful in identifying Damas's uses of sound in his poetry: as both Noland and Hill stress, rhythm is no doubt the primary marker of sound (and history) in Damas's work, but it is one part of a broader use of sound, both as a feature of style and form and as a theme in itself, and again, as a marker of time, its subjective and collective experience.

Sounds in fact figure prominently in Damas's poetry from the opening pages of his first collection, *Pigments*.[18] The poem "Ils sont venus ce soir" evokes the rhythm of the tom-tom as a sonic marker of Africa at the moment of colonial contact:

---

[18] See Carrie Noland's discussion of rhythm in Damas's poetry in *Voices of Negritude in Modernist Print: Aesthetic Subjectivity, Diaspora, and the Lyric Regime*, 148–60. Translations of Damas are mine.

>   They came that night when the
>   tom
>   tom
>   rolled with
>   rhythm
>   upon
>   rhythm (13)

Quite significantly, this moment alters the nature of the dance, and creates a frenetic state that shifts the sensory attention away from sounds and onto vision, as the poem evokes "the frenzy/of the eyes," which in turn are related to the frenzy of the hands and of the "feet of statues," which suggest the ways in which the contact interrupts the rhythm, the flow, and the movement of the dance. The eyes seem able to transfix in this way; the visual contact throws the dancers off-step and diverts attention to the seen world, which controls and deadens the other senses, notably that of sound and its corollary, rhythm. Damas indicates the deadening effects of this sensory-induced transformation in the middle section of the poem, where he wonders "how many ME ME ME / have died / since they came that night when the / tom / tom / rolled" (13). In this early poem then, Damas seems almost instinctively aware that colonial contact involved a sensory struggle in which the "natural" sounds of African rhythms were muted, distorted, or thrown out of step by the colonial interruption, and the sensory adjustment it brought. The eyes have a peculiar power, which in this case marks the beginning of a long and deadly colonial history.

A close acquaintance of Countee Cullen, Langston Hughes, and Richard Wright, Damas was considerably more interested in the question of race in the United States than were Césaire and Senghor. Damas also invokes black American music more insistently and directly than either Césaire or Senghor did, and his poetry is intimately attuned to the sounds, tones, and rhythms of blues and jazz. The sounds of black American music often provide a reprieve from the frustrations of Damas's colonized reality. In the poem "Trêve," for example, it is the musical sounds that seem to create the titular truce or respite from the "toadying," the "bootlicking," and the "attitude of the hyperassimilated" that the poem condemns. The opening lines introduce these American sounds:

>   Respite of the blues
>   of beating on the piano
>   of a muted trumpet
>   of madness stamping its feet
>   to the satisfaction of rhythm (23)

These sounds not only signify contemporary black resistance, but also carry memories of the past, as in the poem "Il est des nuits," which evokes nights "without name [...] without moon" in which the speaker is taken "to the point of asphyxiation" by the "odor of blood / spurting / from every muted trumpet" (25). Interestingly, the sound of the trumpet does not evoke a visual image of the past, but the smell of blood. As with Césaire, history is virtually impossible to access through visual images, and it is only through the other senses, notably through sounds, and in this case smells, that memories seep into consciousness.

Sounds and rhythms are sometimes used to make connections between the Caribbean and Europe, and between the human and the animal, as in the poem "En file indienne," which draws a comparison between the "beasts of burden / who pound in Europe / the still-undecided dawn," and the "strange abnegation / of the morning rays / sated / that enrhythm in the Caribbean / the hips of women porters / carrying in single file" (31). The hammering sound of the animals' hooves is related to the rhythmic movement of the Caribbean women, themselves burdened through work and history to the point that their existence is a form of "abnegation" as he puts it, a state of self-denial that erases and denies identity and relates their status to the "undecided" dawn of Europe, the feeling communicated in the poem of living in a state of uncertain, endless beginnings, and of history being similarly stalled. The idea that there is a rhythmic connection between the European beasts of burden and the Caribbean women is reinforced in the second stanza's reversal of the syntax of the first so that the Caribbean women are evoked initially and then compared in the same terms to the beasts of burden to create a sort of chiasmus, a swinging, rhythmic movement that sets one stanza as the confirmation of the other, and the condition of the animal as a reflection of that of the human. If history is stalled, it is at least in part because of the chiasmic, self-denying, self-negating movement enacted in the poem to suggest a similar negation of the human, its movements—silent in this case—related to the hooves of the beasts of burden, which itself is an apparent metaphor for human existence in industrial Europe. The human exists still in the nonindustrialized world, but is a form of silent echo of the status of the European. It is also stalled as the sounds of industrialization are louder, stronger, more rhythmic even than those of the counter discourse, the sounds of political ideas and movements that may counter the effects of the industrial.

This idea of a relatively unheard counterdiscourse, out of sync and out of rhythm is suggested in the poem "Dans son attente," which evokes the image and sounds of an omnipresent authority figure—"One more cop to fill the ear / with a headache for the jobless" (33). The policeman "fills the ear" of the unemployed, creating a headache and leaving no space for other sounds, which are in any case unheard or without rhythm, as is suggested in the subsequent image of the "bellies that swell / the International / without a metronome" (33). The notion of the song without rhythm or time suggests its ineffectiveness against the crushing rhythms and sounds of order and work and authority, embodied in the figure and sounds of the policemen shouting in the ears of the unemployed workers. The conflict in these poems is therefore enacted, felt, and heard through rhythm and sounds, and history is itself experienced in these ways, as a conflict of forces that impose themselves through sounds; history enters the ears of the workers through either the shouts of the policeman or the rising, swelling words and sounds of the workers' songs so that it is experienced in bodily terms, literally in the guts, and the control of sounds and rhythms is a necessary component of the broader conflict that the poems evoke.

Bodies, sounds, and memory are closely related in the poem "Hoquet," which uses the titular case of the hiccups as a trigger for memories of childhood, notably a mother figure inculcating the importance of good manners to her young son, the recollection of which is followed by the refrain that calls for the mother to speak of the "disaster," the unspoken elements of time and history that are silenced and forgotten. The imposition of French language is part of the mother's (and society's) general culture of silence and forgetting, as is clear in the mother's command to the son:

> Shut up
> Did I or did I not tell you that you had to speak French?
> The French of France
> The French of the French
> French French (37)

The perceived need to speak "proper" French is related in the child's mind to the violin lessons that he is sent to, and which he misses, preferring to learn the banjo, an instrument that is dismissed by the mother in the final lines of the poem:

> No sir
> > You will learn that our kind do not put up with
> no ban
> no jo
> no gui
> no tar
> the *mulattoes* don't do that
> so leave that to the *negroes* (38)

The color- and class-based thinking of the mother is related in the poem to her insistence on the use of proper French, and notions of respectability that promote the violin over the more popular instrument, which, much like the popular language, is seen as the preserve of the lower classes. The sound and bodily shaking of the hiccups triggers the memory, which is itself all about sounds—the hectoring of the mother, the need to speak standard French, and the putatively more refined sounds of the violin, all of which are intended to create and conserve order, while the child hears behind or within it all another sound, the rumbling of history, the great "disaster" as he puts it that no one wants to talk about, but which is nonetheless present, even and especially in the actions and words of the mother.

In a sense, Damas's poetry is the testimony of the disaster that the mother will not speak of, and it has to do with history—he writes of "The inexorably sad days" which "never ceased to be / in memory / of what was / my truncated life," and of the "daze" that he feels still, a sense of being profoundly stunned by history (47). The disaster thus also has to do with present lived reality, and the ways in which history lives and directs present experience. History, as in the poem "Limbé," is considered to be rooted, paradoxically, in "deracination," which relates to colonial life but also to his own experiences in Europe. In the poem, the speaker wishes to recover his "courage" and "audacity," so that he may be, he says, "become myself again / new myself" (44). History has moreover connotations of theft: he writes that "they robbed the space that was mine / customs / life / song/ / rhythm . . . / words / speech," images that restate the importance of sounds, music, and rhythm to the processes of deracination and the wish for an end to the social and personal disaster that he writes of. Indeed, the idea of being out of step or rhythm appears to be particularly significant, as in the same list of lost elements of himself he evokes "cadence" and "measure," terms that relate to rhythm and music but also to a broader sense of life being out of step with itself and with people and the places in which they live. Also, when he does strike a more defiant note, his act of resistance often involves sounds, as at the end of the poem "Pour Sûr," where he writes of all that torments him, "colonization / civilization / assimilation," and that while he waits for their demise his unnamed addressee "will hear me often / slam the door" (53).

Similarly, in his more assured and defiant poems, Damas adopts a prophetic voice that foresees, or rather hears in advance a future state where he will have overcome all that holds him back. In "Bientôt," he predicts that soon he will not only have danced, "I will not only have sung," acts and sounds that are not enough in themselves to free him, but that in the poem at least, through repetition, create a rhythmic energy and sound that suggest impending, inevitable liberation (55). Sounds have this capacity to change time and circumstance as they are not as fixed in time and history as the visual images he evokes, for example, of slavery, the "good negro" as he puts it in the poem "Rappel," whose memory floats in a sense into the present to the accompaniment of a reed flute that plays "on the hills some slave tunes" (63). Sounds are not so imprisoned by time, partly because they can be recreated in the present, while the images of the past remain relatively inaccessible and fixed. The sound of the reed flute, already situated in the poem in the freer space of the colonial hillsides—while below in the fields "zombies roam around" (63)—is an expression of freedom through sound that is timeless, and once it is heard, cannot be unheard. Human sounds, too, echo through time, such as the speaker's "appalling laugh," which he says is made "to repel the specter of the hounds tracking down maroons," and which counters what he calls the "noise" of the colonists' "degeneration" (66).

Ultimately, in many regards, Damas's evocation and understanding of sounds echo those of Césaire, and he largely shares Césaire's idea that dance, music, rhythm, and sound are their racial property; as he puts it in the long poem *Black-Label*: "hip-swaying negro / for dance is negro / and rhythm is negro / for art is negro / and movement is negro" (52). Indeed, it is these elements—sound, music, rhythm, dance—that, Damas suggests, recolonized Paris in a sense, through the presence of black artists and musicians, in a way that ultimately underlines the strategic importance of sounds in reappropriating notions of culture and race, and in rendering place, chiefly the place of exile for Damas, habitable:

> PARIS—Navel of the world
> at the mercy of AFRICA
> of its voice
> its regrets
> of its joy
> its sadness
> at the mercy of the fever of rhythm . . .
> of the muffled trumpet . . .
> "The White Man at the School of the Negro" (53)

Glissant

Sang Rivé/Riveted Blood

In contrast to Césaire and Damas, Glissant rarely if ever evokes rhythm, dance, or indeed sound as markers of blackness or anticolonialism, at least in any straightforward way. Rather, the shape of his poetry is largely fragmented, the sounds muffled, pre-echoes of language and being, but also future-oriented scraps of noise from which a different idea of Caribbean being might one day emerge. The volume *Sang rivé* (1961) is "a collection of fragments, bits and pieces growing out of other works in which the pieces did not belong" (Humphries, "Introduction" xxiv).[19] The poem itself is natural, too, in the sense that it is "mutable and organic," much like Glissant's idea of history, "which is always moving and changing even though it is in the past; *what is past is never finished*, what is done is never complete, what has been lost is always present, and the apparently fixed events of History are subsumed in a perpetual dance of changes" (Humphries xxv). If Glissant is better known as a novelist and essayist, he began his career as a poet and remained attached to poetry throughout his career. As Dash says, "This sustained refusal to abandon poetry or even to recognise the conceptual boundary that traditionally exists between poetry and prose, creative and critical writing, is central to the understanding of Glissant's entire literary enterprise" (*Edouard Glissant* 26). Indeed, Glissant "elevates poetry to primary status in relation to novelistic writing and arguably philosophical writing too" (Coombes, *Édouard Glissant*, 17). As Glissant says, "poetry has always been at the crux of literature, because poetry is the only literary artform which states without stating whilst nevertheless making statements" (qtd. in Coombes, 17). Poetic art, "the only imaginable form of 'exploration,'" Glissant writes, "is a phase of the possible" (*Treatise on the Whole World* 81). Also, poetry for Glissant has a particular relation to time: it is one of the truths of poetry, he says, that it is "always in the future, always marked with the sign of that which is to come" (*Treatise on the Whole World* 89). The sounds of his poetry are, in this sense, a means of exploring the possible, and they echo through his poems, from past to present to future, never dying, forever resonating. They are also the fundamental elements of *langage*, as he explains:

> The poet, beyond the language that he uses, but mysteriously within that very language, on the level of he language and in its margin, is a builder of *langage*. The clever but mechanical game-playing of languages may soon appear outdated, but not the work that churns away at the base of *langage*. The poet attempts to rhizomatically connect his place to the totality, to diffuse the totality into his place: permanence in the moment and vice versa, the elsewhere in the here and vice versa. That is the small amount of divination that he claims for himself, faced with the derelictions of our reality. He does not play the game of the universal,

---

[19] As Dash notes, "Traces of *Un champ d'îles* and *La terre inquiète*, as well as *Soleil de la conscience*, can be found in these collected poems" (*Edouard Glissant* 58).

which would not be a way of establishing Relation. He always supposes, from the first word of his poem: "I speak to you in your language, and I hear you in my *langage*." (*Treatise on the Whole World* 75)

The work that "churns away" at the base of *langage*, as he puts it, has therefore to do with speaking, the poetic work of finding the possible, and just as important, finding ways of expressing the possible. And yet, the poet speaks in one language, that of the other, and hears in his own *langage*, which he defines as "a shared attitude, in a given community, of confidence or mistrust in the [*langue* or *langues*] it uses" (*Caribbean Discourse* 120). As Britton puts it, Glissant's poetics attempts to "wrest [. . .] a *langage* from the colonial *langue*" (*Edouard Glissant and Postcolonial Theory* 47). There is therefore a degree of discord and mishearing in these exchanges: what we read and hear in the work is put to us in one language, and yet any Relation established in and by the poem, he hears, he insists, in his own *langage*, in a way that echoes some of the earliest (mis)communications studied in our chapter on slavery and the unpredictable ways in which words and sounds are expressed and heard.

Dedicated "to every tortured geography," *Sang rivé* "from the outset points to an interest in landscape as well as the secretions, eruptions, deposits and residues produced from the extremes of nature and, by extension, extreme states of feeling" (Dash, *Edouard Glissant* 58). The first, untitled, piece in the collection seems to be a reflection on the nature and functions of poetry, and crucially says that it is "Not [. . .] deaf," but is something explosive and noisy, "eruptions yielding to earth's effervescence" (*The Collected Poems* 5).[20] The work navigates, the poem states, through "matter itself," which suggests that poetry and language precede the work and have substance in themselves, which constitutes something of a radical rethinking of the relationship between language, poetry, and the work. In effect, this confirms the idea proposed in this book that there was poetry in the earliest instances of black life in the Caribbean, and that the sonic culture of those early arrivals as heard by Labat, Descourtilz, and others echoes insistently over time, calling out for skilled listeners like Glissant, Césaire, Damas, and others, including musicians of all kinds, to tune in to those sounds and their innate poetry.

Placing the collection in the context of Glissant's vast oeuvre, Dash notes tellingly that the poems in the collection "are important as sensuous explorations of themes that would be more politically and philosophically focused in the early novels" (*Edouard Glissant* 59). Indeed, chief among the sensory means

---

[20] All references to Glissant's poetry are from *The Collected Poems*.

of exploring themes of time and history is listening, and poetry for Glissant is made up of sounds, "first cries, innocent rumors," the poet writes, which have an almost ocular function in that they are "untimely witnesses to this endeavor" (5). They are paradoxical elements, "perfectly fusing as their imperfections meet," and which persuade one to stop at the point where the speaker situates himself and his work, "at the uncertain—that which trembles, wavers, and ceaselessly becomes–like a devastated land—scattered" (5). The "tortured geography" is not therefore only a spatial, physical metaphor; it also refers to a mode of being, and to poetry, which here is characterized by dispersal and scattering, and language and sounds are not tools as such for the poet, but elements that precede the work, through which the poet and the work navigate in acts of incomplete memory and imperfect recuperation, "always dislocated, always recovered, and beyond completion" (5).

Seeing and hearing are apparently fused in the poem "One Single Season," which is subtitled "Eyes Voice," and which also fuses darkness and light in the opening line, in which "Torches confess to the black colored pond of night," an image that seems to recall a plantation scene (6). The speaker situates himself in a littoral space, and in silence: "Seas, across you my silence patiently awakens" (6). The silence is the quietude of unremembered past times: "The past the past / Ah! stony memory rise up amid the stalks of cane. / Each bush of memory conceals a sniper" (6). The short poem ends with further oblique imagery of the plantation—"Pounding a mill upon our heads/Fires cough in our nights"—and with an affirmation of memory and being, expressed through sound: "Whatever man does, the cry takes root" (6). The cry may in this early poem be related to the Césairean cry, a sort of screaming awareness of history, a memory that lives in voice, and just as seeing and hearing, and darkness and light are apparently fused as one element, so the cry is part of the silence, it can be heard in the silence, just as the silence is a part of the cry, and of the soundscape of memory that the poem tunes into.

History has a silencing effect, in Europe as much as in the Caribbean, as is suggested in the poem "November," in which Europe is presented as "a field of nails. No longer hearing the rusted stream of wild butterflies on a thick day," which suggests the deadening effects of industrialization on nature, but also its silencing, or at least an end to hearing, as if the sound has been turned down on nature as the visual image predominates. Lack of sound spreads, as part of the "mission" the poem critiques, to the Caribbean, where the intention was "to mislead the word through the rich deafness of scorched Tropics. Like a summation of memory-intoxicated fruits in the mute desire of the banana trees" (7). These final images suggest a similar process of industrialized destruction over a muted, silenced landscape, but here the deafness is "rich," a further suggestion that for Glissant silence and muteness are not empty, inchoate phenomena, but have substance, which is related to time and memory, and are not only about the past, but are oriented to the future, in the "mute desire" of the natural object, if desire is taken as a future-oriented state, a silent wish for a different time and state to come.

It is quite striking that some of the most difficult, impenetrable, and perhaps also pessimistic of poems in this collection are those in which seeing and vision are invoked. The eyes do not clarify or elucidate; rather they blur and obscure, as in the short fragment, "Black Smoke," which opens with the image of a "Mad madwoman breadless eyes," which correlates madness with unseeing eyes, which in this case seem related to the woman's hunger or poverty, the state of being "breadless" (12). That visual, unseeing image is immediately followed by a sound that can almost be heard, "the blackbird's cry blooming in its shadow of elderberry" (12). Immediately, there is a contrast drawn between the human—mad, hungry, unseeing—and the animal—sonic, natural, healthy, "blooming." The bird is free, as is its song; the human is seen but unseeing, forever subject to what the poem terms "the master's gaze," its image controlled and defined, yet also blurred and deformed, as is suggested in the final image of the "glazed street engraved upon the dizzying cataract of totems," which reinforces the idea of the visual as a powerful yet flawed cipher for identity, and the lens, the eye, the symbol as elements that blur and render opaque objects and people, so that they never come into full, knowable being, but rather shimmer hazily, unknown, like the madwoman, to themselves or to others.

Sounds of nature and music also feature in the poem "Lavas," in an address to an unnamed creator figure, "You, who have struck up the sarabande and the vertigo of the forests," in whose "forest resounds the musical salvo of daybreak (my unknown life)" (13). The forest emits an almost orchestral sound, which is related in the second image to daybreak, no doubt metaphorically, in that the speaker expresses his lack of knowledge of or connection to his beginnings—nature begins again every day at dawn, but human life has one beginning and separation from it leads to an unending state of estrangement, and a sense that human existence does not move in the timeless cycles of nature. This in turn leads to a sense of living on the threshold of a life about to begin—the speaker says "the land heaves us in imminence," as if without a sense of beginning one's life never truly takes its course, and rather than exist fully in the sonorous forest, the speaker, and perhaps also the writer, "sleep in the river to dig up the silence," the voiceless sediments of time and existence through which they must sift in order to understand what has been lost (13).

The country, the poem says, "pound[s] its hips against the blindness Races races," which suggests a land and a people again on the threshold of themselves, a coming to be driven by sound and dance and working against the visually imposed notion of race (14). The speaker writes "beneath the tambourine drum of baobabs," therefore in or as he says below rhythm, in a poetry that is, he says "flesh" and that defies those who "sew the white-threaded silence," so that his poetry is written against both blindness and silence, states imposed by history and the idea of race and that maintain the poet and the people in the state of imminence that is its historical legacy and their contemporary reality.

There are clear echoes of Césaire's sonically driven, apocalyptic style in the speaker's wish that the poet may "expel [...] the whip the master who entombs and the canes that hiss with waiting, pain and blood, his poetry and fury of poetry" (14). Again, the idea of imminence, of being in abeyance, is suggested in the canes that "hiss with waiting," the sound an almost menacing indicator of the degree of pressure that results from living a suspended, unbegun life. Significantly, the speaker tells his addressee to "listen" to the "trumpetings, / leaning against the silence," therefore the first step is to hear the sounds that do not so much pierce the silence as exist alongside it, and exert pressure on it (14). The silence and the sounds that wait to be heard are related to time, the former being the past and present of slavery and colonialism, while the latter are future-oriented, related to times and sounds to come, when historical wandering and "errancy" will be "ensnared, made obsolete": "when when and when," the speaker asks "the emaciated bells of the inaudible?" (14).

It is not that the state of unhearing imminence places the speaker outside of history, either temporally or spatially. Rather, he is acutely aware of his presence, physically and in time:

> Yet I am present in history down to the marrow. Embedded secularly:
> in this afternoon which I have uttered as vigorously as ignorance: it
> moves its gravel within me. I wait, eating poetry, roses Yes
> I am measured piece by piece
> in nocturnal
> music. (15)

He feels his presence; his time is the afternoon, an in-between time, in which he waits, "eating poetry," he says, while his being is measured in the music that exists beyond the afternoon, in the "nocturnal music" that he can sense, hear, or rather forehear in his state of waiting. As he puts it later, man is "this luminous desire of song," not just desiring but desire itself, a future-oriented being that wants and needs to hear and be heard (15).

The forest remains a repository of sounds: it "howls at life," as if its sounds told a different story to that communicated in the human sounds and silences that preoccupy the speaker. The forest is feminized; it is a "vibrant [...] queen" that resounds to the "tranquil pounding of dawns," and its own "voice of accosted brilliance" (15). Not to hear these sounds, not to know the forest is to the speaker a form of deprivation: "poverty is ignorance of the land," he says, "passion is that which is imagined," and in this poem that imagination is made up of sounds, the natural orchestra of the forest, the beating of drums, the unheard music that is desired, and which is at once a marker of potential future liberation and of the current state of muted imminence (15).

It is also telling that in the section titled "Mirrors," the emphasis is less on reflected visual images than on sounds echoing and reverberating as the terms of comparison and difference. The poem "Cities" evokes a place described as "some object of silence upon the wool of noise," where "thought organizes the display of rags and charm lingers indefinitely" (19). This place is then contrasted with another undetermined site referred to only as "there," where "enormous cats scratch the earth, steel of silence and belief without purpose" (19). This second site appears to be an industrialized country, the enormous cats may refer to machinery, and the "steel of silence" is compared to the initial mention of silence; if the two sites are contrasted, it is silence that relates them and that appears to echo between them as they both are driven to different degrees by a system that as the final words say has a belief in itself but no discernible purpose.

The mirror motif reappears in the poem "Confession," which opens with the statement that "every face is a cry a shattered mirror," a phrase that again fuses the visual with the aural, the face with the cry, and which is followed by a further reference to silence: the face "weighs in its hands the despair / Before it, trembling as silence encroaches" (20). Silence is related to a malignant external force, spread by "one who tortures," who "instills, contaminates / Offends and rises through himself / So he may attack in absolute silence" (21). The speaker situates himself temporally in the aftermath of the attack, where as he says "the vanquished remain, a dispersed and occulted confession" (21). The confession theme suggests historical sin and the need for penitence on behalf of the torturer, while the silenced and vanquished exist unseen and unheard, forgotten but persistent remnants of history.

Un champ d'îles

Where *Sang rivé* is a radically fragmented volume, fittingly so as it chronicles the experiences of historical dispersal and virtual destruction, *Un champ d'îles* (1953) is comparatively a more structured and ordered work, at least in terms of form, which alternates between long stanzas of prose and shorter movements of four-line stanzas, so that the overall effect is of a greater sense of control and order, however much the meaning of the work remains at times uncompromisingly obscure. For Dash, the meanings of the volume are "accumulated" across the poems "and convey a sense of wandering and drifting that establishes a clear aesthetic distance from the Manichean combativeness of Negritude" (*Edouard Glissant* 38). It is quite telling, too, that from the first stanza of this collection, there are numerous references to the "language" of the islands, one that the speaker hears in the landscape, in history, and in the silences to which he is attuned in his early poetic collections, and which in this volume are incorporated into this evolving, more systematized idea of a language of place, time, and being. It is not that the fragments disappear; rather, they are understood as part of an evolving system, where language is forming out of and in the silences, as in this passage: "Oh out of this language that is every stone, enfleshed and raising flesh up over itself, out of this violent and gently obscure language that is the root, endowed with flesh and pushing flesh underneath itself, here is the rough draft" (33). The writing may amount still to a "rough draft," but there is a stronger sense in this volume of substance, of language "enfleshed" with and by itself, constituting something in itself, and growing out of the undetermined "root," a term that is not used at all in *Sang rivé*, but which is introduced here in a way that suggests a more assured notion of the language of place and time that he is striving for, and which remains "violent and gently obscure."

The sudden presence of sound and noise seems to surprise the speaker: he asks "what can be this cry, this shatter of panes in the voice!" and the cry is described as being "coiled around the sails of life," and to be moving "toward this language that loses itself, and then takes itself back again" (33). Importantly, the language loses itself first, and then takes possession of itself, so that absence and loss and silence are constituent parts of the new language. As the speaker goes on to say, this is a paradoxical language, at once sonorous and muted, the "thunderclap of your silence," as he puts it.

Just as the language is born from a process of loss and rebirth, so the sense of place and belonging is understood as a "rebeginning," not a unique, originary moment, but a second, deferred start that follows and is perhaps also concurrent with the historical beginning, and its fragments and silences (33). The speaker evokes a figure, "fearless to enunciate his being [. . .] so that he might be present," which quite clearly draws a link between enunciation and being—the voice announces and instantiates the subject's presence, which is further related to a recuperated sense of "memory and hope, opposite flowers, in this field of flowers (33–34). The same figure is then referred to as "he [who] no longer fears the affection (of naming himself 'I' in this earth)," which further reinforces the idea of the subject's less tentative sense of presence (34). This figure, referred to throughout in the third person ("he"), is compared throughout by the speaker to another, second person figure, addressed directly as "you." The identities of the two figures are never made clear, and any understanding of them is arrived at through the contrasts the speaker draws between them. For example, in contrast to the third-person figure, who is present in both physical and psychological terms, the other is absent: "From this work, however you are absent," but the absence is also a kind of presence, or part of "every presence," as the speaker says (34). The contrast seems also to be between a more human figure, and a kind of ethereal, indeterminate being, a kind of creator at times, not fixed to one place, but which seems to have to do with memory and time, and perhaps also nature, as the poem teems with natural imagery, which does not so much give comfort, or frame the human figure's sense of presence as render his experience all the more difficult to comprehend. The speaker addresses the second-person figure in ways that draw comparisons with the other: "O you, present in this work, yet it is not you who in the plain bewail the rootedness of your solitude, you know not, right down through here, in the leaves, this labor of mutations and legends, the tortured screech owl of language, the wave that unites its seaword with the earth, and the appetite of living in the midst of this fire!" (35). The understanding of both figures is thus created through opposition and negation—saying what one is and is not, and what the other can and cannot do, so that uncertainty and impermanence, and a residual sense of imminence characterize the human figure's sense of presence: "This he pushes his fields toward the stranding sand, the heavy word.—And where now? He asks" (35).

The "you" figure that is often, as in the longer quotation above, addressed in an accusatory tone, may also be related to poetry itself, to writing, and the difficulty the speaker has in making poetry of the indeterminate, fragmented places and times he evokes, but which are at least identified as islands. In what senses can poetry as he knows it be used to imagine these places, their histories, and the memories that are at once omnipresent, invisible, and unspoken? It is telling in this regard that he compares the place to a poem: "Let all this place be mute like an orchardless poem"—a place without sounds is like a poem without nature. The idea of imminence is reintroduced in the image of the poem "hesitat[ing] at the water's edge," the human figure remaining "at the frontier of you" (35), and "the word hesitat[ing] at the poem's threshold" (36). At the same time, even though he has not quite begun his work, he is still behind time in a way: "He who is late in saying what cannot be said, he establishes himself in the dawn" (35). The figure is troubled by "opacity," and grows only "in the assurance of his voice," and yet remains unsure of what to say (35). "What would he say," the speaker asks, and the answer suggests that poetry and language will never quite coincide with the poet figure's being, as he will be "forever the fiber of your gaze, foreign to the fiber of his, forever" (35). Therefore, vision—the gaze—will not, cannot be reflected directly in sound and poetry, and this in turn explains the importance of silence, which is affirmed as the mode through which the poet figure will communicate: his silence will "call to you the foliage of grandeur where the sea is born," and will exist in "spectral layers of silence," as "mute as any splendor" (36).

The first movement of the poem has an almost prefatory function in the way it ruminates on poetry, the poet figure, and the possibility of writing poetry amid a history and a natural environment that are experienced in terms of absences and voids. At the end of this first movement there does seem to be a sense of achievement, that from all the confusion and opacity a poem can finally emerge, and this poem is brought "back yet again to the stubborn faith of this presence, amid the crowd!" (36). The poem is almost conjured out of this shared faith, this crowd that recalls Césaire's muted, absent-present crowd and is also finally established as part of a broader, global history: "O poem born of you, who are born to the world's toil" (36).

The second movement takes on a more recognizably poetic form, in regular four-line stanzas that stand in contrast to the dense prose lines of the first part. The images suggest an island, a bay, the sky, the seas, where "every word is lost [. . .] / In the silence of Waters" and where "the landscape is an abrupt sieve / Of words pushed under the moon" (37). The island has been left behind by its own history, abandoned at once by the "whirlings / Of adventure on the drums," the "wolfpack of words and its prey," and the "immoderation of cutlasses," to leave behind a form of "music [that] is to the heart / Like a hamlet of lassitude" (38). The island is feminized: "the whole island is soon woman / Full of pity of herself by clenching / Her despair in her naked heart" (38). The island itself is "filled with pity" and "pitiable," and "lives on words derived / Like a halo of shipwrecked people / Searching for rocks" (39). In place of these derived words, the island-woman needs "words that last [. . .] words of Moderation," a language that seems to exist in the sounds of the "hardly silenced drum" that "in the innermost depths henceforth stirs" (39). Words and sounds are related to depths, to sediments of time and history, so that "every word is an earth / Whose subsoil must be searched" (40). Drums and rhythm are part of this sedimented, dormant history: "There sleep the tom-toms / [. . .] Inside the subsoil of moderate words" (40). Whereas the first movement of the work sets out the conditions in which poetry might be possible in such a historical context, so the second movement suggests the particular ways in which language and sound can be heard so that they can transmit memory and history, but also speak of the current time. "Of pain have we made a word / A new word which multiplies," the poem says, before evoking an image of the drummer: "He who arranges his drums and cloths / In the sandness of words," so that the drum, and music, and rhythm are in the language, the new words that are like sand, and through which time, memory, and meaning sift as if through a filter of words and sounds.

The drummer "accepts the noise of words," the "storm full of words" and that the speaker says will "lead you to your threshold" (42–43). In this coming linguistic storm the drums become part of the noise of the sea, "streaming / Awaiting the sudden crash of billowblades / The awakening of dancers on the water," which is part of the "noise of fraternity" that the poem has been reaching toward, and that it hears finally in the drum, the new words, the sounds of nature and history that are part of the clamorous noise to the threshold of which the poem gradually advances (43).

It is not that the sound and noise revivify the island; immediately after arriving at the clamorous threshold, the speaker insists that "all this place is dead" (44). He does so as he returns to the dense prose and long paragraph structure of the first part of the poem. There is nevertheless a sense of having crossed a threshold into a new time or situation, which is communicated in the phrases "Nevermore shall the wind go by the word," and "Nevermore, oh never shall dawn go forth saying dawn, 'I am the awakening of eyes and the light of depths'" (44). This second phrase in particular is important in that it suggests that the dawn or rebirth will be less about opening eyes and clearing vision—he writes later of "extinguished gazes"—than a phenomenon that is heard, in the "fissured voice" of the poet, which "no longer touches anything except the ramshackle houses of this noise around the streets where the grass grows," and which is emitted from a "wound whereby the word oozes from the trunk, splitting the bark" (44). Language itself is taken apart, "the word comes undone," and this is part of a broader movement whereby "all that was pure becomes confused and choked with brush," and the poet shifts "toward that chaos to carry thunderous words" (44). Likewise, the regular cadences of poetry no longer hold, as is suggested in the image of the poet struggling to keep time: "in vain would he keep the rhythm of paddles in the current" (45). His rhythm, his word, is "awkward, its colors exhausted," while the cry he gives out "is that of the only disentwined country," so that there is a concordance—however fleeting and provisional—between form and content, place and language, and sound and being (45).

It is perhaps this aspect of sound-related meaning that Dash refers to in his argument that in Glissant's early poetry, "the land *vibrates* at a more symbolic level with the accumulated meanings of language, poetry, knowledge, otherness and desire itself" (*Edouard Glissant* 41). Dash's notion of vibration reminds us of Gallagher's idea of Caribbean literary criticism as "registering some of the major vibrations and gravitations of French Caribbean writing," through listening to which "we can move closer to a sense of the Caribbean in general" (6).[21] To sound Caribbean poetry in this way, particularly in Glissant's work, is also to sound the nature of language, and indeed of writing. Drawing again on Walter Ong, Gallagher argues that to write (much like to see) is "a 'particularly pre-emptive and imperialist activity'" (*Soundings* 114). That is, much as seeing "present[s] surfaces ready to be mapped, 'fixed', explored, colonized, and ultimately, dominated," so writing reinforces the visual culture of the colonizer (4). And if sound, like time and history, turn around the Caribbean author, then the oral is also ever present in the literary, and reading is always also listening.

One important final implication of this is that when Glissant refers later to his well-known "prophetic vision of the past," it is not only vision that he is concerned with: for Glissant, the past echoes and resounds across time, in rhythms, reverberations, so that, as indeed for Césaire and Damas, sonic markers are sonorous parts of what he calls in *Poetic Intention* the "continued movement [. . .] of our past" (qtd. in Dash, *Edouard Glissant* 52). If, as Dash argues, "consciousness is a slow, patient and painful process," characterized by repetition, the continual movement of the past, then the Caribbean poet is always a listener, sounding the past, hearing history, and ever attuned to the echoes of the future.

---

[21] For a discussion of vibrations and pulsations as primary sonic materials, see Steve Goodman, "The Ontology of Vibrational Force."

2
Time Out in Trinidad
White "Expatriates" in the Late Colonial Period

How can one listen to a painting, a silent movie, a postcard, a photograph, or any other soundless, "visual" object? And, perhaps more to the point, *why* should we? Such are the questions that will guide the following two chapters, in which the primary materials are amateur, or home movies of different kinds made in and about the Caribbean. In effect, these chapters return more squarely to the sound–vision node around which Kei Miller's *The Cartographer* turns, ever wary of the imperial eye, and in his own way attempting to listen to an apparently silent visual object, the map.

The work of these chapters draws initially on that of the art historian Michael Gaudio, specifically his book *Sound, Image, Silence: Art and the Aural Imagination in the Atlantic World* (2019), in which the author, as Mary Gallagher does in her study of Antillean literature, presents his analyses as "soundings." In Gaudio's case, the focus is on the ways in which the "spatial, cultural, and socioeconomic distances of the Atlantic world were managed through the creation and dissemination of visual images," specifically, engravings, paintings, portraits, and kinetoscope film (ix). Thus, his work complements and reinforces that of this book, in that it asserts the importance of the visual in crossing, surveying, portraying, managing, and ultimately controlling non-European spaces, cultures, and people. Gaudio writes, for example, of the "extraordinary confidence in visual representation that developed in tandem with the expanding markets and inequalities of European and American colonialism," and of how "visual practices that include linear perspective, natural history, ethnography, exhibitionary methods, landscape painting, cartography, and portraiture helped put the world at empire's disposal" (x). The primary product of this "representational machine" was, Gaudio says, alterity: "Against the human, this machine produced nature; against reason, it produced superstition; against civilization, it produced the primitive" (x).

Gaudio chooses the term "soundings" to describe the work he does, "for its suggestion of an experimental testing of depths, and for its particular relevance to the crossing of oceanic distances" and because he is interested in the "sounds, as well as the silences, that are conjured by pictures" (xi–xii). What connects the diverse range of materials he analyzes is the way in which each work disturbs the "privileged domain of vision by an appeal to the ear" (xii). There is in visual material, he says, a "potential to be heard" that indeed disrupts the imperial eye, and by paying attention to the unheard elements of visual materials, such disruptions may be identified and amplified (xii). Gaudio is aware of the broader field of sound studies, and he quotes Leigh Eric Schmidt's argument that the story of modernity is "almost always one of profound hearing loss in which an objectifying ocularcentrism triumphs over the conversational intimacies of orality" (qtd. in Gaudio xii). Yet, Gaudio is also as interested in the "stubborn silences" of visual materials, the ways in which they will not or cannot "open our ears to the sounds of the past" (xiii).

To begin to answer the question of how one would "sound" a silent picture, Gaudio suggests we develop an "aural imagination," a term used in literature on music and poetry, to stimulate an imagined experienced of sound from written material. His own work builds on that of other art historians, who have begun to apply the concept of the aural imagination to the visual arts. At the same time, he insists that the aural imagination is not a "mental prosthesis for uncanning the sounds of silent pictures" (xiii). The aural imagination does not offer a "smooth trajectory" between seeing and hearing; instead, it is about the "productive friction" between the two senses (xiii).

Importantly for the material this chapter engages with, Gaudio grounds his own study in the aspirations of early film, and Thomas Edison's wish to make reproductions that would "Awaken both the eyes and the ears of audiences, uniting sound and the moving image in an experience 'without any material change from the original'" (xiii–xiv). If "silent" film did include musical accompaniment and in-house commentators to interpret the intertitles, what it could not do was create a synchrony between visual and aural experience. It is into this gap that Gaudio's work slides, and in which he sees/hears great potential for the aural imagination to do its work. "How do we respond to pictures that really want to speak to us" he asks, echoing the installation artist Fred Wilson (xiv). It is not that the sounds he hears in the visual work complement the intentions of the diverse artists; rather, when the pictures speak it is through "those exemplar sounds of the Atlantic world that intrude upon the hushed domain of visual contemplation as disruptions of propriety and reason, sounds that are normally kept at bay for the sake of peace and civility" (xv). Gaudio's project, indeed any such attempt to listen to silent objects, is "not an entirely rational enterprise," but it is a necessary and potentially fruitful one that allows us to "sound [. . .] historical distance, seeking the words that can simultaneously open and abolish it" (158).

The works to be studied and listened to in the following two chapters—silent home movies made by expatriate workers and tourists, and other, more official, tourism movies—cannot be considered as "art" in the sense that Gaudio's works are: that is, they are not made for public exhibition, or to be held up as visual means of promoting ideas of empire and civilization. Except that, remarkably, in their own ways, they do convey those sorts of ideas, though they do so through more "everyday" means—recording the daily lives of expatriates, the vacations of individual tourists. For Gaudio and for the material studied in this and the following chapter, "silent" visual media contain sounds, and the task of the viewer-listener is to imagine those sounds and the ways in which they relate to the visual image, and to situate the work in the gap between seeing and hearing, which is often also the space in which meaning becomes blurred, fuzzy, indistinct, and the latent but living sounds of the works crackle into life, reverberating into the present.[1]

In trying to imagine the auditory qualities of apparently silent, visual phenomena, we should recall Glissant's tendency to converge the (Western) visual and the (Caribbean) sonic in his sound-image of "The flash of the cry, the arduous opacity of parlance," in which the cry and speech appear in visual terms, respectively as a sudden, ephemeral flash and as a visually obscure dense and hidden language (*Poetic Intention* 180). Also, such an attempt to fuse sound and image relates to Sterne's notion of the "sonic imagination [. . .] a deliberately synaesthetic neologism" that is about sound but "occupies an ambiguous position between sound culture and a space of contemplation outside it" ("Sonic Imaginations" 5). We can think about sound even where it appears to be absent; a sonic imagination extends beyond the purely sonic, and sound may be contemplated and imagined at least in part visually, as Gaudio, Glissant, and Sterne suggest. In this regard, we should also acknowledge the work of David Toop, notably *Sinister Resonance*, in which he addresses the "challenge of representing the intangibility of sound" in, for example, Marcel Duchamp's *Nude Descending a Staircase, No. 2*—"In her descent, she clatters, freezing a sequence of moments both sonic and kinaesthetic" (70)—and in works of Italian Futurism: "Maybe we can't hear hearing," Toop says of the latter, "but we can certainly observe the act of hearing" (71). Though painting is, as Toop says, a silent practice, "the representation of listening and sound

---

[1] On the history of sound in the cinema, see Rick Altman, "Introduction: Four and a Half Film Fallacies."

through visual arts is an ancient history" (72).[2] In a later essay, Toop writes of how in the time before the existence of audio recording, the desire to "archive intangible and transient phenomena" was served through painting, "a medium developed to represent through illusion tangible objects alongside those states of flux taken for granted as fit subjects for an artist: movement, presence, air, depth, tactility, dimensionality, the sensorium" ("Entities Inertias Faint Beings," 246–47). Veering more closely to the primary materials studied here, Toop raises the idea of "audentia":

> To be part of an audience is to experience audentia, a hearing and a listening, and every audience, whether for theatre, opera, cinema, television, video, webcams, and even media that may be "inaudible," such as written texts, painting, sculpture and site-specific installations, is a listener or eavesdropper. (*Sinister Resonance* 83)

The particular material studied in this and the following chapter—amateur or home movies—is not conventionally considered worthy of scholarly interest; its audience would be nothing like what Toop imagines for the works of art that he writes of. As Patricia R. Zimmerman writes, "home movies too often have been perceived as simply an irrelevant pastime or nostalgic mementos of the past, or dismissed as insignificant byproducts of consumer technology." And yet as Zimmerman says, amateur film "provides a vital access point for academic historiography in its trajectory from official history to the more variegated and multiple practices of popular memory, a concretization of memory into artifacts that can be remobilized, recontextualized, and reanimated" ("The Home Movie Movement" 1). She further notes that such amateur film artifacts "present a materialization of the abstractions of race, class, gender, and nation as they are lived and as a part of everyday life [. . .]. Home movies provide vectors into the processes of racialization, race relations, and the imaging of racial difference" (4). Similarly, as the work of Heather Nicholson shows, this kind of material poses some intriguing questions about history, memory, visual archives, and the place of the everyday in analyzing historical periods. Scholars often lament the absence of oral testimonies of those who existed before the invention of technologies that could preserve their voices—we wonder how those people must have sounded, how they lived day to day. Yet, when those technologies are available and the images disseminated, scholars tend to overlook them in favor of "legitimate" sources,

---

[2] See also Fred Moten's argument that "neither language nor photography nor performance can tolerate silence. [. . .] The meaning of a photograph is cut and augmented by a sound or noise that surrounds it and pierces its frame" (*In the Break* 205).

such as professional films, and published written accounts, including ethnographies, biographies, novels, and poems. As Nicholson points out, there is much to gain from treating amateur movies seriously:

> For some it is the uncensored visual testimony taken by people at a given moment—a persuasive lens through which to adapt historical events and experiences unmediated by subsequent memory. For others, its appeal lies less in what it offers as evidential history and visible proof of observable details: what it does not show in its selective chronicling of past experiences is instructive.[. . .] Alternatively, amateur footage might attest to the experts' objectifying gaze, and the unequal power relations of those framed by the lens and those holding the camera [. . .]. Aesthetic interests [include]: how did cine-camera users negotiate the visual novelty of motion capture, and what lingering influences of still photography may be discerned in the camera technique of the enthusiast? ("Looking beyond the Moving Moments" 200)

Thus, our interest in the films studied in this chapter lies in what they show and do not show, silences and sounds, the relations between the person filming and those filmed, including Trinidadian people, and the ways in which music is used to complement the visual images to add the sound of the local to the images, as if the visual representation of the place cannot exist without hearing this music. Also, if we relate the *aesthetic* element mentioned by Nicholson broadly to the term's etymological sense of pertaining to sensual perception, we can begin to think of the ways in which the films visualize the sensory, corporeal experiences of their subjects, and thereby challenge the "discursive normality of the visual" in narratives of travel (Forsdick, "Travel and the Body" 68). A focus on the sensory, bodily aspects of the narratives helps understand the ways in which the corporeality of travel is never smooth or without conflicts or clashes: the friction of people and cultures coming into contact leads to the erosion and transformation of travelers and the sites they frequent (69). How do the people represented in the films change? Who stays the same? And to what extent does the moving, at times intrusive and all-seeing camera record or actually instantiate the changes in the expatriated travelers themselves?

The expatriate is a particular kind of traveler, one who generally undertakes a longer term of displacement than a tourist, but who, unlike the exile, can normally return home once the period of expatriation, often the end of a work contract, is over. While there is a significant body of academic work on the theme of exile, expatriates are rarely given much attention by historians or cultural scholars. In Peter Burke's definition, the term "expatriate" refers to "individuals who are not forced to move away from home but choose to move, often because they are attracted by working conditions abroad. Some of them migrate on their own initiative, but many accept invitations from the host country" (Burke, *Exiles and Expatriates* 82). In the Caribbean, there is a long history of what Burke calls "commercial expatriation," the condition of living overseas for reasons of commerce or work. Most obviously, the colonial period involved the expatriation of diverse groups of Europeans to the Caribbean to work on the plantations, or as merchants, tradesmen, doctors, surveyors, soldiers, missionaries, and other occupations. In some cases, there were extended periods of expatriation for these individuals, while for others the time in the Caribbean was short, or involved frequent returns to the country of origin. In the rest of this chapter, I focus on a particular island—Trinidad—and a particular subset of the expatriate workforce there, the British engineers who worked on various projects related to the island's oil industry, which dates to the beginning of the twentieth century, and the first successful oil drilling at Guayaguayare in the south of the island. Although this location was eventually abandoned, in the nine years of its operation, the site had seen the construction of bungalows to house the workers, a railway, and various other buildings. In addition to constructing industrial plants, housing, and providing ancillary services, "the pioneer oil companies also contributed to the construction of access roads throughout south Trinidad" (Brathwaite and Boopsingh, "The Social Impact" 285). As Bridget Brereton points out, Point Fortin became the first major center of oilfield operations, "as a port and developing town ship. In 1907 Trinidad Oilfields Ltd. set up base at La Fortunee Estate, Point Fortin [. . .] and buildings and clay roads were built in a region that had been wild bush and abandoned estates. [. . .] Point Fortin was, in fact, 'the town that oil built,' growing up in the space of fifty years from a forest clearing with a few rough huts to a modern town of about 30,000 people" (*A History of Modern Trinidad: 1783-1962*, 203). It is important to note that the expatriate workers involved in these and related projects were not only white British or Americans—there was a notable presence of other Caribbean islanders, men and women, who worked at different levels of the economy, in the oil industry itself or as domestic workers in the households of the white expatriates. That said, almost all of the managerial and technical staff were white expatriates; even the skilled workers were Americans (Brereton, "The White Elite of Trinidad, 1838–1950" 41).

My main interest here lies with the white British expatriates, and with a particular family whose experiences are chronicled in a series of short films available on YouTube and which provide a revealing insight into Trinidad at a crucial time—the late 1950s, just before independence, and at the time of the

Caribbean Federation, the ill-fated attempt at regional self-governance that fell apart after Jamaica and Trinidad withdrew from it and opted for independence in the early 1960s. The films thus provide insights into a world in transition, as colonial rule comes to an end, and with it the privileged status of white expatriates begins to shift. As the films show, however, those privileges are still intact in this late colonial period: access to secure, well-paid employment, comfortable housing, and good education is taken as a right for the expatriates, who are presented as a form of technical elite, differentiated from the old island elite, the group known as the "French Creoles," whose lineage can be traced to the earliest days of plantation slavery on the island, and who by 1960 made up barely 2 percent of the population.[3] The expatriates enjoy a form of immediate social promotion on arrival in Trinidad: coming from the lower-middle class in Britain, they are through their race and employment promoted into a privileged social class in Trinidad, and take full advantage of this new status.

The political context of 1950s Trinidad was quite complex. Twenty years before the arrival of the expatriate family, there were labor riots in Trinidad that involved black and Indian workers, led by T.U.B. Butler (a migrant worker from Grenada) that shook the colonial government and led to the founding of the modern trade union movement. Butler was actually a pipe fitter in the oilfields of south Trinidad, and therefore something of an expatriate worker himself. The riots were principally to protest at working conditions in that industry, and then spread to the sugar factories. Butler was jailed from 1937 to 1939 and was rearrested and imprisoned for the duration of the Second World War.

The war brought the American "occupation" of Trinidad, and the presence of more than 25,000 U.S. troops, who "represented a formidably armed police force and thus contributed materially to the defense of a preexisting white supremacist social order," which in the wake of the labor riots, was "already desperately struggling to stage their superiority before an increasingly restless, disbelieving nonwhite audience" (Neptune, *Caliban* 9). On the other hand, however, the occupation unsettled the white establishment in ways that would never be reversed and that would lead finally to independence. Released from prison in 1945, Butler set about reorganizing his British Empire Citizens' and Workers' Home Rule Party, which won a majority in the general elections of 1950, only for the British establishment to install the less radical Albert Gomes as the first chief minister of Trinidad and Tobago.

---

[3] On the history of the white community in Trinidad, see Bridget Brereton, "The White Elite of Trinidad, 1838–1950."

Writing of the great disruptions in Trinidadian society of the period, Harvey Neptune states:

> The Colony was a veritable theater of social battle in these years. By the time the dust cleared, the result was indisputable: those dominant groups fighting to turn back the hands of time, to restore the society to its prewar mores and conditions, ended on the side of futility. The island's subaltern set, seizing the moment occasioned by base installation and operation, had wrought irreversible social unsettlement. (*Caliban* 9–10)

American presence would further impose itself in ways directly relevant to the films that are the subject of this chapter. During the second decade of the twentieth century, there was a surge in oil exploration and production in Trinidad, and the petroleum industry depended heavily on American expertise. Seeing their jobs as "a combination of masculine adventure and enterprise," and themselves "as men embarking on manly missions in the tradition of Theodore Roosevelt," the American oil workers disrupted colonial racial and class behavioral norms, so that:

> In a caste-like world where these elites obsessively took care to deport themselves at a respectable distance from the dark, poor, and dangerous classes, white American men embodied deviance. Yankee sojourners, moreover, seemed not indifferent to but frankly contemptuous of established colonial codes of comportment. [. . .] As one unrepentant petroleum industry pioneer declared, "You just can't make oil men adopt British customs." (Neptune, *Caliban* 57)

Culturally, too, this was a time of ferment and change. The Trinidad Theatre Workshop was founded in 1959, by the Walcott brothers, Derek and Roderick; Derek would be its director until 1971. V.S. Naipaul's literary career was starting, with his masterful novels on Trinidadian life, *The Mystic Masseur* (1957), *The Suffrage of Elvira* (1958), *Miguel Street* (1959), and *A House for Mr. Biswas* (1961). As one of the short films studied below shows, Carnival was the most striking and powerful expression of Trinidadian culture by this time, a dazzling visual display, and a great popular cacophony of noise, sound, and music, fueled by the classic calypso music of the time, and the steelbands. Some of this music is used to accompany the films, though virtually all of the films themselves are silent, have no sound, and to listen to them with no sound is a quite different experience to having the music played. The soundless films seem generally more poignant and affecting, and to capture better the silences that were part of the expatriates' lives, living in detached bungalows on company compounds in a remote part of south Trinidad. Silence was a significant part of the mothers' lives, given that they are the ones confined to the home, and to spending the long days there alone, apart from when they are in the company of other mothers or their domestic staff. The silence of the films highlights the ways in which each individual figure lives in their own silent world; we gain a stronger sense of how the experience of expatriation and isolation leads each one to confront their individuality in ways they would not have done before. For all that the experience brings them together as a family, it also highlights their differences, and brings to the fore questions of identity they would not have had to face previously, concerning their relations with each other, with places new and old, new people, new ways of speaking. Identity becomes a kind of secret, to be kept close, guarded in the interior life of the individual, and known most intimately in silence. There is also a power in the silence, a refusal to give up identity through language, almost a return to a primordial state of being, outside of or before language, in ways that recall Heidegger's notion of "primordial silence," which he says is "more powerful than any human potentiality. No one, on his or her own, has ever invented language—that is, has been strong enough to break the power of this silence" (qtd. in Agamben, "Image and Silence" 95). However subtly the films show this, and however banal the family's everyday experiences may be, there is a sense in the films of the individual family members living in forms of silence that predate and have no language, the silence of being alone, being free in a sense, but also confronted with themselves in wordless ways.

There is a feeling in the films of the family living in forms of silence that remind us of Agamben's reading of Kafka's parable on Ulysses, and how, according to Agamben, "the silence of the Sirens represents a zero degree of song and, following a stubborn tradition that sees in absence the most extreme form of presence, also represents an at once zero and ultimate degree of reality" ("Image and Silence" 96). "The silence in question," Agamben continues, "is [. . .] merely the impossibility of saying" (96). Clearly, these films were not intended to be viewed as anything other than naive recordings of the family's life in Trinidad, but there is throughout a discernible sense of silence that has to do with the move to a different country, the shifts in the family dynamics, the way the experience pushes them together yet drives them into their interior worlds, and it is there that their silence is heard most clearly, in echoes and reverberations of themselves.[4]

---

[4] In this regard, the silence of the figures in the film relates to Jennifer Solheim's definition: "silence is not an absence of sound or voice. Silence has both form and content; silence arises from that which goes unheard" (*The Performance of Listening in Postcolonial Francophone Culture* 6).

The silences in and of the film bear comparison to Agamben's notion of silence, which is not separate from language, but is of language, "the silence of language itself" ("Image and Silence" 96). Agamben is interested in the relationship between image and word; he finds that in painting "the word and its silence are visible," and that silence may be represented visually:

> Painting silences language because it interrupts the signifying relation between name and thing, returning, if only for an instant, the thing to itself, to its namelessness. But this anonymity of the thing is not one where something is lacking, it is not a distressing impossibility of saying. It is, instead, the presentation of the thing in its pure sayability. Separating name from thing, painting does not cast the thing into the abyss of Sigē, but, instead, allows it to appear in its luminous, beatific sayability. (96)

In a similar way, the silent film seems to return its subjects to themselves, their namelessness—we never learn the names of the family members. Perhaps this explains the unbearable nature of the silence, the desire for some kind of sound, usually music, to reduce the heaviness of the silent encounter with the self, which to some degree transfers to the audience, the viewer, who partakes in the silence and in the expatriates' wordless meeting with themselves.[5] The films differ, however, in that they do not share painting's desire, as ascribed to it by Agamben, to present visually the "sayability" of its subjects.[6] Instead, the films seem to guard their silences, not to bring them into the light and sound of knowability, but to insist on the unknowable aspects of the subjects' experiences.[7] Whereas, as Gaudio points out, the well-known image of "Nipper" the confused dog looking for the source of His Master's Voice, represents the "disembodiment of sound by the phonograph" (*Sound, Image, Silence* 145), the films studied here rather embody, or reincorporate the silence of the filmed subjects: the silence reinhabits them, as if the body is its rightful home. In one sense, the figures represented in the films may be read in Gaudio's terms as "symptom[s] of a modern, technologized, and fragmented self" (146), but at the same time, the silence denotes not only loss or disembodiment, but a way of seeing and hearing the silence that technology considers to be a lack but which has a presence and meaning that would be

---

[5] Alain Corbin alludes to the unbearable nature of silence for the modern (Western) subject: "Silence is not only the absence of noise. We have almost forgotten it. [...] The fear, indeed the terror incited by silence have intensified" (*Histoire du silence* 9).

[6] See also, Alain Corbin's remark that in the West, painting was considered "silence speaking" (*Histoire du silence* 9).

[7] This brings to mind Maurice Blanchot's well-known phrase: "To keep our silence, that is what, without our knowing it, we all seek, when we write" (*L'Ecriture du désastre* 187).

lost if, for example, it were ever possible to add the original sound recordings to the films. In Gaudio's words, referring to the kinetoscope, "it is precisely in the sensory limitations of this new technology [. . .] that the possibilities behind the imitative magic of cinema become apparent" (155). This "magic" has to do with silence, and the way its meanings remain tantalizingly out of reach, out of earshot, however much we seek to touch them, to hear them.

These are portraits of a kind, self-portraits, and in the films the filming subjects and objects coincide at times, as if two bodies become one, while at other times there is a curious separation that does not confirm identity as one and unified, but maintains the split, fractured self and the fluid, uncertain subjectivities that emerge from it, so that there is no idea of a permanent, unchanging identity, and consequently no name that can be attached to the experience. Again, the faces of the family tell the story, convey the silences. For Agamben, "true silence" is to be found only in the face, which is a kind of home: "Character marks the human face with all the words not said, all the intentions never acted upon; the face of an animal always seems on the verge of speaking; but human beauty opens that face to silence. The silence that prevails is not the simple suspension of discourse, but the silence of the word itself: the idea of language. For this reason, in the silence of the face, and there alone, is mankind truly at home" ("Image and Silence" 97).[8]

The silent films thus lead us to pay more attention to visual cues, to smiles or frowns or other facial expressions that reveal much about the individuals' particular experiences of living in Trinidad. The father is seldom filmed, but when he is he appears the happiest, the most satisfied—a smile spreads most readily across his face, and his happiness is constant, from the beginning to the end of the experience. The two boys by contrast appear pensive as they arrive in Trinidad, but they gradually adapt and seem to enjoy living there, to the extent that by the end the elder boy in particular looks unhappy as the ship pulls out of Port of Spain. The mother is in many ways the most difficult to read, and the most interesting figure. She does not appear to be unhappy, but neither is she as carefree as the father. She is virtually always filmed with her two sons, and is protective of them. She seems to have limited interactions with other families or other women, and no connections outside of the expatriate circle. On the other hand, it is the mother who is a kind of mediator between the family and any local people they encounter—she is there at the markets, dealing with the local women who work there, or at the store, buying the groceries. She also seems open to using local ingredients in her cooking, to experimenting in

---

[8] On the history of "silent" films and the cinema in the United States, see Rick Altman, "The Silence of the Silents."

that way and as such is a force for integration with the local community. The mother is however the most inscrutable of all the family members; her smile is not as open or unreserved as the others'. One senses she is holding something back, that she is not completely at home in Trinidad, and this appears to be confirmed at the end when, in contrast to her sons, she looks finally to be content, and as the ship pulls out her smile is the broadest. Thus, the silent nature of the films leads us to read them in a certain way. The silence is real in a sense, in that it suggests the way in which memory is retained, as imagery rather than sound, feelings caught up in visualized memories, and that silence is also a component and sign of the loneliness of the expat existence. Read alongside the great political and cultural happenings of the time, the films constitute an important archive of a world that is at its zenith in many ways, but which will soon fade quickly, as independence is gained, and the privileged status of the British expatriate is gradually diminished. The films are also "artless" in the sense that they are not conceived of as anything other than means of retaining a family's memory of a time spent abroad. As such they have qualities of directness, naivety, and spontaneity that are not always features of "proper" art.

They are also forms of travel narrative, though here the subjects are not intellectuals or artists, but engineers and other workers whose travel is driven not necessarily by the desire to visit other places and write about them, but to live and work there, and most importantly, earn salaries that are often higher than those earned at home. There is refreshingly none of the self-reflexive introspection that is often found in travel narratives on, for example, the relationship between writing and traveling. Instead, the medium—film—is embraced and taken as a naturalistic means of recording and retaining an experience of travel that is again quite particular, and is determined by the length and terms of the contract. The films are "authentic" in these ways, and provide still a valuable window onto a privileged group in late colonial Trinidad, into a world that was fast disappearing, in a landscape that itself was changing quickly. The films are also markers of the privileged access enjoyed by the white expatriate community to new technologies, specifically the home camera, which allows the family to record their experiences in ways largely not open to the local community. The films were likely made in 8 mm format, which allowed for smaller and more portable cameras, and made filmmaking more affordable and practical for everyday use. Most amateur film formats did not record audio; and this is the case with the majority of the films in this archive. Access to the technology also confers a significant degree of power to the expatriates, as they are able to portray the island according to their own experience of it. Somewhat like the French Creole surveyors of the plantation era, they scan and map out the land, as a means of getting to know it, and more subtly to control it, and impose themselves on it. Or even, theirs is a version of the "imperial gaze" that Pratt talks of (*Imperial Eyes*), and which is evident in earlier chronicles of slavery by Labat, Moreau, Descourtilz, and countless others. Somewhat like their white predecessors, the expatriates become masters of memory in a sense, capturing a moment in island history that is largely untold from the perspective of the working-class Trinidadian. Also, the memory is largely produced from a male perspective, as the father appears to film virtually every clip, and the mother and children remain the objects of the camera's gaze. The father films scenes of work and industry, and one wonders how different the films would be if the mother had access to the camera, how her perspective would differ from that of the father. In the following sections, I work through each of the films, analyzing them in turn, and mapping out the narrative of expatriate life that is gradually built throughout the series.

Time out in Trinidad
Pt. 1, Arriving at Piarco and drive south to Penal
[https://www.youtube.com/watch?v=VMjtBd6gtww]

In this nostalgic sequence, a British family arrives in Trinidad in 1955, via New York on a Pan American DC6B. The camera lingers on the beautiful airliner as it lands and taxis to Piarco's quaint wooden terminal building of the 1950s. Note the ground crew unloading baggage and a later shot of the flight crew returning to their cars, the stewardess in her semi military PAA uniform. After loading the car the family begins their drive south to their new home in Penal. Note the practically empty roads! A far cry from today.[9]

The plane's arrival is filmed, presumably by the father, who must have been in Trinidad for a period of time before the rest of the family traveled. The Pan-American flight would most likely have come from Miami, so the family will have flown to the States from Britain. The Trinidad flight is the last leg in a long journey. The airport buildings are small and the cars are parked directly behind the small terminal building. Two American sailors wait by the runway, apparently to greet a passenger. Well-dressed passengers disembark, mostly men in suits, ties, and some with hats. The first sight of the younger son shows him wearing a jacket and carrying a suitcase. Passengers, pilots, and flight crew go quickly to their cars, and the father packs the suitcases in the truck. A map of Trinidad shows the journey they will make southward to Penal.

---

[9] At the beginning of the discussion of each film, I cite the text that accompanies the film on YouTube.

A sign with "Southern Road to San Fernando" sits in front of some dilapidated buildings with a Pepsi Cola billboard beside it. A concrete sign with a crown symbol indicates that the road is the "Princess Margaret Highway," and the road stretches into the distance, lined with coconut trees. The car speeds by the flat countryside, with sugar cane fields on either side. Another Pepsi Cola sign marks the entrance to Penal; its market building is shown, before the car pulls up to the family home. It is interesting that we see none of the family's reaction to the new place, that all that is shown is the place itself, as if it is seeing them and has its own presence. The new arrivals would understandably feel overwhelmed by the place, its unfamiliar sounds and sights, the heat, and the general strangeness of arriving in a new country. We can only imagine their thoughts as they arrive and drive south. The term of the contract must stretch out before them and seem like a long time to be away from home, in a strange and unfamiliar country. Also, as they arrive in colonial Trinidad they take on new identities: that of the expat, the itinerant worker on a sort of secondment, a traveler with the security of going home, and most likely a physical home to return to; also, perhaps more fundamentally, the family *becomes* white, and thus highly privileged in this context. Whiteness confers on them a status that they would not have enjoyed as an everyday middle-class family in Britain. They are immediately promoted to the higher echelons of this new society, and we do not know how they feel about this, or even if they think about it, or take it as how things are and should be. As the series of films advances, we can pay attention to their relationships to each other, and with other people like them, and think of that in comparison to the presence or absence of local people in the films. Will the films be, as in this first instance, more about the place and the people, or will they be about the family and the white expat group they fraternize with? At this point, we get a sense of the shock of the arrival, the silence of the family as they contemplate the time ahead together and as individuals, for just as the expatriate experience brings them together as a family, so it also highlights their individuality and forces them to rethink their relationships with each other, with the new place and people, and, crucially, with themselves. What kind of people are we in this new place? Are we the same people that left Britain? Can we stay the same? Should we stay the same? Who are we and who am I in this new place?

Pt. 2, Los Iros, Morne Diablo, Mayaro
[https://www.youtube.com/watch?v=DnL9UCIfa_Q]

This sequence shows three of the beaches in South Trinidad as they appeared in the mid 1950s. Beginning with the drive to Los Iros, behind a Shell tanker, our visitors can be eventually seen unloading the trunk of their Opel Kapitan. Note the bottle of Fernandes Rum amongst the "supplies" in the old "Flit" box! Included are shots of a beached jellyfish and water lilies. One of the boys displays a shark's head. While their parents picnic, the children enjoy climbing on the branches of a fallen tree. Note the mounted policeman in the Mayaro sequence. Notice the saga boy and the craft crossing the bridge at 2:00.

Trinidad is no preindustrial paradise: the family car drives closely behind a Shell oil truck on its way to the three beaches. Los Iros does have the coconut trees and vistas that the family might have been expecting as they contemplated coming to Trinidad. It is notable that it is to the coast that they travel first, as if the views they find there are familiar in a way—the sea, the sun, the coconut trees swaying in the breeze all must have been a stark contrast to the Britain they left behind. The picnic box they packed into the trunk of the car contains no food, just a flask and bottles of alcohol, including a full bottle of Fernandes rum. This introduces a key element in the social life of the expats: the alcohol that is freely consumed and that is a key component in enjoying the "time out" from work. The boys and mother go into the sea, their skin pale still. A jellyfish is filmed, as are ripe green coconuts on the trees by the beach. The boys enjoy the rough surf, while the mother changes back into her regular clothes and pours a drink from the large flask, most likely tea, which suggests that the alcohol is drunk mainly by the men. The boys change back into their t-shirts in the car, which over the course of the films becomes like a motorized home for them, almost a companion that is ever present as they move around the island. Natural phenomena such as water lilies seem to fascinate them—the beauty of the flora is again no doubt in contrast to that in Britain, which must figure heavily still in their minds, given their recent arrival on the island. Places are new to them, they shift around quickly from one spot to the next, eager to gain a sense of the place and get their bearings.

At this point, the family sticks to the south coast, visiting next the beach at Morne Diablo, where the boys climb the bare branches of a fallen tree. The boys are usually filmed in close proximity to each other, the elder one leading the way and the younger one following behind. One senses the closeness of their bond, and also the way in which the move to Trinidad has thrown them together and made them spend more time together than they would have done at home. Sometimes, it seems like the elder boy in particular is trying to escape from his younger brother, while the younger one tags along, always wanting to catch up with his sibling. There is possibly four or five years' difference in age between them, so they are at different stages in their development—the elder one would be about eleven or twelve years old, and is thus more of an individual than the younger one, who seems more content to be in the security of the family context, to be guided by the mother in particular or else by his brother. The adventurous elder boy fishes out a shark's head from the sea and holds it toward the camera. The mother and two boys are filmed together, the mother handing the younger boy his shoes, thinking always of them and their well-being.

Mayaro is a longer stretch of sandy beach, fringed with coconut palms and, like the other beaches, virtually empty. Clearly, at this point it is white people who would be interested in visiting the beaches as places of leisure and relaxation, or who would have the means—the transport—to take advantage of the beaches. As the car apparently drives along the beach, a policeman on a horse passes by. Although they are the only people on the beach, there are beach houses at Mayaro, Creole-style buildings with shutters open to the sea breeze and shaded by the coconut trees. A sign attached to one of the houses says, "Why worry, this is the life." There are more people in the next beach shot, which shows a group of white people behind the mother, who swings a cricket bat. The father is rarely filmed, though here he appears in the frame holding a bat and with a wide smile—he seems to be the most at ease in Trinidad and to enjoy the beach. He laughs and smiles freely in a way that the other members of the family rarely do. He appears settled here, comfortable with the place and himself. The elder boy, by contrast is alone in the next shot, his head down in the shade by the car, and kicking a football on his own. The mother and father sit and enjoy the picnic, as the afternoon sun catches the sea and creates a golden light. The waves crash while the camera fixes on the horizon, and one wonders if they are thinking of the sea and the distance that separates them from Britain, and whether the sea is to them a sign of the proximity or the remoteness of their home.

Pt. 3, Navy Base, Stauble's, and Kingfisher to St. Mary's Bay
[https://www.youtube.com/watch?v=BO2HTv0bwUY]

This is the first time I've seen a picture of the guard house at the U.S. Naval Station at Chaguaramas since 1960! I remember it well as early in the 50s we managed to wreck it when the brakes failed on the family car! The launch, Kingfisher, forms an integral part of my childhood as it was our transport to the Company Island House at St. Mary's Bay on Gasparee. Finding these films evoke bittersweet memories of a childhood long since past. Once, Harold, our boatman, had to be awakened in the middle of the night to return a very sick me to Port of Spain. I will never forget that night. Even though the two blond boys in the film are not my brother and I, they almost could be as they happily play in the same place we did.

The sign that greets the Family in Chaguaramas, "U.S. Naval Station, Trinidad, B.W.I." indicates the doubly occupied status of Trinidad in the postwar years: a British colony with an American naval base, the island is still very much a possession of foreign countries, and at the same time a strategic site for those countries. The entrance to the base is guarded, the guard seems to hand the family a set of keys. The next shot is from a boat leaving the quayside. An unsmiling man is apparently the one taking the family to St. Mary's Bay on the island of Gasparee, where there is a house owned by the company. The mother smiles as the father films her, the younger son sitting behind her. The house is perched by the edge of the sea and is surrounded by vegetation. The boatman guides the boat in, tying it up as the family disembarks, apparently with another family. The mother sits with another woman on a plank, both of them with their feet in the water. The mother is rarely filmed with other women, and when she is, it tends to be with women of other expatriate families. The two boys play on a rowing boat, while in the distance a large naval or commercial ship passes by. The young boy fixes the camera, his face unsmiling as the sky darkens and the sun goes down behind the other islands. The company house is further evidence of the importance of leisure to the expats, the ways in which life for them is to a large extent based around "time out," either with other families or alone in the single-family unit. The family is never filmed apart, which again shows the ways in which they are rather thrown together by the circumstances of their new lives. They are free but also restricted in what they do: the boys in particular seem to have no lives outside of the family or to be able to do anything on their own.

Pt. 4, Chinese Laundry Burn Down!
[https://www.youtube.com/watch?v=g9umjHIZCD8]

In this sequence the San Fernando Fire Brigade responds to a fire at a Chinese Laundry. It appears, of course, that the laundry has already burned flat to the ground, which is not surprising as most buildings at that time were of wood construction. Note the crowds running back and forth, real pandemonium, almost on an epic scale! Try to find the old lady in the blue dress with the white polka dots. She looks completely lost. There are also several big bamsies in the crowd! The sequence ends with some shots of the damage caused by the huge fire on Frederick Street in Port of Spain in the late 1950s.

This is one of the rare films in which the focus is not on the family but on the Trinidadian people, specifically their reaction to a fire at a Chinese laundry. The crowd gathers closely to the fire, watching it and the fire brigade closely.

While most stand watching the scene, closer to the blaze men run back and forth at pace as the building apparently burns to the ground. The scene moves abruptly to Frederick Street in Port of Spain, which appears quiet with only a few motor cars and men on bicycles. A caption states that this is "six days after the shopping centre had been ruined by fire," before the camera focuses on some ruined buildings, with a sign that reads "Salvatori." The fires must have been big news stories, and it is interesting that these are some of the very few current events that are recorded in the films. In most of the rest of the films, it is as if the family is cocooned, isolated from political and social events, as if the expat life allows them to do that, partly because of the limited social circles in which they move, and partly because of the limited time they know they have on the island—a two-year contract is short enough for them to think of their time there as an extended holiday, and for them not to become involved or interested in local life, beyond freak incidents like fires. There is also something in the way the laundry fire is filmed that makes the reactions to it appear almost comical or caricatural—the men rushing back and forth, the large crowd encroaching on the scene, as if the people are foolish in some way, inherently different in character and temperament to the white expats.

> Pt. 5, Union Park Turf club and San Fernando
> [https://www.youtube.com/watch?v=KllRLohiOaY]
>
> A horserace at the Union Park Turf Club. Some city shots of San Fernando including the Colonial Hospital, High Street, Woolworth's, Debe and a Hindu Temple.

One of the aspects of expat life in colonial Trinidad, with its social hierarchy linked so closely to notions of race and color is that white incomers find themselves immediately promoted to the higher echelons of society and granted access to privileged activities, such as in this case, the turf club, where the sport of horse racing seems to thrive. There is a large grandstand and other buildings, a wide racetrack, with many local people in attendance, watching from the side of the track rather than the grandstand. The grandstand is apparently reserved for the privileged classes. The family seems to mingle among the lower classes in this case, filming the crowd as a kind of curiosity. Streets of old San Fernando are filmed, with Creole-style houses and narrow, steep paved roads. Living in the south of the island, San Fernando is far more important to the family and presumably the other expats as an urban center—they rarely go to Port of Spain. San Fernando appears as a pleasant, quiet town, with a few motor cars in its streets, churches and parks, and a monument to Ghandi. The old colonial hospital is the largest building that is shown, while on the main street there is a large branch of Woolworth's. A market scene shows something of the mixed nature of the population, a Creole town with people mixing freely. There is a Hindu temple, and scenes of modern cars juxtaposed with images of men on rickety wooden carts, and a sense of Trinidad as a place that must fascinate and confuse the new arrivals: modern and traditional, pastoral and industrial, exotic and familiar, Christian, Hindu, and Muslim, but also British and colonial, a bewildering mix that at once welcomes visitors and retains a kind of opacity so that we never sense that the expats truly get to know the place, its culture or people.

Pt. 6, Carnival 1957
[https://www.youtube.com/watch?v=2ccbF4DMqHU]

These wonderful 8mm colour home movies capture Trinidad Carnival of over 50 years ago. Note the beautiful art deco Queen's Park Hotel and the unmistakable American influence on the revelers' costumes. At that time, the Chaguaramas Naval Station was still in operation, with thousands of American servicemen stationed there. Look for the Coat of Arms of the Federation of the West Indies and the Anchor Special cigarette head gear! A beautiful troupe of Dakota "Red Indians" dance by among others. The camera work is good and the colour is still relatively stable on this old film that captures a Trinidad that has long since disappeared.

What could be more bewildering, more inviting and confusing than Carnival, an occasion to which the family seems drawn but that also reminds them of their foreignness, and the unknowable otherness of Trinidadian culture, its resistance to easy classification or colonial containment? It is interesting that this is the only piece of footage in the whole series with its own ambient sound—in the other films, calypsos and other contemporary music forms are played over the images and one never hears, for example, the family speaking, the sound of the car, the noise of the sea, or the sounds of birds.

In this piece of film, you hear the sounds of Carnival before you see the masqueraders. Carnival announces itself as sound—the voices of men talking in the background, over the noise of various bands, whistles, percussion instruments that beat relentlessly and that sound remarkably modern and contemporary—the rhythm is fast and played with a kind of fury that makes it impossible not to be moved by it, like it is a force inside the people. People stand on the balconies of the art-deco style Queen's Park Hotel, while others sit on the roofs as the parades pass by. The camera is at street level, and focuses first on a small group of white people, apparently tourists or else expat friends, who seem fascinated with the spectacle. It must be Carnival Tuesday, as that is the day of "pretty mas," when the bands wear their full costumes and seem to be charged with extra energy. The music is, again, like a force, the steelbands like an army of sound, so powerful they are together, playing off against each other, playing so fast and beating so hard.

One senses that on this day the streets belong to the people, and that they move at their own pace. It is a shaking sound, the shac-shacs filled with peas that are shaken to a quick beat, creating a kind of base for the pan men, who come by in American sailor costumes, all in white, some doing the off-beat sailor dance that is deliberately out of step and awkward, a knowing way of mocking the Americans and their way of dancing. There is a French or French Creole voice off camera, one man telling another to say hello. Then there are other bands, men dressed like American footballers, all padded up and with helmets. One man smokes a plastic pipe, another points a plastic rifle. The leaders of the bands have great elaborate costumes, butterflies or dragons. Little Chinese boys look on. Then there is a Red Indian band, more pan men, styled on cowboy movies, a great chief with huge antlers coming out of his headdress, two men in an open-top car, dressed like American generals, medals pinned to their chests and pointing guns, a band of Roman centurions. Then come some women dressed as Red Indians, walking in step, "chipping" as it is called, and the men in the crowd whistle and shout at them. Donald Duck, some harlequins, another great wave of pan men, beautiful women dressed in the Creole, femme-jardin style, Egyptians, more sailors, Dakota Indians with great headdresses and tomahawks, a Three Musketeers band, the women dressed like French aristocrats, others with moustaches painted on. It is not entirely clear if the father filmed the scenes, as the camerawork seems different and the family itself is not filmed. Also, again, the use of ambient sound is unique to this clip. One assumes, nevertheless, that they did indeed attend Carnival, and that their experience would have been similar to that presented in the film, of a bewildering visual and aural spectacle in which men and women seem to participate equally, and that provides evidence of a thriving local culture, full of verve, color, and energy that stands in contrast to the rather muted images of local people and their lives that feature in some of the other clips.

Pt. 7, Ram Lila in Penal 1958
[https://www.youtube.com/watch?v=LSLNrBx9nlI]

Ram Lila (Rama's Play) is a dramatic Hindu folk re-enactment of the life of Lord Ram, ending up in a ten-day battle between Lord Ram and Ravan. A tradition that originates from the Indian subcontinent, the play is staged annually in Indian communities across Trinidad to this day. This humble Ram Lila was performed in October of 1958 in Penal.

While Carnival is the most popular and most anticipated of Trinidad's festivals, there are many others that the family must have been aware of during their stay on the island. Ram Lila in Penal in 1958 is also announced in sound, chiefly percussion and rhythm, the tassa drums of the East Indian community. The battle reenactment is carried out by men and boys dressed up colorfully. The barriers between performers and audience are quite porous, and young schoolboys stand by the stage where costumed participants watch the battle scenes. The men, including at least one Afro-Trinidadian man, play the music, which drives the performance, and gives it its tempo. A young white boy stands chatting to an Indian boy, who wears a school uniform. It is likely the young East Indian boys wore their school uniforms at most times in public. Clothing marks the white people as different: they have changes of clothes, t-shirts and shirts with colorful designs, while for the local children and adults dressing up is for festival times and of course, parties.

Pt. 8, Drive from Siparia to Port of Spain
[https://www.youtube.com/watch?v=HmOKS5quJV4]

This fairly general collection of shots depicts a drive from Siparia in South Trinidad to Port of Spain along the Princess Margaret Highway and the Churchill - Roosevelt Highway in 1957 or 1958. There are a few stops along the way, notably, the transmitting stations for Radio Guardian and Radio Trinidad and the Moslem Mosque at Curepe. A massive crane passes by slowly at the junction of the two highways and the journey finishes at the Port of Spain docks with the Compagnie Generale Transatlantique's beautiful liner "Antilles" in port. This shot was taken before the "Antilles" was fitted with her taller funnel. A beautiful liner which sadly met her fate at Mosquito Island in 1971 where she hit a reef, caught fire and broke up, fortunately with no loss of life.

The ability to travel round the island with ease also marks out the expat family from many of the local people. It is not only the *ability* to do this that is unique to the expats and other nonnatives, however—it is the desire to do so. Their sense of space and place appears different to that of many of the locals, who tend to stay in their communities or regions more than the expats, who move around, feeling their way, marking out their coordinates, in a spirit of discovery that is typical of new arrivals. Siparia appears as a sleepy provincial town, along the way there is a church, some local boys playing football, the mother goes to a fruit stand, and as the drive continues, the low hills of the Northern Range come into closer view. The road is quiet, with only a few landmarks, including the Radio Guardian and Radio Trinidad buildings. The hills are dry, a white mosque stands in Curepe, which is at this time largely undeveloped, as is the surrounding area, in sharp contrast to how it is now. In Port of Spain, the French transatlantic liner *Antilles* sits in the port, a further sign that Trinidad was very much part of the cruise liners' itinerary.

[Pt. 9] Princess Margaret's Visit to Trinidad 1958
[https://www.youtube.com/watch?v=DP17L--O3rc]

This 8mm film marks an important passage in Trinidad's history with the arrival of Princess Margaret to open the parliament of the newly founded Federation of the West Indies. It fell apart some two years later. We see her arrival in a magnificent BOAC Bristol Brittania with Piarco done up for the festivities. She meets all the dignitaries and heads of state and inspects the Trinidad Regiment. The Jamaica Regiment makes an appearance as does the Trinidad Police Force. Note that the film is shot from the Control Tower! On a Royal Visit no less! In an early shot you can see British Pathe at work filming the events. HRH leaves in a Daimler semi drop head limousine. Later shots of the Governor's Residence and Red House fill in those visits and the camera returns in force to Piarco as HRH arrives from Tobago on a Vickers Viscount. HRH is presented with a painting from a Trinidad artist and three cheers are given HRH boards the Britannia to carry her to her next destination, British Guiana (Guyana).

Colonial connections ensured that Trinidad was part of the tourism network in the Caribbean, and brought visitors including members of the royal family to the island. Princess Margaret's visit to Trinidad in 1958 was for more than mere tourism, however: she was there to open the parliament of the newly formed Federation of the West Indies. Although the Federation was a first step in some sense toward independence, the visit was still marked by colonial pomp and circumstance—marching bands in white and black uniforms, military displays, flags, and music. A large part of the crowd is made up of white people, at least those invited and who were able to stand in closest proximity to the events. Curiously, the father seems to have gained access to the airport control tower to film the proceedings, and in one of the first shots the mother looks up at him smiling and waving, with the younger boy in front of her in khaki shorts and white shirt. A camera crew waits on a makeshift podium, while a worker applies a final lick of paint.

A caption lists some of the dignitaries' names: Lord and Lady Rance, and the "West Indian Heads": Marryshow, Bustamente, Manley, and Grantley Adams. Two Royal Navy captains walk around aimlessly, while the Jamaica Regiment band plays. The official party is led by "Lord Hailes, Sir Edward Beetham, and their ladies." As the princess walks across the tarmac there is a scramble of photographers, followed by an inspection of the Trinidad Regiment. The guest leaves in an open-topped car, waving faintly to the crowd. The scene then shifts to the capital city, and a uniformed guard standing outside the Governor-General's House, where the guest is apparently staying, and then there are shots of H.M.S. *Stourbridge* docked and festooned for the occasion. A shot of the front page of the *Trinidad Guardian* shows its headline: "Parliament launched," along with a photograph of the royal visitor. There are shots in town around the Red House parliament building, and then footage of a slow drive through large crowds, apparently near Pointe-a-Pierre. Another newspaper headline announces a "Gay farewell for princess today," and that her "Tobago stay ends with a barbecue." The arrival in Tobago is greeted with similar pomp. A caption states "after Tobago holiday, lunch, and on to British Guiana." The Trinidad Police Force band plays as she leaves, receiving a painting by an unnamed Trinidadian artist and the crowd's three cheers. The departure is muted in comparison to the excitement of the arrival: the visitor's power resides partly in arriving as she does surrounded by pomp and a certain mystery; the other part of her power lies in her ability to leave. She comes and goes as she pleases, and one senses as the white dignitaries bid her farewell a degree of sadness at their being left behind on the island. The princess arrives and disappears, her aura undiminished. She has something in common with the expatriates—the privileged status of being white and British—but her presence implicitly reminds the expats that they are subjects, too, that they are closer to the Trinidadian people on the social scale than they ever will be to the princess. The expatriate condition allows them the illusion of escaping the strictures of the British class system for a while, but the princess' visit, however much it seems to be enthusiastically welcomed by them, serves as an implicit reminder that there are gradations of white people, and that they are closer to the bottom of that scale than the top.

Pt. 10, Drilling operations at Fyzabad, Pitch Lake, Forest Reserve turntable, Point Fortin, and Pointe a Pierre
[https://www.youtube.com/watch?v=P7J3fQ_KV1U]

This noisy film recounts the old days of drilling for oil in Trinidad's southern oilfields. I'm going to say that this is Apex Oilfields as you can see an ATO (Apex

Trinidad Oilfields) lorry delivering bags of cement. However, the original film opens with shots of Shell operations in Point Fortin. The derricks do look Apexian but I cannot be 100 percent sure of the location, although I hardly think Apex would be delivering concrete to a Shell operation. Nonetheless it is a marvelous sequence that clearly shows how wells were drilled "back in the day". The shots may not be in the correct order and the soundtrack is lifted from current films of drilling and may not be accurate. It has been almost 50 years since I witnessed a well being drilled. The film continues with amazing shots of a Turntable at Forest Reserve. These massive flywheels with eccentric cams fixed at their hubs powered up to 20 pumping jacks at a time through a system of steel cables known as "jerk lines." These lines criss crossed the oilfields and woe betide the unfortunate bush creature that got caught in them. The pitch lake at La Brea follows. It is the largest natural deposit of asphalt in the world and pitch and asphalt from here covers most of the roads in North America. At the time this was filmed it was mined by Trinidad Lake Asphalt. Note the Trinidad Automobile Association's sign over the La Brea sign. The film ends with some shots of the Point Fortin and Pointe a Pierre refineries and some shots of the Texaco fields at Forest Reserve.

The need to work is the fundamental difference between the princess and the expats, and is one connection between the expats and the local people, however much their working conditions differ. The American "occupation" of Trinidad had been a kind of watershed in this regard: the sight of white Americans carrying out manual labor was a shock for a society in which such work was exclusively carried out by nonwhites. The power of the whites and the mystique of whiteness lay in large part in their ability to reap virtually all of the rewards of manual labor, while carrying out none of it. Although the expats do not seem to be involved in manual labor, they do work for their salaries, and as such they occupy a singular position in the society—coming from cultures in which it is social class rather than race that determines the kind of work that one does, they constitute an in-between class that expects and needs to work and at the same time enjoys many of the privileges that history confers on any white person in Trinidad. There is sound in this footage of various oil-related work: early in the film a white man stands by as an onshore drill turns rapidly, later two local men in helmets are shown assisting the operation. Work thus to some extent brings the expat men in closer contact to local men than would be the case in broader society. The local men carry out the heavier manual work while the white man supervises. Given the nature of the work, however, there is little heavy manual labor, and more attention is paid to ensuring the smooth running of the machinery. A caption states: "After striking oil, top of well is sealed, Xmas tree fixed and gas is drawn off."

The power for drilling is provided by the turntable that is connected to the drills by a series of steel cables. Views of the Pitch Lake show people spreading pitch on the roads by their homes, and a sign that mentions "Sir Walter Raleigh 1595." Another sign for "Shell Trinidad Ltd, Penal Division" implies the long connection between the early European arrivals and the latest newcomers— the expat workers, working not for a specific government, but for the multinational oil company that in some regards takes on the roles played by the old colonial powers in commandeering natural resources and extracting the profit from them. A third sign for "Helena Discovery Well, Forest Reserve, No. 1" indicates that the well was first drilled in 1914, that it produced over the next three years a total of 226,000 barrels of oil, and that it now produces only three barrels per day. It is a kind of historical landmark, and a reminder of the finite nature of the natural resources of Trinidad. Shots of the Shell refinery at Pont Fortin are followed by a caption that states, "Point a Pierre. Trinidad leaseholds oil refinery sold to American company for 65m pounds," and images of the large Texaco plant. In effect, the oil companies are new colonizing forces, appropriating the natural resources and setting up on the island not in order to improve the lives of the everyday people, but to stay only as long as the oil is there, and then abandon the place as quickly as they arrived.

[Pt. 11,] Life and Schooldays at the T&TEC Power Station Compound 1955–58
[https://www.youtube.com/watch?v=HnHyyIwOr34]

This is a lovely, almost idyllic sequence in which the camera captures the simple delights of daily life at the T&TEC (Trinidad and Tobago Electricity Commission) compound in Penal in the late 1950s. Beautiful shots of the staff bungalows, the reservoir, a pick up game of footy in the backyard, tea next door and mother kissing her two boys goodbye as she sends them off to school leave us in no doubt that this was indeed a special time in this family's life. Both boys attend an unnamed local, fully integrated school and several shots detail the bustle around the school, with some local ladies obviously selling sweets to the students. Later on in the film the older boy's school uniform changes to that worn by boys at Presentation College in San Fernando. The film finishes with some shots of local flowers found at the camp.

This is an important film in the sequence as it focuses on the domestic, everyday life of the family, including the boys going to school. The expats' homes are comfortable, generally in the bungalow style that is itself a colonial import. There are gardens with tropical trees and plants, though again the work in the gardens would not have been done by the white families. The homes have large garages for the modern motor cars. The boys leave for school at 7 a.m., the mother kissing the younger boy as he leaves in his shirt, tie, and khaki shorts, while the elder son wears a white shirt and khaki shorts. They smile as they leave the mother, and walk down the road from their house. Interestingly, it is in school and through the boys that the most extensive contact with local people seems to take place. Outside the school, local children wait, while the younger boy buys sweets from a vendor. The schoolyard shows very few other white faces among the pupils; the younger boy poses for the camera with a friend, a local boy. Returning home at 4 p.m., the boys climb the hill back to their house, smiling still, and are greeted by their mother, who is having tea with another woman and her young child. The next image in the sequence is of the elder son returning from school wearing a different uniform—the navy blazer, tie, and long pants of Presentation College in San Fernando, a prestigious school in the south, and apparently the institution of choice for older children in the expat community. The boys are adaptable, even as they are at the frontline of the contact between the communities and have to negotiate the difficult business of integrating into the school system and in the case of the elder boy, moving from one institution to another in a short period. He strolls more languidly to the mini bus that will take him and other white boys to the school. The school building is modern, and houses the Catholic boys' school that was founded around 1930, though admission to the school seems to have been open to non-Catholics. Subsequent images of the home suggest an idyllic lifestyle for the families: the boys play football; the closeness of their bond is evident as they play together. It would be interesting to hear how the boys speak, both with their friends at school and at home, as there would no doubt be a degree of code switching between the different contexts, and this would contrast with the parents, whose accents would most likely remain the same, as markers of their whiteness and Britishness. The boys' identities are more fluid, and they seem at ease among their friends at school, and more liable to think of themselves as equals to the local people.

[Pt. 12,] The Longstaffs at Apex Oilfields 1956
[https://www.youtube.com/watch?v=1yMp_BLWuso]

This very short clip shows one of the families I knew at Apex Oilfields, the Longstaffs. I've slowed the film down to 40% of its speed as the original clips were very short indeed. What a handsome family they are! I only remember Richard, the boy leaning on the window of the Opel Kapitan. I knew he had an older brother, Eric, but have no memory of him. I do remember Richard's father, Bill, slightly. His Mum, Belle, is truly a beautiful woman and so very British. The clip opens with the older boy at the Point Fortin club pool and continues at Bungalow 14 in Apex, where they lived. Bungalow 14 looked out over No. 1 Dam, which can be seen in the background of one of the shots. Noticeable only if you freeze the frame is Singh, the barber, smoking a cigarette and cutting a lad's hair with a pair of hand powered clippers. Singh was a legend in Apex. Once his cow got loose and got into one of the Camp Senior Staff's gardens. He complained loudly to Singh. Unmoved, Singh threated to "slit he belly if he touch mih cow." Sigh. Only in Trinidad.

These shots of another British family show first an older boy, a teenager who, interestingly, seems to be up to date with contemporary fashions: the hairstyle, the checked shirt, and the jeans. A younger boy stares longingly out of a car window, while a mother smiles for the camera. A barber cuts a boy's hair, a cigarette hanging from his mouth, while a mustachioed father walks proudly by. The nuclear family is clearly the predominant model for the expats: two married parents, the father working, the mother at home and, curiously, all of the children seem to be male, of various ages. This familial structure is in effect the backbone of the expat community, which provides security and familiarity in the foreign country, a kind of continuity with life in the homeland. Interestingly, too, this family structure seems particular to the expat community, as the glimpses we see in the films of family life outside the expat sphere show women working in and out of the home and a more fluid, less rigid idea of family life than exists with the expats.

Pt. 13, Maracas Bay and North Coast Road
[https://www.youtube.com/watch?v=s04e-P4hxjM]

The music is curious—like parang and with a gently driving rhythm over which the high-pitched, almost operatic singing seems to hang, like two musical styles coming together, the singing like an echo of a Spanish past.

The road is quiet: built only a decade before, it opened up the North Coast to the people of Port of Spain, especially those with motor cars, who could escape the city at the weekend and go to the beaches. Two pillars stand to mark the entrance to the North Coast Road; the camera looks below to a swimming pool and then across the valley to the city and the bay, the houses to the west where the Port of Spain expat community has traditionally been housed. The hills are still heavily wooded. The camera operator stands on the opposite side of the road as a single car approaches: there is a degree of thought and planning in the filming, a story being told of the place and its landscape, and the expat family's relationship to it. There is a sense of wonder and perhaps awe as the road reveals the first glimpses of the sea and the dark green fingers of the land reaching out into it. There is danger, too, as the camera seems almost to have to lean over the vertiginous cliffside to catch the image. The same car reappears, now with more people in it, stopped by the roadside to look at the sea far below and into the distance. A white arm hangs out of the window, waving at the camera, a sign of relaxation and feeling at ease. The beauty of the coastline is further displayed through some trees that frame a scene of rocky islets against which the sea washes in little sprays of white, and then there are multiple shots of the thickly forested hills stretching into the hazy distance. The road is not busy; only one other car is filmed on its way to Maracas Bay, which is first filmed briefly from above, and then on the car's final descent with the first view of the white sand and coconut trees, the dark blue-green sea.

There are only a few visitors to the beach, their cars parked in the shade of the coconut trees. The beach area is completely undeveloped, with no hotel or food outlets and the forests in the surrounding hills are thick and green. The only modern building is a kind of pavilion, designed perhaps to shelter from the rain, apparently at the eastern end of the beach, where there are more cars, and more families, all white, apart from local woman selling corn, her children sitting in the shade of a tree. The beach looks beautiful in the sun, which catches the tops of the waves, making the whole scene shine. A man jogs on the beach, while children and dogs play in the shallow water, the waves crashing against them. The untanned bodies of the visitors suggest that they do not visit the beach regularly. Mothers hold their small children close as they venture into the water. Everyone is smiling, happy, and a rainbow cuts across the bay. A local police or other officer in uniform stands alone, watching the rainbow and the children, his hand on his hip. Later, preparing to leave, the mothers take care of the children as the bathers dry themselves, cars are packed, and the day ends, the music still playing and giving the whole short film an air of nostalgia. The music in fact is virtually the only Trinidadian human presence in the film, apart from the one or two vendors or officers, as otherwise it is only white people who use the beach as a site of leisure, a family day out. Clearly, the use of a motor car is essential to reach the bay from the cities, and the bay is finally like an enclave, a "safe" and exclusive place for the families of expats and perhaps some white Trinidadians to socialize and unwind. In this way, the scene perhaps anticipates the later exclusive resorts that would come to characterize Caribbean beach tourism, where visitors are kept apart from locals and the beach is a site to which only certain groups have access. Life is idyllic for the expats—family groups appear strong and the links with other expat families form a sort of extended family that is also their community;

people know each other and are interested in socializing only with others in the group.

Pt. 14, Mount St. Benedict
[https://www.youtube.com/watch?v=kL0QUrOpFps]

Set to some of Lionel Belasco's music this pleasant sequence brings us memories of the Benedictine Monastery at St. Augustine. Almost a self contained city in itself, the Benedictine monks administered a Seminary, a boarding school (The Abbey School), their monastery, a senior's residence, a guest house, a farm, beehives, bakeries and the like. Today it is but a shadow of its former glory, with the boarding school closed and recently, the Seminary closing, sending its few remaining seminarians to Jamaica. Mt. St. Benedict was a popular destination for day visitors as well and many locals came here to picnic. Note the Indian family relaxing with their lunch just behind their two tone Ford Consul with the wide whitewall tires.

Mount St. Benedict is first filmed from an elevated position to the west. The low hills are covered in green forests and the land around is largely uninhabited, which makes the forest seem isolated. Trees sway as if in time to the upbeat calypso tune that plays. The perspective then shifts sharply to the mount itself, a view of the car at the edge of the car park, looking over the large plain below and south to San Fernando. The buildings appear at first virtually deserted, so the camera focuses on the plants, the flowers and bushes blowing in the breeze. Some boys cross the courtyard before the main monastery building, then a vendor woman is seen under a tree, which indicates she knows there will be at least some visitors liable to be interested in what she is selling. A nun walks down the road, as a woman watches her from behind. It must be towards the end of the rainy season, the end of the calendar year, as the immortelle trees are in flower, and their orange flowers stand out against the foliage turned deep green by the rains. The mount must have been a popular spot for weekend picnics, as a local family group is filmed under the trees, the women seeing to the children and the men chatting or standing alone, looking over the scene below. The family is well dressed, the men are in khaki trousers and white shirts, as if they have come from church to picnic or lime. There does not appear to be any alcohol involved. There is a sense of serenity and peace as the camera takes its closing shots, focusing on the hillsides and the vast green plains below—Trinidad on a sleepy Sunday near to Christmas time.

[Pt. 15, Sunday Afternoon around the Savannah
https://www.youtube.com/watch?v=poedhR-rzol]

In contrast to Mount St. Benedict, where there were only a few visitors, the Savannah in Port of Spain is the place to go following church or for recreation on Sunday afternoons. This film opens with piano music playing, which gives an air of gentility and order that is at first reinforced with the sight of three young girls in white dresses, Sunday churchwear that is intact except for the white hats that they hold in their hands. The girls walk closely together, in time, and look to the camera directly, without smiling, as if they know they are being filmed as a curiosity. One can sense a certain distance between the person filming and the girls, as if the camera and its operator are intruding into a private experience, and as if the girls can tell the operator is foreign and not to be trusted or engaged with. There is almost a sense of defiance in the girls' stares, as if they are returning the gaze in a sense, asserting that it is the man who is a curiosity, and disrupting the fixed subject-object positions on which the entire series of films depends: the girls subtly yet powerfully become subjects, the ones looking, staring, resisting. The girls disrupt the easy, harmonious atmosphere that the films generally portray, the sense of a colony at ease with its situation. It is remarkable that one of the few disruptive moments in this regard should come from some of the youngest people filmed, the girls that did not look away but stared the camera down, shifting the gaze subtly yet so powerfully. The camera seems almost to shake, unsettled by the returned gaze.

More commonly, the films' subjects do not look at the camera and are filmed as in the next scene without their consent or knowledge. On the eastern side of the Savannah a white woman walks alone, and cars pass sedately along the broad avenue. There are numerous cricket games taking place on the Savannah, local men in their whites, set against the green of the grass, the trees, and the hills that act as frames in scenes that appear almost painted. The white of their uniforms recalls that of the girls in their Sunday outfits—white as a marker of purity and respectability. The rules of the game limit in many regards the extent to which the cricketers can rebel or return the gaze in the way of the girls, who appear free to walk how and where they wished in the city. Set against each other in sporting competition, the men play out an odd ritual, a game of imitation that is not completely unlike Carnival, in that there is behind the play a serious political and cultural intent—to appropriate the game to a degree, so that bowling is a form of attack and batting a subtle form of defense that involves a wide range of responses, including deflecting, blocking, leaving, and when the bowling is weak, driving it back at or beyond the bowler. Black skins, white games, white uniforms.

The white of these uniforms is further related to that of a guard, filmed almost surreptitiously from behind a small tree, standing rigidly, looking to the left, in his white coat and pith helmet, a picture of colonial order, apparently guarding the Governor's House, which is set against the hills, behind iron gates and stone pillars. Everything else in and around the Savannah is relatively open—anyone can go anywhere and as such different social groups can encounter each other there, even if they do not seem to engage each other too directly. The Governor's House is by contrast set away from the road, and half-hidden behind trees, it appears as a symbol of power, real power out of reach and even the comprehension of local people, a self-created mystery that seems also strangely vulnerable, in that it needs to hide itself away to retain that mystery, as if it knows its power is based on illusion and deception.

Another guard in white uniform marches in front of a hedge, with the Governor's House more visible and cars passing by. This guard carries a rifle on his shoulder, an unusually open display of potential violence in this colonial setting where control is exerted largely through more subtle codes of play, dress, and comportment. The guard marches awkwardly—in fact, it is more like a regular walk with longer strides, as if he is straining to keep to the rigid tempo of the march. He looks fleetingly at a local man as he passes, almost as if he is searching for recognition or acknowledgment, but the man passes by as if the guard is invisible, and the guard speeds up his walk, strangely alone on his own island.

A sign indicates the arrival to the Royal Botanic Gardens, quickly preceded by an almost Edenic scene that sets the gardens against the green hills falling into the distance. Interestingly, the visitors here are uniquely white, and are dressed in white, in khaki, dresses, shorts, and hats. Flowers and shrubs, red, yellow, pink, sway in the breeze, while a piece of text announces the next image will be of the Australian Sausage Tree, a sign also that the gardens are composite sites in which the local flora encounters that of the broader colonial world—plants, like people, are transported and planted, expected to grow, though in the gardens the effect is harmonious—plants can be grown, trimmed, controlled in ways that people cannot.

An elevated view of the city presents some of the popular districts, possibly Belmont, while the Savannah appears as the heart of the place, the site that connects and brings together the disparate parts of Port of Spain. Beyond the seafront, there are large ships in the bay, signs of industry and of connections to broader commercial markets, other port cities in the Caribbean and farther afield. A drive down the hill to the town ends with views of the so-called Magnificent Seven houses that line the western side of the Savannah, the first of which appears as a baronial Scottish castle and is followed by others in French Colonial, Indian Empire, and Mediterranean styles, each one out of place but also part of the composite visual imagery of the Savannah—the dizzying set of signs that might appear chaotic but is part of the creolizing city, a place that is forever becoming, that unsettles and returns the filmmaker's gaze, in ways that recall the opening images of the girls staring down the camera.

> Pt. 16, Yacht Club, Goodwood Park, Blue Basin Waterfall
> [https://www.youtube.com/watch?v=uiTqIexOkNU]

An upbeat calypso tune accompanies the first scene at the Yacht Club, with two young white boys on a jetty, and then a local man in a speedboat trying to start its engine. Farther out at sea the R.M.S. *Mauretania* passes by, its twin funnels visible in the distance. A long-serving ship on the Cunard Line, by the 1950s the Mauretania was used for Caribbean cruises in the winter months. Closer to shore, catamarans catch the strong breeze and cut across the choppy waters. On shore, the car park is full of motor cars, and young white boys walk with a local woman, no doubt a nanny, while on the shaded jetty white men, women, and children have tea and ice cream. Men in white uniforms, possibly from the Mauretania or else Royal Navy officers, come ashore and are greeted by a driver.

Views of Goodwood Park show the early development of this middle-class area to the east of Port of Spain; there is still at this point a large area of swampy forest that separates the suburb from the city. There are modern, American-style houses with low roofs and large glass windows, a nanny carries a child into one of the houses, and a game of cricket takes place, apparently with local players.

Two young white boys in khaki shorts and white shirts run up a path to the Blue Basin waterfall, where a large group of local people bathes in the waters below the fall. The mother follows the boys up the hill to the fall, which contrasts with the Yacht Club, where the patrons are overwhelmingly white. The fall, by contrast, is visited mainly by local people, and we do not see the white boys or woman actually go into the water, though one of the boys does appear to be in the water; the camera remains at a distance as the local people enjoy the swim. Thus, there is no scene in which locals and white adult foreigners mix as equals—at the Yacht Club and in the short scenes at the houses, the local people are in various roles of servitude—maintaining boats and looking after children. At the waterfall, there is a sense that the white family is intruding, that this is not their natural space—the men stand with their backs to the camera almost like guards, and none of the people look to the camera. The insouciant lives of the white expats contrast subtly but also sharply with those of the people, who seem constantly aware of the power dynamics in late colonial Trinidad.

Pt. 17, Shell Camp Club, Point Fortin
[https://www.youtube.com/watch?v=JerT7GmGfs0]

All footage contributed by Sooty 1312. This film is not to be copied without the express consent of the operator of this channel. Central to expatriate life in the southern oil camps was the Club. Each camp had its own and as Jennifer Franko mentions in her book, each club would advertise its events at other camp clubs across the oil belt. By far the largest were the clubs at Pointe-a-Pierre, Forest Reserve and Point Fortin but the other camps, no matter how small, each had its own and together they provided a vibrant and exciting social life for company employees, with any excuse used to put on another "club event." This sequence details pleasant days around the pool at the Shell Camp Club and what a beautiful place it is! At the beginning, note the wrought iron grille with the initials "UBC" from the early days, before Shell, when the Point Fortin fields were operated by United British Oilfields. There is also a shot of the Forest Reserve Club, which looks much the same today, some 55 years later. Christmas Day, 1957 was spent at the club as well, with the children playing with their toy boats in the pool.

The UBC initials on the iron grille refer to the United British Oilfields company, one of the early operators of the Point Fortin oil refinery. Adults, mainly men, gather round the bar, while children play round the pool, with mothers in attendance. It is Christmas 1957, and two boys stand in front of a Christmas tree with model boats that are most likely gifts. They play with the motorized boats in the pool. The campgrounds are green and well maintained. After swimming, the mother looks briefly at the camera, which then diverts its focus to the two boys, which is interesting as it suggests the modesty of the mother and the importance to her of her sons, as if they are the important people here, and she is not worthy of attention independently of them. Returning to their car, they smile constantly, as if the day, indeed their lives, are charmed and carefree. There is a brief shot of the Forest Reserve Club, followed by a caption that reads "Club Beach Bar under the banyan trees" and a shot of a few people in the shade of the trees and a tiki-style bar—"Another day at the club," a caption reads, while a man sits alone in the bar and a few children play in the pool. Boys leap into the pool from the high board. There is overall a degree of repetition in this film, a sense of doing the same things time after time with the same closed group of people, and of the novelty wearing off, inevitably. There is also more of a sense here of physical isolation, of being away from the city and the main centers of population. The club is a focal point set up to serve every subgroup in the expat community: the men go there for drinks and relaxation, the women tend to the children, who spend most of their time in the pool, playing, and working off their energy. While the men socialize together the women seem to lead more solitary lives, preoccupied almost completely with the raising of the children.

Pt. 18, Shell Penal, Penal Market, Shopping at Allum's Grocery, Forest Reserve [https://www.youtube.com/watch?v=5Fliw5hlBk8]

All footage contributed by Sooty 1312. This video is not to be copied without the written consent of the operator of this channel. Number 17 [sic] in this series takes the viewer to the Shell Camp in Penal around 1957 with some shots of the Club and in what is becoming a regular sight in these films, the trunk of the Opel Kapitan is once again being loaded with booze! Included is a visit to Penal Market. I think these shots are beautiful as they capture an integral part of life in Trinidad in the 1950s—the market. Look at the shots carefully. Our family picks up their greens and we see the boys unloading some melons at their bungalow at the T&TEC Camp. Follows a short trip through Forest Reserve Camp and a stop at Allum's Grocery store where mother does the shopping. I don't remember Allum's but our camp, Apex, had Grell's grocery at the entrance to the field. After the amalgamation of most of the fields, Grell's became HiLo, a very well known grocery chain in Trinidad.

The Shell Trinidad Club at Penal is a low, colonial style building, clearly part of a network of clubs that were important focal points for the expat community. Alcohol is again a key part of the social life; an East Indian man smiles as he loads the car with a crate of Carib beer, and a view of the car's trunk reveals a selection of other drinks, including rum and Coca-Cola products. Perhaps ironically, there follows a quick shot of the Shell Clinic, the medical facility for staff and their families. Views of Penal Market show the mother and sons engaging with local vendors, mainly East Indian women. The mother and son leave the market laden with produce, as a policeman stands watching. Back home, the boys unload the car. A visit to Forest Reserve Oilfield begins with a view of the Post Office, no doubt an important site for the expats and one of the primary means of communicating with friends and family. The mother and sons do more grocery shopping, this time for tinned goods in a store, Allum's. A local man helps them to the car with their boxes of goods. This film is useful in that it shows the daily life of the expat, the need to carry out banal, domestic tasks, and the ways in which this becomes the domain of the mother—she is the one who thinks of and plans for meals, and it takes some effort for her to stock up to feed the family. There seems to be little by way of imported goods, and the family eats predominantly local produce. Alcohol is again an important part of the adults' lives—the culture of the camp seems to rely on it to facilitate social bonds between the expats. The mother is throughout strangely silent, even if in this film we sense her presence more strongly; the domestic domain clearly belongs to her and she takes her role there seriously. There is also a strong sense of the closeness of her relationships with her sons, particularly the younger one, who accompanies her everywhere, and helps her in completing her tasks. The father is presumably there filming, but he does seem to be on the outside looking in to the daily lives of the mother and sons, the mundane, quiet, potentially lonely side of the expat life that the men tend not to see when they are working or spending time with other expat men. Significantly, too, the mother seems not to have many of her own friends, and to spend virtually all of her time with her family, principally her sons. The camps seem to cater for the men and the children; the mothers hover in some in-between space between the men and the children, caring for both, and almost erased as people. The men and boys smile readily for the camera, but she holds back and remains inscrutable, as if the camera is in a way a confidante, a partner in silence that sees her as she is and to which she does not put on any false cheeriness. Neither smiling nor frowning, she appears always in-between, negated, alienated from the expat women as much as the local women she encounters at the markets and who inhabit fully the public sphere, while she is restricted in the places she can inhabit: the home, the car, the club, each one of which is never truly her own.

Pt. 19, Opening Day, Penal Power Plant
[https://www.youtube.com/watch?v=mHXZAM-UeZA]

In 1958 construction of the Penal Power Plant was completed. This film contains footage shot on opening day showing the plant and some of the preparations for opening ceremonies. The colony's governor officiated and the Trinidad Police Band provided the music. This short provides a wonderful glimpse of the workings of T&TEC at that time.

The power plant is presented as a sign of Trinidad's modernity, its progress as a colony. Local workers are filmed, unsmiling, which contrasts with the broad smiles of the white woman at the beginning of the film. By a lake, there are staff residences that appear new and to offer comfortable accommodation. A caption reads that the official opening took place on February 26, 1958, and was carried out by the governor, Sir Edward Beetham. At dusk, 6 p.m., there is a "sound and light programme for V.I.P.s." The Police Band plays close to the power plant, the white and black uniforms recall the guards at the governor's house in Port of Spain. The invited guests are almost all white, mostly men in suits, with some women wearing hats. As the sun goes down, the show starts: an illuminated image of a kettle, lights flashing as the band plays.

> Pt. 20 - Loading Cane. Erin Dairy. Rural Trinidad
> [https://www.youtube.com/watch?v=OrJGMf3tTno]

> No. 20 in this series brings a tear to my eye. The lilting love song and the idyllic images of rural Trinidad bring to mind happy memories of a land I left 50 years ago. Beautiful in their simplicity, these scenes tell more than meets the eye about the backbreaking sugar industry in Trinidad. Note the donkey powered crane lifting massive bundles onto waiting railway wagons. Look carefully at the shot of the donkey as it pulls its cart onto the road. Note the hive of activity in the background and the railway crossing. This crossing is the Usine Ste. Madeleine track across the main road just entering Debe from the north. Continuing on in this episode we visit the Erin Estate, a dairy farm, and we stroll along the byways of a Trinidad that disappeared a long, long time ago.

The modern power plant contrasts with the scenes in this film of the sugar cane industry, the canes filmed first swaying in the breeze against the blue sky and then on the back of wagons pulled by donkeys driven by workers. A donkey pulls a crane that lifts large bundles of cane onto waiting railway wagons. Two white boys in colorful shirts chew at bits of sugar cane, while the mother sits in the car, her face shaded and only semivisible. Following a short clip of some wooden shacks, the camera pans across the cane fields, which stretch far across the low, rolling hills. The Tate and Lyle factory has two large chimneys and, set against a darkening sky, appears a foreboding industrial site that contrasts with the following scenes of pastoral simplicity—a water buffalo bathing in a mud pool, and a man sitting on a cart being pulled by a cow. The Erin Estate is a dairy farm, with various animals filmed apparently in slower motion, as is the closing shot from behind of the man driving his cart down the country road. The mood here is nostalgic, as if the family senses the coming end of the apparently simple life of the agricultural worker: electricity and oil are ushering in modern ways of living that the white family very much enjoy, but in this film it is as if they would like to keep the people living the simple lives they lead, which are most likely not simple at all, but difficult and relentless, tied to the cycle of the sugar cane and the back-breaking work of planting, weeding, and harvesting, which is not presented in the film: the cane goes from field to cart apparently without effort or toil. Notably, too, the people work constantly, and leisure and "time out" are possible only for the white family, which tours the island making these little postcards, memorializing itself instantly through the films, which are nostalgic even as they are made. Memory and nostalgia are thus luxuries that the family is afforded through their privileges of race, class, and wealth—by contrast the local workers filmed here appear to turn in circles of time, like the donkey turning the crane, or in cycles related to the sugar-cane crop, which tie them to the past in ways that suggest different experiences of time to those of the family. The expats are aware of moments, of time passing quickly, ruptured by the modern technological advancements they help bring about. Their days are different from one another, they are able to travel by car to different places, so that their experience of time is closely related to place, their ability to move around, and conversely their experience of place is determined largely by their conception of time as quickly changing, advancing, things changing. This contrasts sharply with the ways in which the local workers seem to experience time and place as far more fixed, unchanging entities, tied to cycles of work, nature, and history that act on their lives with the force of fate, turning relentlessly even as parts of the country enter into a distinctly modern experience of time and place. Finally, the possession of and access to the camera is also a marker of these different experiences of time, space, and modernity. The camera gives its holder the power to record specific forms of memory and to act in a sense as a guardian or keeper of time—each snapshot of the family acts as proof of their existence in a certain time and place, one that can be accessed still sixty years later. With regard to the workers it records, the camera fixes subject and object positions: the workers exist only as objects of the camera's gaze, as distant and undifferentiated beings that stand as markers of the place and its uneven movement into modernity. Of course, the workers are remnants in a sense of a previous, distinctly modern mode of working—the murderous intensity of the slave plantation—but they are increasingly detached from the technological modernity represented by the oil industry, the power plants, and the camera itself, and appear marooned in a certain, unchanging time and place. These are crucial images, as they record a critical time in Trinidadian history, the point where the different classes in society become increasingly detached, where an uneven modernity imposes itself, splitting the society in ways that reinforce previously existing divisions and that determine each group's fate in relation to their access to the modern life and its various technologies. Caught at the high point of colonial rule, the film has a prophetic quality, a sense that the relations set in place by the new technologies would be the foundations of the new society, or even be hindrances to creating any sense of a new society that would be in any meaningful way different from the colonial model that the film represents so briefly yet tellingly.

> Pt. 21, Produce of Trinidad, Fresh fish at Mosquito Creek, Shrimp at North Beach, Rice Paddies
> [https://www.youtube.com/watch?v=WwEOUTuMy8I]
>
> Set to the tune of the original "Man Smarter" sung by King Radio, this sequences details some of the produce of Trinidad. It never ceases to amaze me how bountiful Trinidad was. Oil and Gas and Sugar have been covered already and this sequence details some of the lesser products of the colony, like calabash, cocoa, bananas etc. For an island only 60 miles by 40, the number and variety of products exported is truly amazing.

For all that she often appears to be limited in the social spheres in which she can move, the mother is also the one who mediates any contact with local people, for example in stores or markets, or as in this case in buying fish directly from fishermen. The calypso that plays in this film, "Man Smart, Woman Smarter," by King Radio complements the images of the mother engaging with the fishermen, and providing the boys with an example of how to interact with people. "The women of today smarter than men in every way," the song goes, and the mother shows how she is the connection between the family, its sequestered expat lifestyle and the daily life of Trinidad. She is the contact point, the one in the middle, in-between, and it is her role as mother and cook that brings her into contact with the local people. This is still not in any way an equal relationship, but in contrast to how she appears in expat company—marginalized, in the shadows and sidelines—she is often at the center of the exchanges with local traders. A country scene shows a man, a woman, and some young girls growing rice, then the rice drying out before finally being packed into boxes. At home, the rice is poured into a bowl with water and put into an electric oven. Coconuts are shown at various stages of growth, and the boys try to break through the hard husk of a ripe nut to get to the milk and flesh. Coconut husk is shown drying and then used to stuff mattresses. The calabash fruit grows green against the blue sky, the boys shake some fallen fruit for the sound, the hard, hollow rattling that makes the fruit ideal as a musical instrument, the shac-shac that gives rhythm to parang and other bands. Cocoa fruit hang in roadside trees, and ripe pods are shown at home, along with tonca beans, and spice bark. Grapefruits and bananas grow freely and abundantly, and there is overall an appreciation for the natural riches of Trinidad. Though there is a limited sense of integration with local people, food is for the family a means of being local in their own way. The mother appears to use local produce in her cooking, and to be innovative in her use of ingredients. There is not an excess of foreign imported goods available, but this does not seem to be a problem as the family, led by the mother, eats a varied diet of fresh produce. Food and the search for it brings together not only the family as a unit, but it also forces them to interact with local producers and to get to know the people and place in ways they could not do if they limited themselves to the expat lifestyle of the camp and the club.

Pt. 22, San Fernando Hill, PoS Docks and USAF at Piarco
[https://www.youtube.com/watch?v=h2FvzgQx5CU]

A few of these shots may have appeared in earlier sequences where they were not the actual focus at the time. In this clip I've compiled those locations in more detail. I'm sure that viewers in Trinidad will see a very different San Fernando in this film than exists today! At the Port of Spain docks, we view the liner "Antilles" at the wharf and if you look in the foreground you can see several TGR goods wagons waiting to be loaded. The video concludes with two aeroplanes belonging to the United States Air Force landing at Piarco. The calypso is "Seditious Law" by Growling Tiger.

San Fernando Hill is one of the few natural landmarks in the south of Trinidad. The mother is filmed climbing the 320 steps to the top of the hill, the boys in front of her. She is dressed as ever modestly, in a long skirt, and wears heels for the climb, which is interesting as it indicates a certain rigidity in her choice of outfit—she would wear the same thing if she were at home, the club, the beach, or the market. As such, her identity as it is expressed through clothing and shoes is quite fixed—she is the white woman, the expat, wife of the worker, and perhaps most importantly, mother of her two sons. She has standards, and whether in public or at home she dresses smartly, as do her sons. Of course, the clothing and footwear options for any woman would have been limited in the 1950s, and the idea of wearing more comfortable shoes may not have occurred to her, but there is a certain stoicism about her in that she is always moving ahead, getting on with things, and never complaining. The view from the top of the hill reminds us of the similar view from the St. Augustine Monastery, only here the hinterland is even more empty, and stretches far into the distance. The view to the west includes the greater part of the urban area, the development reaching to the sea and that includes the extensive oil refinery with its chimneys and towers. The film switches rather abruptly to the Port of Spain docks, and views of some large sheds with rusty roofs. A cruise liner sits at the docks, the *Antilles*, another sign of the burgeoning tourist industry. The film ends with two large USAF airplanes landing at Piarco airport, which indicates again the ways in which Trinidad was connected to the outside world—through ships and industry, but also increasingly through aviation and its enduring strategic importance for U.S. interests in the region.

Farewell to Trinidad, 24 October 1958
[https://www.youtube.com/watch?v=IqzhEwp4HBA]

All footage contributed by Sooty1312. This video is not to be copied without the consent of the operator of this channel. Sadly, this brings to an end the Time Out in Trinidad series. There will still be a few more videos coming as I cull the three hours of files to find anything I've missed. Also stay tuned for more exciting films as the Camito sails from Port of Spain, through the British West Indies, to Britain. One cannot adequately describe the Expatriate in the Colonies. They were a migrant group of people from Britain who fanned out across the British Empire to engage in and contribute to her prosperity. Trinidad provided a wonderful life for these families with housing, medical services, provisioning and in some cases, vehicles provided by the companies that hired them. For most, as surely as they arrived, they would eventually leave. Some stayed for many, many years. Some even took up permanent residence. Most, however, returned home at the completion of their contracts. Remember that these families had built a life for themselves in the colony and many grew very fond of that lovely island called Trinidad. Parting was sweet sorrow for them. More so, their departure also brought sadness, and in some cases, unemployment for the household staff these families hired. In many cases, the servants and yardboys grew very attached to their employers and their departure brought an uncertain future for them. In this film you can see a somewhat lost servant standing as this family bids their farewell to their friends, to T&TEC and to Trinidad. The two boys in this film, David and Graham, still fondly remember the land where they spent three happy years at T&TEC. David returned to Trinidad in 1988 with his wife and two sons to find an independent Trinidad that bore little or no resemblance to the beautiful colony he once knew. With its wealth of natural resources, Trinidad has struggled throughout the 1990s and the 2000s to curb its massive crime rate and rampant corruption. The roads in these films bear no resemblance at all to the traffic choked multi-lane motorways that exist today. The railways are gone. Oil production has moved offshore. The sugar industry has long since collapsed. The beautiful countryside cannot be enjoyed by tourists as robberies, murders and kidnappings continue to rise. With the election of Kamla Persad Bissessar, hope has returned to Trinidad and only the years ahead will tell us how successful her government will be in solving some of Trinidad's problems.

Everyone knows that one cannot return to Colonial days. The past is the past. But every Trinidadian living there today deserves a life that includes the peace and security evident in these films.

"We say goodbye to all our friends and the land of the hummingbird, 24th October 1958." For the first time, the family's "help" is shown, a woman who stands modestly, smiling and not smiling in turn, not unlike the mother in that regard. It is interesting that they should ask her to come outside for the camera, as if they did not want to show her working, doing their chores, and at the point of their leaving they wanted to show that they recognized her as a person. It is almost as if the woman has been hidden away while they have filmed the rest of the footage, and that they take her out as a kind of prize, to show their friends back home—the intended audience—that they had a black maid and that is how you could live in Trinidad. In this regard it reminds the viewer of the Sembene film, *La Noire de* (1966), in which an African maid is taken to Europe as a kind of prize and shown off as a curiosity. The clip is very short, and the camera lingers longer on the family saying goodbye to a young white couple from the inside of the car. The ship "Camito" waits at the dock for them, as the family packs up, the two boys looking downbeat as they see their mother walking toward them. A mixed group of passengers boards the ship, while onshore various workers go about their business, and other men work at the family's car, preparing it to be lifted onto the ship. Leaning over the side of the ship, the boys look apprehensive still, while the mother smiles and waves, apparently relieved to be leaving. A small group of friends stands at the dockside as the walkway is raised and the ship pulls away from land. The friends wave—the men in shirts and ties and the women in dresses. Moving farther into the bay, there are shots of the low forested hills and of the elder boy alone, his gaze fixed on the island, sadly it seems, his face set against the gray sky and sea. The contrast between the elder boy in particular and the mother is striking—in Trinidad the boys appear at all times happy and carefree, while the mother is often quiet, apprehensive-looking, and in the margins. On the ship, it is as if they have switched states—the mother is happy and relaxed, and the boys are quiet and reflective. This points not only to their different experiences in the island—the nonstop fun and adventure for the boys, the isolation and separation from home and family for the mother—but no doubt also to their different experiences of time: two years for the boys is a large part of their lives and they perhaps wonder how they will fit in again to the place of origin, while the mother is able to see the two years as part of a longer pattern, a short interruption of her life spent at home. While the boys are more likely to think of the island as their home, the mother never seems to commit to the place in that way. Ultimately, this underlines one fundamental aspect of expatriate life—its temporary, provisional nature, the knowledge that one can leave at the end of the contract, which for some means the period spent abroad is carefree and full of social events, while for others, it is a profoundly insecure period, longer than a holiday but too short to put down roots, to acquire one own's house or to think of a long-term future there.

Ultimately, the representation of the expats' lives in these films also contributes to the broader understanding of "whiteness" in the Caribbean, and underscores the idea that this category is far from homogeneous and is made up of a wide variety of subgroups with varying degrees and kinds of attachment to the islands. Whiteness was for a long time in scholarly discourse an "unexamined norm," to use McCusker's phrase ("The 'Unhomely' White Women of Antillean Writing" 274). As McCusker argues, however, there has been a great surge in works on whiteness, many inspired by Toni Morrison's call in *Playing in the Dark* to discover the manifestations of whiteness in American literature in particular (274). These studies emphasize, McCusker says, the "slipperiness of 'race', its scientific invalidity, and its constructed or imagined status" (274). McCusker is chiefly interested in the Francophone Caribbean islands, but her remarks on the continued privileged position of island-born whites in the French Antilles can also be applied to Anglophone islands such as Trinidad. To be sure, Trinidad's complex ethnic composition is reflected in its class structure, which is arguably more fluid than that of the French islands, but whiteness and paleness of skin still have considerable social currency. The whites' position of being a "dominant minority" is "paradoxical" according to McCusker, and sets them apart from white majority population in Western countries, from "what we might call the 'banality' of racial privilege, or from the naturalization of whiteness as an unmarked category" (275). Rather, she says, the descendants of the white plantation-owning caste,

> experience if anything a heightened visibility, and an amplified sense of racial identity. [...] Their desire to maintain racial purity (*préserver la race*) was to become a historical and socio-cultural counterweight to the impulse among non-whites, famously analysed by Fanon, to "whiten" or "save" the race, or, in more colloquial terms, to *chaper la peau* (literally, to save or to escape one's skin): that is, to marry partners of a lighter skin tone, and thereby facilitate social ascension. Given their minority demographic status, it is unsurprising that white characters have also been diegetically marginal in literature. Whiteness could be said to figure primarily as an absence in much twentieth-century writing, or perhaps more accurately, as a powerful absent-present. (275)

McCusker proceeds to examine the representation of white women in prominent Francophone Caribbean novels. She is primarily concerned with the particularly French Caribbean ethnocaste of the *Békés*, the small, endogamous minority descended from the planters. There is little consideration in these or other novels of other, later white groups, such as the expatriated workers in these films. While there is much that distinguishes the expats from the old planter classes, they are connected by their whiteness and the privileges that status affords them. Whiteness in the films is indeed, as in McCusker's terms, "a powerful absent-present," and it is also a "blank" category, not just in that it is underexamined or ignored, but that it is also in the case of the expats lived and represented through forms of silence and unknowing. The mother in particular bears comparison to some of the women discussed by McCusker, who are seen as alienated figures, even as they inhabit the home, and yet bear the burdens of the family. The more she is there, the more the mother's burdens seem to weigh on her, and these are not just to do with her family, but they also relate to history and place, the ways in which those elements inevitably infiltrate the family, drawing them further into the Trinidadian class and color system. But, as said before, if the one part of her and their power as white expats is in arriving and assuming their privileged position, the other part is in their leaving, their ability finally to leave it all behind. And for the mother that final movement is also a form of reconnection with herself, as if her two, separated bodies come back into one. In her smiles and laughter, we sense that the departure from the island is also a decisive break with the silence in which she and the family existed and which is the defining aspect of the expatriates' condition.

3
Sound Touristics

At sunrise on December 31, 1820, the Scottish traveler Mrs. A.C. Carmichael arrives at St. Vincent and is immediately struck by the view, which she says is "of the most captivating kind" (*Domestic Manners* I. 3). Quite tellingly, though, she resists being seduced by the visual beauty of the place—she says she is "not about to enlarge in the way of description," as if she is wary or mistrustful of her eyes, which might betray her purpose of observing "man, rather than nature," as she puts it. Thus, something interesting happens to her European vision at the moment of encounter with the island—a form of blinkering that allows her to see what she wants to see and to shut out elements of the place, chiefly its visual beauty that would challenge her largely preconceived notions of the people ("man") there. The visual appearance of the environment, what she calls the "awful convulsions of nature to which these tropical regions have been subject," seems moreover to disturb her notions of natural order, of everything and everyone in its place (4). She, and no doubt other Europeans, see in certain ways: this is not a neutral way of seeing, but a trained eye that expects and desires to see things in ways that would reinforce existing ideas of the people she is there to observe. As such, she is an earlier version of the twentieth-century European traveler or tourist that this chapter will consider, partly in terms of vision but mostly with regard to music or sound "touristics," the complex, recurring encounters of Caribbean people with travelers and tourists, and the ways in which these encounters reflect and sometimes undermine established notions of class, race, gender, and culture. Carmichael is an example of an early sound tourist as she also, perhaps despite herself, is drawn to sounds, those of the people she says she is there to observe but must also listen to.

Just as the unaltered vision of the place might challenge her preconceptions, so its sounds also disorient her and upset her idea of natural order. Visited onboard by "several of our own people," by which she means slaves belonging to her family, she finds she can understand little or nothing of their speech: "for though it was English, it was so uncouth a jargon, that to one unaccustomed to hear it, it was almost as unintelligible as if they had spoken in any of their native African tongues" (5). The people speak freely and appear "full of life and spirit," but she is perceptive enough and good enough a listener to realize that such a show of affection may not be as innocent as it appears—she says they "seemed overjoyed to see their own master," which suggests an awareness that the speech and broader verbal culture of the people may not be as direct or guileless as they appear at first to be (5). Already her visually driven desire to see the place and the people in a certain way is disrupted by the speech of the people—the "uncouth" language and the suspicion that what they say is not what they mean. Almost instinctively, then, her ears seem to prick up, and she is sensitive to sounds in ways that again challenge her desire to *see* order and structure in the place and among the various groups of the society. Nocturnal sounds particularly unsettle her, and she records that half of the night "is frequently passed in listening, rising out of the bed, and ascertaining whether or not all is quiet" (58). Sounds are thus difficult to judge and decode for her and other whites. Accordingly, she writes of a man and a boy who row out to their ship to sell them fruit, and how "they accompanied the motion of their oars with a song, or rather a sort of chorus, the words of which were only a repetition of 'Shove her—shove her up,' but repeated so quickly, that to me it appeared like any language on earth but English" (6). The rhythmic movement of the oars, along with the repetitive chant seem intended to lull her and the white sailors and to distract them from the boy's attempts to cut one of the ship's ropes. It is a fascinating example of the ways in which sounds and music are used by the captive people to seduce the whites and to use sounds as ruses to cover acts of resistance big and small.

In general, she identifies herself as a "traveller" (8), and as such is again an early version of a tourist, a temporary visitor with the means to come and go as she pleases, and there to sample the sights and sounds of the place. For all that she says she is not there to observe nature, she cannot help but see the place as a tourist would—climbing into the hills behind Kingstown, she says that the hilltop "commands one of the grandest views imaginable," and eulogizes the beauty of the place (7–8). Similarly, she is charmed by the Creole town, the features of which "at first sight arrest the eye of the traveller," and she is "struck" by the tropical flora (8–9). The people, by contrast, appear to her to be "disgusting" in their ragged clothes (10), while in the town she concedes some mulatto women were "elegant and graceful" (11). She becomes rather unwittingly and involuntarily a form of sonic tourist: invited to a gentleman's house on the first evening, she finds that the custom among the whites is to drink tea between seven and eight, "and music making up the remainder" (12). Her appreciation of the music is interrupted when, as it begins, she "heard a noise" coming from the hall. The lady of the house reassures her that it is "only the little negroes; they are dancing there; and are all extremely fond of it." Feeling an urge to go and watch the dancers, she stops herself, fearing they would stop and remarks she should not have been concerned "for negroes are not at any age at all abashed by the presence of a stranger." More broadly, that first evening in the house sets up some of the terms of her sonic tourism: she and the other whites sit to listen to music, while the black people dance to the sounds, and the whites are in turn drawn to the performance, which itself is in contrast to the relatively restrained, repressed customs of the whites.

Quite tellingly, she notes that over time the whites tended to host fewer large formal dinner parties in favor of small social events, and that card playing was replaced by dancing, while music "first became tolerated, then listened to with some interest" to the extent that by the time she left St. Vincent for Trinidad "if there were no musicians, there were at least many who liked music and encouraged it; and finally the piano forte, and quadrilles, to a great extent banished cards and scandal" (41). In subtle but profound ways, then, the whites adapt their ways, and rather than sit and listen to music passively, they will dance and listen attentively to it. The longer she is there, the more her proclivity for music and dance increases, so that she seeks out these events and takes pleasure in the quadrilles in particular (42), and in her own way becomes to some degree "creolized," as she says of those whites who have adapted most to island ways (53). Attending a great ball, she writes of a naval band playing quadrilles and country dances, which she describes as an "extraordinary advantage in the West Indies," for in the islands, she says, the only musicians are "negro fiddlers, who play merely a little by the ear: they know neither sharps nor flats, and when such come in their way, they play the natural instead, so that it is very difficult to find out what tune they are playing" (45). The "only comfort," she says to those annoyed by such "discord" is that the music is always accompanied by a tambourine and triangles, "so that the discordant tones are pretty well drowned" (46). In addition, the musicians "keep time with the foot, and move their head and body backwards and forwards in a most ludicrous way," so that it is the rhythmic effects that most draw her to the music, and which are relatively absent in the music played by the naval band (46). There is also the distinct possibility that, far from being unaccomplished musicians, the black players deliberately produce a sound that they know will irritate the whites, and frustrate their desire for melody and recognizable tunes. In offering a "discordant" sound that grates, and displeases the whites, the black players nonetheless draw in the whites with the rhythmic aspects of their sound, so that in very subtle but profound ways they use the music to manipulate the feelings of the whites and to demonstrate their mastery of sound and the way it can be used to determine mood, comfort, and humor.

Her final comment on the ball relates to the "presence of the negroes," which she says must be permitted with "no interested motives" on behalf of the proprietor: "it must proceed from pure good will, and the wish to see them happy" (47). She returns to this point when she writes more exclusively on the "negroes' holidays and amusements." On this point, she notes that it is common for "negro slaves to give parties" (285). Further, she writes that "the negro holiday entertainments are very grand indeed," in particular Christmas but also Easter (286–87). She finds that the "amusements of the native Africans are much of the same kind as those of the creole negro," though the Africans dance to the drum, and the Creoles "consider a fiddle genteeler." Moreover, although of an evening they will sing and dance to a drum, they would not take the instrument to a grander party: "Fiddles and tambourines, with triangles, are essential there," she says (292). Similarly, they will dance quadrilles and waltzes at an organized party, while less formally they will dance their own African and Creole dances. Therefore, it seems clear that the Africans and Creoles have at least two modes of music and dance, one more genteel for the grand parties and white ears, and another for themselves, with the drum as a particularly cherished instrument, a marker of their own identities, expressed and kept alive in sound. Moreover, the people use music and dance strategically, to break up the monotony of work—"they will dance at any hour of the day," Carmichael notes, taking this propensity for dance to be simple merriment, when it appears also to be a form of detour, a means of owning their own time and using it as they please (293).

Carmichael not only is drawn to the music and dance of the people but also engages in close conversations with several "native Africans" that constitute a partial record of the oral history of the people. Again, she actively seeks out aspects of the sonic culture of the people in ways that the permanent residents do not. Interestingly, the first woman she speaks of, named simply as "F," wants little to do with her, or to share her testimony—"Let me be," F says, which Carmichael takes to be one of the many "Scotticisms" that the people have learned from the Scottish managers and overseers (303). On the other hand, the "principal enjoyment" of F was "in telling old stories to the family," and so she is a kind of storyteller figure, wary and selective of her audience (305). Stories, like music and dance, are to be performed, but differently, again according to the audience. As such, they are another part of the cultural property of the people, communicated through sound. There is a strong sense that each of the interviewees tells her what she wants to hear—essentially that the white masters in the islands are better than the African masters they knew. Each is laconic, except for Q, who turns her back and laughs every time before speaking to the whites, and speaks more freely, apparently as a means of asking for favors from the white woman (308). The last interviewee is Y, who was "uncommonly handsome," and a "first-rate dancer, both of creole and African dances," admired by Carmichael for the "grace, gravity, and majesty of his demeanour," which again shows how she is drawn to the dance, music, and sounds of the African and Creole people (319). The knowing nature of the captives' communications is underscored in a proverbial phrase of one man who tells her that "monkeys could speak well enough if they liked, but 'dey cunning too much, for dey knowed if they do speak, massa would soon make them work,'" which suggests that language use is a strategy of resistance and detour, a means of not being consumed by work and thereby retaining a sense of being and identity that escapes the strictures of the plantation and its white overseers (I. 322).

For all that she is at pains to downplay the occurrence of the physical punishment of the enslaved, she does acknowledge that its threat is ever present, and indicates that it is the sound of the whip being cracked "three times loudly" that awakens the people and acts as a reminder of their situation, for "as the crack is heard distinctly at the negro houses, this is a warning to go to labour" (II. 4). A bell sounds at the approach of a heavy rain shower to clear the field (II. 24). The boiling house is full of sounds, and she says, "scenes of great merriment," with people singing songs and "telling the jokes of the day" (II. 29). Again, she is drawn to such scenes and spends time among the people, and takes in the sounds of work, music, and revelry as integral elements of her experience as an early sound tourist. At the same time, it is fair to say that she is most acutely aware of sound in her earliest accounts of the island and the longer she is there (she stays in St. Vincent for over five years), she seems less struck by the sonic culture of the people and more interested in justifying slavery and determining the character of the "good negro," by which she essentially means a quiet person. By implication, the ability in the longer term to live with and justify slavery involves a certain deafness to the people and the place. It is only when she and her family, along with their slaves, relocate from St. Vincent that she comes into intimate contact with the people, and that she mentions again their "noise and boisterous fun," which prevent her from taking in fully the "beautiful panorama" as they sail close to Trinidad (II. 48). The new island strikes her visually—the views to South America, the sights of the hills, the woods, but also of the people, who appear to her as "singularly varied and many-coloured," as a result of the long connection with Spain and South America, and extensive foreign trade links.

Some measure of the common interisland sonic culture of the people is given in the "great ball" that is arranged by the Trinidad slaves to welcome the St. Vincent people (II. 55). That this culture is also multilingual is confirmed in her statement that in the market of Port of Spain she hears a "great diversity of tongues spoken," which "bewildered as much as it astonished" her: "There might be heard, the languages and dialects of English, Scotch, Irish, French, Spaniards, Dutch, Germans, Italians, Chinese, and Turks," the polyglot sounds of a "motley population" (II. 69). Later, she complains about the effects on her slaves of visiting Port of Spain, from where they "return heated with liquor, and of course with exaggerated stories in their heads; these they retell to all their comrades at night, as they sit eating their suppers," and which subsequently leads to numerous absences from the fields (II. 194). Again, "good negroes" are the quiet ones, those seen and seldom heard. Therefore, in contrast to the sounds of St. Vincent, with its less varied population, the human soundscape of Port of Spain is immediately confusing to her, almost disorientating, and she recoils somewhat from it. By contrast, she appreciates the skill of "Trinidad taught musicians" and the "masterly vocal performances" she hears at a formal dinner at Government House (II. 74). Also, she takes with her a pianoforte, which requires tuning so that instead of playing her own music she spends her evenings on the plantation "chatting over the events of the day" (118). To her ears, sounds of nature are generally jarring: mosquitoes buzz endlessly in the evenings, parrots "make a horrible chattering," and she notes that "the handsomest shape and the gayest plumage are poor compensations for the melodious song of birds; and how one's heart would have bounded, could one have heard the note of a blackbird, or a sweet Scotch mavis!" (II. 122). Settled in her plantation home in the country, and far from the confusing, polyglot sounds of Port of Spain, she tunes in once more to the sounds of the people; or more accurately, she attempts to train their ears to appreciate the European music she plays on her pianoforte: "The youngest negro," she notes, "almost as soon as it can stand, begins to dance and sing in its own way. As they get older, they improve in both of these native accomplishments: some of them have very quick ears for music." When she plays the piano forte, those others in earshot listen, and "if it happened to be of a kind that admitted of dancing, they were sure to avail themselves of it," so that over time "they had a large addition of tunes added to their stock of negro airs; and I have heard sundry airs from Haydn and Mozart, chanted by the boys when cleaning their knives, with astonishing accuracy" (II. 152). Also, she and her husband attempt to stop the people drumming on Sundays and dancing late on Saturday night, saying that the activity "was breaking a positive command of God" (II. 206).[1] Therefore, the more time she spends with the people, the more she tries to train their ears, as part of her overall program of improvement,

---

[1] She also writes of the Methodists' attempts to forbid or limit dancing among the enslaved (II. 245-46).

which includes her Bible teachings, reading lessons, and attempts to reduce the number of fights among the people. Also, just as is done in the fields, she uses sounds to control those who work in the house: she rings a bell repeatedly for glasses and water to be brought to her and an English visitor (II. 154). For all that they seek to control and "improve" the enslaved, notably through seeking to limit and delineate their sonic culture, the planters' efforts come to nothing—Sunday drumming and dances continue, religious instruction falls on deaf ears (II. 223–24), and they hear of plots to kill them, which lead them to realize that "all instruction from the master was useless" (II. 219). More broadly, as she writes near the end of her narrative, "negro recreation is comprised in one word, dancing," and the drum often provides the only musical accompaniment; Christmas and Easter are the two feasts most widely celebrated, and are marked by singing, dancing, speech-making, and merriment (II. 285-97). Ultimately, for all that she writes of scenes of merriment and the sounds that accompany them, the sonic culture of the people remains largely unheard by her and other whites, as is suggested in the words of an "insurrectionary song" she inadvertently overhears:

> Fire in da mountain,
> Nobody for out him,
> Take me daddy's bo tick (dandy stick),
> And make a monkey out him.
>
> Chorus.
> Poor John! nobody for out him, & c.
>
> Go to de king's goal,
> You'll find a doubloon dey;
> Go to de king's goal,
> You'll find a doubloon dey.
>
> Chorus.
> Poor John! noboby for out him, & c.

The explanation of this song is, she says:

> that when the bad negroes wanted to do evil, they made for a sign a fire on the hillsides, to burn down the canes. There is nobody up there, to put out the fire; but as a sort of satire, the song goes on to say, " take me daddy's bo tick" (daddy is a mere term of civility), take someone's dandy stick, and tell the monkeys to help to

put out the fire among the canes for John; (meaning John Bull). The chorus means, that poor John has nobody to put out the fire in the canes for him. Then when the canes are burning, go to the gaol, and seize the money. The tune to which this is sung, is said to be negro music; it is on a minor key, and singularly resembles an incorrect edition of an old Scotch tune, the name of which I do not recollect. (II. 301–2)

The song, its words, and its insurrectionary tone and intention are final reminders of the ways in which the sound culture of the people is a repository of and vehicle for their deep, silent, yet resonant desire to be free. It moreover delineates in this early account some of the limits of later sonic tourism—the ways in which sounds become sites of contact and conflict between visitors and locals—which will be discussed in the rest of the chapter.

Twentieth-Century Sonic Tourism

>Tourist, don't take my picture
>Don't take my picture, tourist
>I'm too ugly
>Too dirty
>Too skinny
>Don't take my picture, white man
>Mr. Eastman won't be happy
>I'm too ugly
>Your camera will break
>I'm too dirty
>Too black
>Whites like you won't be content
>I'm too ugly
>I'm gonna crack your Kodak
>Don't take my picture, tourist
>Leave me be, white man
>Don't take a picture of my burro
>My burro's load's too heavy
>And he's too small
>And he has no food here
>Don't take a picture of my animal
>Tourist, don't take a picture of the house
>My house is of straw
>Don't take a picture of my hut

> My hut's made of earth
> The house already smashed up
> Go shoot a picture of the Palace
> Or the Bicentennial grounds
> Don't take a picture of my garden
> I have no plow
> No truck
> No tractor
> Don't take a picture of my tree
> Tourist, I'm barefoot
> My clothes are torn as well
> Poor people don't look at whites
> But look at my hair, tourist
> Your Kodak's not used to my color
> Your barber's not used to my hair
> Tourist, don't take my picture
> You don't understand my position
> You don't understand anything
> About my business, tourist
> "Gimme fie cents"
> And then, be on your way, tourist.
> —"Tourist," Félix Morisseau-Leroy[2]

Morisseau's well-known poem is useful in further introducing this chapter, in that it writes of the often fraught and uneven relationship between tourists and natives long after slavery has ended, especially when the latter have visibly poor living conditions. For the visible is crucial in this encounter, as the poem realizes: judgments are made as they were for Carmichael above based on visual impressions and on conceptions of difference. In the modern touristic relationship, these judgments seem to reinforce the identity of the tourist through the power they have to define the native other, and to effectively erase the identity of the latter by reducing them to an image, voiceless, subdued, and passive.

The poem also suggests that refusing to be photographed is a way of resisting the tourist, and that even if they are photographed, the local subject will "crack" the tourist's Kodak, by not conforming to touristic ideals of a passive, exotic, beautiful Caribbean object. The basic problem for the

---

[2] https://pen.org/tourist-and-boat-people/ accessed April 14, 2023. Edwidge Danticat reads the poem on the same web page.

native voice in the poem is that the relationship set up by tourism leads to misunderstandings and misapprehensions. "You don't understand my position / You don't understand anything / About my business," the speaker says.

Voice is important in the poem, as in contrast to much of Carmichael's narrative, it is only the native voice that is heard—the visitor or tourist is silenced, their power lies in the visual, the ability to define through voiceless images. Of course, the fact that the poem was first written in Creole further reinforces the verbal-linguistic resistance of the speaker: photography gives the illusion of truth, but the speaker insists that the images finally are unable to convey any kind of true reality, which is hidden behind the images and lies and exists at least partially in sound, voice, and language, again much like Carmichael's narrative reveals, however inadvertently.

In a phrase that could easily be applied to Carmichael, Mimi Sheller writes of the "privileges of moving through the Caribbean" long enjoyed by travelers and tourists "that allowed them to construct local people as rooted to the place and natural scenery as an unchanging tropical backdrop" (*Citizenship from Below* 210). Modern tourism, she says, "can be understood as a form of embodied encounter between foreign travelers and local people that involves corporeal relations of unequal power" (210). Sheller emphasizes the embodied nature of these encounters, as she says, "the physical materiality of the bodies brought into proximity in such moments of encounter matters in particular ways" (210). Sites of such bodily encounters may include, for example, beaches and resorts, where local and tourist bodies come into contact through, for instance, braiding hair or massage therapies (211). As she states, "The way tourists and local people face each other, look at each other, hear each other, smell each other, or touch each other are all part of the power relations by which forms of gender and racial inequality are brought into being along with national boundaries of belonging and exclusion" (211).

Such an interpretation of the relations inherent to Caribbean tourism relates closely to Morisseau-Leroy's insistence on the bodily and the sensory—the hair, the dirtiness, the ugliness the speaker mentions—which are markers of unequal wealth and living conditions, but also in the case of the poem, potential means of resistance through a refusal to conform to a touristic stereotype. Tourism is after all, a further vector of colonial presence in the Caribbean: long a "hot spot for travelers, both in terms of actual travel and in terms of the tourist imagination," the region's tourist industry began in the nineteenth century and has since "developed myriad and idiosyncratic ways of tailoring encounter and experience to desire and expectation" (Rommen, "Introduction" 1). In the British context, the attempt to re-present the islands as picturesque paradises began in the late 1800s. This was no mean challenge, as to that point the West Indies had been seen by outsiders as a deathly place, plagued by tropical diseases such as yellow fever, malaria, and cholera. As Krista Thompson writes, early promoters of Caribbean tourism "had to radically transform the islands' much maligned landscapes into spaces of touristic desire for British and North American traveling publics" (*An Eye for the Tropics* 4). To reinvent the islands in this way, the colonial government and British and American corporations in Jamaica and the Bahamas enlisted a small army of photographers, artists, and lecturers. Together, as Thompson says, "through photographs, postcards, photography books, illustrated guides, stereo-views, and lantern slides, these image makers created a substantial repertoire of visual representations of the islands. These pictures were instrumental in imaging the islands as tropical and picturesque tourism destinations" (5). These models of visual representation were adapted by other islands as tourism spread through the region and have been vital in shaping European and North American perceptions of the place and its people. As such, the islands have undergone a process of visual "tropicalization," which is defined by Thompson as "the complex visual systems through which the islands were imaged for tourist consumption and the social and political implications of these representations on actual physical space on the islands and their inhabitants" (5). Tourism is thus for Thompson a predominantly, almost exclusively, visual phenomenon: people and places were able to be captured, framed, and packaged in photographs, postcards, slides, and films. Although she does not make the connection, there is a clear continuation in such pictured representations of the colonial regime of the eye, of the desire to frame, control, and profit from places and people through visual power, in this case the cameras wielded not only by professional photographers, but by virtually any modern tourist—the first mass-marketed cameras were produced at the beginning of the twentieth century, and "put travelers in charge of visually recording their experiences" (8). These innovations were thus part of the modern visual culture that Nicholas Mirzoeff and others write of, and which for Mirzoeff begins with the major shift in the mid-seventeenth century in the "European division of the sensible." The new sensorial order of things was produced by the needs of European expansion and encounter, "above all in the plantation colonies" (*The Right to Look* 49). The processes described by Thompson relate closely to the term "oversight," which is used by Mirzoeff to describe the visually based system of control in the plantations, "the regime of taxonomy, observation, and enforcement that came to be known as 'economy'" (50). Surveillance and discipline are two fundamental objectives of the visual regime in both cases, explicitly so in the case of plantation slavery, and only slightly less overtly in the "parade of the picturesque" that Thompson writes about, the "picturesque natives" who featured in some of the images, "who seemed loyal, disciplined, and clean British colonial subjects" (6).

The ability to record, preserve, and disseminate visual images preceded the capacity to record sound, and music in particular, by at least a decade. For instance, the first Trinidadian recorded music was by Lovey's Band, a string band popular with the island's elite, which went to New York in May 1913 and recorded titles for both the Victor Talking Company and the Columbia Phonograph Company. Lovey's Band was also the first musical unit to encounter a foreign market; its Spanish titles were marketed through Columbia's popular Spanish-American series, and not only in the United States (Cowley, *Carnival, Canboulay and Calypso* 183–86). The Victor Talking Machine Company came to Trinidad in August 1914, with the specific aim, as the *Gazette* reported, "of recording a complete repertoire of Trinidadian music including the Pasillos Spanish Waltz and Two steps by well-known Bands; also Carnival and Patois songs and East Indian selections by local talent" (qtd. in Cowley, *Carnival, Canboulay and Calypso* 191). The "Calipsos" were sung partly in French Creole, while the Kalendas were accompanied by the rhythms of the stamping tubes and the bottle and spoon, vernacular elements that were sanitized to some degree and now made their way into recorded sound, and hence into the musical consciousnesses not only of the island but also of the larger listening audience abroad. Just as it was doing in the United States, the advent of recorded music in Trinidad destabilized the relationship between seeing music performed and hearing music. The technology of sound tempered the visual elements of music and disconnected the music from the people who produced it. Recorded music allowed the commuted and sanitized sounds of blackness to permeate further into middle-class culture, and to be disseminated to Europe and North America in much the same way that the visual images of postcards and brochures presented "respectable" Caribbean citizens, good, dependable subjects of the British Empire.[3]

As Thompson realizes, music was by the 1930s considered useful for tourism purposes, as a sonic accompaniment to the "tropicalized" images that drew visitors to the islands and catered to tourists' tastes for "black cultural performances that provided a mix of Africa, the primitive, and exotic in various doses" (148). The increasing global fame of black performers led the tourism industry to reconsider, Thompson says, "what they had until that time referred to as 'noise' or 'racial instinct' as culture, a marketable product"

---

[3] For an excellent analysis of contemporaneous developments in music and the recording industry in the United States, see Gitelman, "Recording Sound, Race, and Property."

(149). In the Bahamas, "Native Nights" were introduced in tourist hotel clubs, featuring dancers, conch shell blowers, and other local instrumentalists, "signaling a new era of acceptance of black cultural expressions on the island and interest in their traditions for the sake of tourism" (149).[4]

Indeed, the sonic aspects of tourist desire and expectation have tended to be related to "music touristics," sounds packaged for performance and sale to visitors, and which are "often intended (and interpreted) as a sonic signifier of otherness (as a marker of difference), and consumed as such both locally and translocally" (Rommen, "Introduction" 7). Jocelyne Guilbault proposes that tourists and tourism be taken as a "critical starting point" in the modern history of Caribbean musical encounters and be "consistently woven into the analysis of the colonial and the postcolonial, the local and the global, the national and the transnational" ("Afterword" 314). Steven Feld similarly argues that it is impossible to separate the history of tourism from that of slavery and colonization, "the history of gaze, the history of reproduction of power relations of tourists and touristed" ("Prologue"). In her revealing study of sound in a Barbados all-inclusive resort, Susan Harewood pays attention to the unwanted sounds beyond tourist music, those that jar with the sounds of paradise and escape: the silences, clocks chiming in ways that appear to her as "disturbing noises of persistent coloniality," and the "noisy viciousness of imperialism" ("Listening for Noise" 109, 124). Similar work done by Jerome Camal in an all-inclusive resort in Guadeloupe tunes into the rhythms and repetitions of everyday life, so that he finds the resort to be "a repeating machine, which is itself the repetition, or more precisely a remix, of the plantation machine" ("Touristic Rhythms" 82). There is perhaps no other region where music and tourism are so closely entwined, where music is offered as a marker of both exotic otherness and comforting familiarity: as noted in the introduction to this book, most modern visitors will have heard the Caribbean (or at least its music), before they have seen it. To hear the music in situ is to confirm one's presence in the place, and the reality of the place is apparently confirmed through its music.[5]

For all that the scholars cited above criticize touristic ties as repetitions of colonial relations and sites such as resorts as repetitions of the plantation, in other crucial ways hotels have been important locations for the

---

[4] Thompson writes later of the Atlantis resort as an example of the contemporary "experience economy" of themed resort, and how the visual images of underwater adventure are accompanied by "'ethereal' background music" (200).

[5] For excellent case-study analyses of "music touristics" in the region, see Timothy Rommen and Daniel T. Neely, eds., *Sun, Sea, and Sound: Music and Tourism in the Circum-Caribbean* (Oxford: Oxford University Press, 2014). See also, Ian Gregory Strachan, *Paradise and Plantation: Tourism and Culture in the Anglophone Caribbean* (Charlottesville: University of Virginia Press, 2002).

development of music and musicians. In his memoir, the founder of Island Records, Chris Blackwell, writes that he discovered his first recording artists while working at the Half Moon Hotel in Montego Bay, Jamaica at the end of the 1950s. While he ran the hotel's water-skiing concession, Blackwell heard the Bermudan jazz pianist Lance Hayward, whose *Lance Hayward at the Half Moon Hotel* was Island Records' first album, released in 1959. Hayward was, Blackwell says, "very much in the mood of Oscar Peterson and early Nat King Cole. Nothing too troubling or distracting for the well-heeled, cocktail-sipping hotel clientele" (*The Islander* 44). Most of the copies were sold to tourists in the hotel, "as a holiday souvenir," he says, one that would take the listener back to a "sunny, easygoing 1959 Montego Bay in an instant" (47). Blackwell's next record was also by a musician he had met while both worked at the hotel—the guitarist Ernest Ranglin, who had played on "mento records for tourists," but who was also adept at jazz and calypso (47). Perhaps somewhat estranged from the emerging sound system culture—he mentions Coxsone Dodd's contemporary recordings of exclusive songs for his own sound system—Blackwell's search for talent extended to other hospitality venues, specifically the Ferry Inn, the restaurant and nightclub he ran for a short period. For Blackwell, the touristic sites where he discovered many of his early artists did not make them any less authentic—he says that he would use the "versatile and melodic" Ranglin as his "secret weapon" when he wanted to bring "Jamaican realness" to any record, and that the record they made was "a sonic blast of optimism, the sound of Black Jamaican musicians breaking free of the colonial grind" (48). Nor was this "realness" a quality that he found only in Jamaican-born musicians, as he writes of The Caribs, an Australian band who played calypso and mento on the Gold Coast before relocating to Jamaica, where they backed Laurel Aitken on his first Island release (51). The Caribs became the house band for The Glass Bucket, which "catered to tourists and the local upper class," and where local musicians would often play with visiting stars—Don Drummond is mentioned as one of these musicians (51). The Caribs would thereafter move on to the "elegant Myrtle Bank Hotel, where Ian Fleming stayed when he first visited Jamaica in 1942" (52). In all of this, therefore, there is a curious mixing in touristic sites—Blackwell writes of the "polyglot" Jamaican music scene, "drawing participants of Cuban, Panamanian, Trinidadian, Lebanese, Chinese, Indian, and European origin" (51)—that also cuts across divides of race, class, and nationality: the hotels and clubs brought together upper-class Jamaicans and tourists, and crucial to those encounters was the music of a diverse set of musicians defined less by race or nation than by time and place, their coming together at a specific place at a particular point in its history (Blackwell writes that these were not "normal times" for Jamaica, which was "on the cusp of major social and political change," 57).

In addition to the social skills and confidence that such encounters would no doubt have enhanced for the musicians, the hotels allowed singers and musicians to improve as artists and to gain experience in playing for foreign audiences, "learning stagecraft, earning foreign exchange, and also exposing them to a life and environment quite different from Western Kingston."[6] As Timothy Rommen has shown, similar patterns of touristic contact with multiple, complex effects for the performers also occurred in the Bahamas, where hotels were again prime sites for local musicians to learn their trade, though in the well-established tourist scene in the Bahamas there appeared to be more of a tendency to "exoticize" the local, and to stage fire dancing, limbo, and other performances that were "designed to showcase 'native' (and not-so-native, but spectacular folkways" (*Funky Nassau* 87). Even here, though, as Rommen notes, the hotel environment did create a space for international encounter in certain clubs, and the "fluid spaces [...] contributed to a great deal of musical exchange" (*Funky Nassau* 88).[7] In similar vein, Matthew J. Smith explores the 1950s hotel scene as a site for exchange and contact between Haitian and Jamaican musicians. As Smith writes, musicians were far from static or immobile, and traveled as the music did, "the length and breadth of the Caribbean region" ("Wanderers of Love" 126). For example, the guitarist Ernest Ranglin, spotted by Chris Blackwell in a Jamaican hotel, also worked in the Bahamas. As such, musical contexts were "shaped by travel, both the physical travel of tourists and people [...] and the migration of music around the region" (126). Foreign tourists are not passive in these encounters: as the "most visible category of traveler," tourists were the "most tangible representation of North American culture," and as such the evolving musical forms of the region were shaped to some degree by the encounter with the tourists and their expectations (126). Musicians themselves constitute "a special category of tourist visitor," in that they travel to experience "the novelty and thrill of the visit," but they are also there to work and to learn (126). Hotels feature widely in Smith's analysis: he writes of the early Haitian traveling musician Professor Arthur Bonnefil, who performed at the Hotel Cecil in Kingston and at the Metropolitan Hotel in Port-au-Prince, and of the famous Haitian nightclub Cabane Choucoune, a popular destination for musicians and tourists alike (135–36).

---

[6] Matthew J. Smith, personal communication, July 10, 2022.
[7] See also Rommen's analysis of contemporary all-inclusive resorts in the Bahamas in "It Sounds Better in the Bahamas: Musicians, Management, and Markets in Nassau's All-Inclusive Hotels."

Popular films from Jamaica attest to the importance of hotels in providing contexts for musicians to perform in ways suggested by Smith and Rommen. For instance, the 1976 film *Smile Orange* is situated almost entirely around a hotel and is concerned in a largely comedic and parodic way with the relations between tourists and locals, and music is a constant presence in these uneven, often discordant exchanges. As the hotel staff prepares for the tourists' arrival, the Jamaican flag is taken down from a pole and replaced by the Stars and Stripes, an early sign that the hotel will undergo a sort of occupation, shaped and determined to some degree by the tastes and desires of the tourists. Appropriately, a generic island-style music accompanies these scenes, with locals rushing to bring about the changes to the place, losing themselves and playing up to stereotypes of themselves in the desire to accommodate the tourists. As the tourists' bus draws up, a mento-style band plays at the hotel door. The tourists play little heed to the musicians, and the music seems barely to register with them, as they are more interested in voicing their many complaints. Music is established as a sort of auditory background, there but unheard, unacknowledged but also ever present and essential to these encounters. Indeed, in virtually every formal setting that brings tourists and locals together, music is played, as for example in the dining room, where a woman plays guitar and sings in a similar folk-mento style to the musicians that welcomed the tourists initially. Clearly talented, she sings and plays well, though again is apparently unheard—appropriately she is framed in front of the room's wallpaper, as her music is the auditory equivalent of wallpaper, part of the décor, there to provide local color. In a different but related vein, music is also played in a sort of cabaret-disco scene with bikini-clad dancers performing to the sounds of another talented band, playing trombone, guitar, trumpet, and saxophone. This time, the tourists do engage more with the music, smiling, and imitating the dancers, as tourists and locals dance in a more intimate space, brought closer together by the music. A saxophone solo demonstrates the skill of the musicians, yet it is the rhythm that beats throughout the scene and that the people seem to engage with most. For the musicians, the event is a sort of practice session, where they momentarily interject solos into the rhythmic overall sound. The main character, Ringo, has his own theme tune, that plays half-ironically, and echoes near-contemporary works such as "The Theme from Shaft." More generally, incidental music plays regularly, and most prominently in scenes where locals and tourists mix, as if it is necessary to fill in the silences or discordant sounds—the complaints, the grating accents—that would otherwise characterize those relationships. Accents more generally are part of the touristic soundscape—the Americans do not adjust theirs, but some of the hotel staff do, whether to mimic the

Americans or to adopt a British-style accent that denotes formality and real or imagined class differences. As such, music and sound both amplify and muffle social, national, and racial differences in the film, and musicians are key actors in the encounters between tourists and locals—though they remain largely unacknowledged and unheard, they nonetheless bring people together, chiefly through rhythm, and they use the events at times to practice, to learn how to play to foreign audiences, and to adapt their styles accordingly: they give the people some of what they want, and in the improvised solos cut loose a little, expressing themselves and their musicianship more expansively than is normally expected in the touristic environment.[8] In general, hotels have remained important sites for musical performances and exchanges, as Matthew Smith writes, "The aspect of talent scouting at hotels did not end with Blackwell's era. In recent years some well-known singers in the island were 'discovered' while performing open mic or karaoke sets at city hotels. Much like the swarm of athletic coaches from the US who come annually to Jamaica and trawl the local high school meets in search of the next Usain Bolt or Shelly-Ann Fraser, so too do talent scouts make their way along the hotel circuit in time for showtime."[9]

Sound Touristics in Haiti

In the rest of this chapter, I engage less with music touristics than with what may be termed "sound touristics," the broader sounds and silences of tourist and traveler experience in the Caribbean that are present in earlier accounts such as that by Carmichael but that seem to be amplified in modern encounters between tourists and locals in the Caribbean. I take tourism seriously in the ways recommended by Rommen and Guilbault, who refuse to hear the sounds of tourism as "inauthentic, unauthorized, or otherwise spurious," and ask if the "overwhelming focus on the visual and material aspects of tourism has silenced the importance of the political economy of music and sound in sites of leisure?" ("Introduction" 9). I discuss filmed representations of Haiti, many of which were made at the time Morisseau-Leroy wrote his poem, in the early 1950s, that is, before the Duvalier dictatorships, a time of relative prosperity and hope, the later part of the "postoccupation period" that Matthew Smith describes as "modern Haiti's greatest moment of political

---

[8] There are similar scenes in the 1978 Jamaican film *Rockers*, for instance when a reggae band led by Jacob Miller plays to a white crowd, one tourist remarks, "Hey, that's no calypso." See also, for comparison, *Club Paradise* (1986).
[9] Personal communication, July 10, 2022.

promise" (*Red and Black in Haiti* 2). As in the previous chapter on the filmed lives of white expatriates, the tourist and tourism films analyzed here offer further evidence of the power of the white, outsider gaze that runs through the history of the colonial Caribbean and is a fundamental element in the construction of ideas of racial difference. The rest of the chapter is also interested in how silence affects the way in which the memory of the past transmits itself into the present. The silences of the people and the place seem to take on a new poignancy with the passage of time, as one watches the films and realizes that the people and to some extent places will by now be largely gone. The silence of the films thus highlights in some ways the workings of time, the movement from life to death, voice to silence, so that the films are like moving postcards, snapshots that remind us that voices fade and die just as bodies and places do.

The films also bring us back to the truths with which the book begins and which shape its development: that the sonic is always intimately connected with the visual in the Caribbean, and it is often in silence that the two domains meet, clash, coincide, and relate.

* * *

These films, made by individual tourists and official bodies such as the Canadian National Film Board are found online, mostly on YouTube and the Travel Film Archive, and are in general, again like the expatriates' films discussed in chapter 2, largely *artless* in nature. Their interest lies in the relations they set up between tourists and locals, and the various intentions of the filmmakers, some of which conform to the perspectives critiqued by Morisseau-Leroy, Sheller, Rommen, and the other critics, and some of which do not, at least not in direct ways.

The latter is the case with the first film to be analyzed, which was made in the 1950s, the so-called golden age of Haitian tourism, when, for example, the waterfront area of Port-au-Prince was redeveloped to accommodate cruise ships and their passengers, to allow easy access to the city and its attractions. The American occupation of 1915–34 had "opened up" the country to the outside and, given its close proximity to the United States, it became a convenient and popular destination, particularly with the growth of Pan-American Airways, which had started in 1927 as an airmail and passenger service between Key West and Cuba and which by the 1950s had long established regular connections to Haiti and other Caribbean and Central American countries. Cruise ships continued to dock regularly in Port-au-Prince until the late 1980s, when tourism "declined dramatically" in the wake of Jean-Claude Duvalier's departure (Largey, "Hello New York City! Sonic Tourism in

Haitian Rara" 101). While I focus first here on an American visitor to Haiti, it is important to note that intra-Caribbean tourism also developed during this period, and as Matthew Smith has shown, there were particularly close ties with Jamaica ("Wanderers of Love").

The title of the film—"Come to Haiti"—clearly indicates its intentions—to promote Haiti as a place to visit and encourage others to go there. It is not clear who made the film, and it is interesting that a private individual would put together a film of this kind. Clearly, Haiti has made a very favorable impact on the filmmaker, and he has been moved to promote the country through making the film. The audience is not entirely obvious, either—who would have seen this film? Was it made for friends and family? Was it perhaps made by a returning soldier, who had been in Haiti during the occupation?

"Come to Haiti," 1950s

The film[10] starts with a long focus on a tourism poster, a visual means of encouraging visitors: "Come to Haiti" it says in English, clearly directed at the North American market. A brightly clothed woman carries an oversized basket laden with tropical fruits. The font used for the word "Haiti" suggests already a subtle kind of exoticism mixed with a cartoonish idea that Haiti will be a fun place to visit, unthreatening and ready to greet you. The image of work shows that the people are ready to serve and could even carry a message of black people engaged still in agricultural toil, connected to the land and to a history of servitude.

The next frame focuses on the means of travel. "Pan-American World Airways, Port-au-Prince," reads the sign on the landing steps, which shows potential visitors that they can travel by modern means, in comfort, and directly to the country. Haiti is part of this pan-American network, not threatening but Americanized, safe and clean. You can travel there safely, and if you need to you can leave quickly.

The film suggests something of the experience of the first-time visitor arriving by air, the surprise of being in a new place a mere hour or two after leaving the home country. Unlike the cruise ship visitor, the air passenger does not necessarily have the same place to retire to every evening, or even in the day, as the aircraft naturally lands and leaves again, while the ship stays in the port as a kind of refuge, a floating home for the visitor to return to. The air passenger is on land for the duration of their stay, and this affects their

---

[10] https://www.youtube.com/watch?v=fulluXEnMcQ.

experience of the place, the attention to detail, the heightened curiosity, the unspoken mix of trepidation and excitement. The first images of the city are reassuringly modern—the motor cars, the electricity poles, the people quietly going about their business. Mixed with this is a sense of the picturesque, the old Creole houses set against the deep blue sky.

The visitor is almost inevitably drawn to the seas, the shore, and there he sees the Luminous Fountain, built in 1949 for the World Exposition, and the camera focuses on the neat surroundings, the paved roads, the electric lighting. The next shot sees the visitor overlooking the bay. He is dressed as a visitor, in white linen shirt, though it could be he is there to work. He stands in silence, scanning the scene below, the sea, the valley, the mountains. There must be more than one visitor on this trip, as he is being filmed. Next, it shows the Cathedral of Our Lady of the Assumption, famously destroyed by the 2010 earthquake but which stands here in all its splendor, and as a reassuring sign of Christianity in a country so notoriously connected to non-Christian religion.

Scenes of order and civilization are then abruptly juxtaposed with images of a popular market, where items of clothing are being sold, low down in the city, close to the shore, which is associated with the urban poor. Here, too, however there is a degree of order, a healthy sort of bustle that suggests that commerce is very much part of daily life, a kind of glue that connects the poor to the storeowners who share the downtown space in the adjoining shopping arcades. Rows of motorcars suggest that the bourgeoisie work and shop here, and that business is relatively profitable. There is energy, a commercial spirit, and a degree of cohesion in these commercial spaces.

The visitor soon runs out of conventionally touristic sights to film and focuses on a dry fountain by some administrative buildings, some with neat gardens, again down by the shore, which is apparently still a desirable location for offices and businesses. At the same time, there is an almost voyeuristic interest in filming poverty, as if social deprivation is part of the attraction for the tourist, a sort of confirmation of popular ideas of Haiti. Roadside shacks and other areas of lower-class accommodation are filmed, and what is remarkable is the almost complete absence of people, as if they have left the area to work for the day. The old abattoir is shot briefly before the film switches to a view of the bay and some largely unmanned fishing pirogues. Fishermen fix their nets on the quayside, while on the streets behind, a popular market is installed by a Texaco gas station. It is notable that the cameraman shoots from across the street, at a safe distance from the bustling market. He takes a more central position when filming the entryway to the Marché de Fer, though again buildings and people are shot from a distance, as if the cameraman wishes to remain unseen and detached from the world he is recording. There is apparently less reticence in filming the statue of Christopher Columbus with its prominent cross facing the city, Columbus with his back to the sea, to Europe, to the past. The statue marks a beginning, a point of departure, while the rest of the city plays out like a long sequel to that initial conquest. The statue is naturally fixed, as apparently is its meaning, while the city moves ceaselessly, its meanings in constant motion and flux: the compression of the popular areas, the open spaces of the commercial and administrative zones. It is interesting that this apparent tension between the various sectors in the city—broadly, the popular and the bourgeois, the developing, Americanized city and the Creole, the African—is played out in the lower part of the city, by the sea, which is a sort of crossroads, a place of arrival and potential departure, the sea a historic site, the land here a form of in-between space between the sea and the mountains that frame the city. At this point, the lower part of the city seems to alternate between the order of the neat gardens, fountains and monuments and the uncertain disorder of the popular areas. It is as if the city could go either way, as if it is at a crossroads in its history.

The absence of sound is perhaps felt most acutely at 7.32, where drummers play and a couple dances, apparently in some arranged performance. The man sits and smiles as the performance plays out. He seems to be residing in a guest house in a more elevated part of town, as cars and people pass on the road outside. Without sound, the scene loses the energy and vitality it must have had. The same can be said of the entire film: the lack of sound in a way seems to pacify or domesticate the images. Sounds are less easy to control than the visual images, which are apparently more important to the filmmaker—the place can better be represented through how it looks than how it sounds.

Outside of the city, he visits small farms, sees mango trees, an old plantation mill, a river where people swim, and two old churches. Here, the emphasis is on simplicity of life and the timelessness of the people's existences, as some women pass by on donkeys and others carry laden baskets on their heads. In contrast to the modern city, life here seems unchanging, if precarious, as the camera focuses on the hills denuded of trees, the barren beauty of the place.

At 13.00 he relocates to Cap Haïtien, which appears as an altogether sleepier city, its streets almost deserted, its old Creole buildings still standing but dilapidated. The white paint on the Notre Dame Cathedral is faded and gray in parts and adds to the sense that the city is forgotten, secondary, bypassed by modernization, haunted still by the ghosts of colonial times. The streets are narrow, the old balconies hanging over them, creating a sense of intimacy that is largely absent in the images of Port-au-Prince, where the roads and avenues are paved and widened, and relatively full of life, cars, and people. If

Port-au-Prince appears at a crossroads in its development, Cap Haïtien seems by contrast at a dead end or a cul-de-sac, with little of the frenetic energy of the capital city and with less evidence of foreign presence, either of tourists or the businesses and embassies that are based in the capital. The waterfront has none of the statues and monuments that were shown in Port-au-Prince; instead, the quayside is virtually empty, with no fishermen or boats of any kind, apart from a small boat loading sacks of produce.

The general feeling of dilapidation and of living in a fading, half-forgotten history is compounded when he visits the magnificent Sans-Souci Palace, where it seems that one does not need sound to appreciate the visitor's experience. The Palace is visually remarkable, a monument to the time of the revolution, the glories and follies of history. One imagines the voiceless, breathless reactions of the visitor, the shock and surprise of the place. The camera pans across the scene, unable to fit the whole place into one frame, to quite capture the scale and wonder of the palace. It then turns 360 degrees, which gives a spinning effect and suggests the dizzying sensation felt by the visitor. The camera focuses on details, the steps, the intricate stairways, before zooming out to try and capture the effect of the palace as a whole, but again it does not ever present the whole edifice in one frame. Unlike in other scenes, where the camera flits quickly between shots of various scenes, here it slows down, pauses, and tries to take in the whole vista. In other scenes it is like the visitor is controlling what he wants to see, as if the place is passive, the object of his view, but now faced with the palace it appears as though he is the object, that suddenly the power dynamics are reversed and he is being seen. One can sense that this unsettles him as the camerawork is the least assured, never able to capture the whole scene and always shooting from below the image, never dominating it as it does in other scenes. This is not picturesque tropicality; it is something far grander and more threatening and imposing than that—a statement and affirmation of what Haiti is, of the suffering it went through to even exist, of the grand ambitions it had for itself. The palace is defiant in this sense, its visuality is eloquent, full of meaning that the visitor seems to be sensitive to, and again the absence of sound does nothing to diminish the experience, as one senses the visitor's wordless reactions, the way the sight of the palace registers internally in contrast to his engagement with other scenes, which is by comparison superficial and unthreatening.

Similarly, when he visits the Citadelle Laferrière, the views are from below, and the sense is of awe and wonder, of the place visiting and taking control of him rather than the reverse. He almost has a feeling of vertigo on reaching the citadel, as the dirt road crumbles into the deep valley below. The closer he gets to it, the more his perspective is limited, as he is almost face to face with the thick stone walls, unable to gain a broader view of the place. Remarkably, then, the final shot is from overhead, apparently from an aircraft, which allows him to regain the all-encompassing perspective that he has not been able to achieve the closer he got to the palace and the citadel. Interestingly, too, the overhead shots are in black and white, which perhaps underscores the age of the building, the sense of a long, difficult history. From above, one sees the scale and form of the citadel, and here it appears almost unreal, like a scale model, and as the aircraft passes overhead the camera fixes stubbornly on the scene, as if the visitor is trying to comprehend the work and ambition that must have gone into its construction. As if to emphasize the visitor's new appreciation of Haiti's history, the next scene switches to a flag, flying against the blue sky, on which the camera lingers until the end of the film.

The film is finally of interest as it does to some degree conform to Sheller's notion that tourism depends on a "dominant gaze that determines unequal relations of looking between tourists and those they define as locals or natives of the place they are touring" (*Citizenship from Below* 212). Yet it also in parts shows some of the ways in which the dominant gaze can be disrupted, even reversed. As in the Morisseau-Leroy poem, the local is not without power in this relationship, even if that power lies in refusing to smile or act out the role of insouciant Caribbean native. As Sheller says, "Every embodied encounter is a moment of improvisation, role-playing, and interaction in which a re-scripting of power is always risked" (212). And just as the native person, the local, can redraw the relationship of power, so can the native place, the locale, which particularly at the end of the film, at Sans-Souci and the Citadelle, almost becomes itself the source of the gaze, an all-seeing presence whose scale dominates the tourist and his camera and whose voice seems ultimately to speak of the history of the place and its refusal for its meanings to be appropriated by outsiders, or diminished by time.

"Come to Haiti" is actually unique in its extended presentation of the perspective of an interested tourist in the 1950s; the perspective is more precisely that of a traveler than a conventional tourist—there are no scenes of beaches or swimming pools or other common tropes of Caribbean tourism. The film also focuses on Haitian places rather than people; come to Haiti it seems to say, for the variety of views and sites to be visited—the people are of secondary interest. Haiti in the silent film is shown rather than explained. In this regard, too, the film is unique, in that other films of the period tend to use voice-overs as means of directing the viewer in a certain way, forming their understanding of Haiti for them and toward certain ends. It is notable in this pre-Duvalier period that there is a distinctly sympathetic view of Haiti that is promoted, and an overall sense that the country is being rehabilitated, reassimilated and domesticated, presented as less threatening or unknowable, particularly to the North American audiences that are the primary public for some of the more official films.

Such is the case with "Introduction to Haiti by Mary Darling, Presented by The Office of the Coordinator of Inter-American Affairs," in which the emphasis is firmly on information, on giving potential visitors sights of Haiti but also a sense of the history and contemporary reality of the country.[11] The tone is measured and nonjudgmental in the main, and there is a variety of scenes that are described in a straightforward, factual way.

The film begins at sea, a ship's horn sounds as it rolls in the choppy waters of the Windward Passage, making its way to the second largest island in the "romantic archipelago." The first sight of Haiti is of its mountains, and then the focus shifts back to the sea from an elevated position above Port-au-Prince, which shines in the sun, framed by the blue sea beyond. The Notre Dame Cathedral and the National Palace stand out above the low houses of the capital city, and both are described approvingly. Remarks about the density of the population prompt the presentation of the market, apparently held in the lower part of town, close to the shore. It is a food market, and the vendors speak Creole in this, "one of the few independent Negro nations in the world." The food seems plentiful, and the vendors stop at lunchtime for a "snack and a snooze." The narrator draws a parallel between Americans and Haitians, saying they are both "blessed with liberty." The history of popular struggle is preserved in the people's culture, in the music and the maypole dancing that is shown. Children dressed as "Indian aborigines" wait to join the carnival parade. The narrator talks of the history of slavery, how in 1517 "Negro slaves" were taken to repopulate the island, of the French arrival in 1697, which led to the creation of the large plantations and in turn the enrichment of the planters. Carnival characters that he describes as "grotesque figures" are he says memories of the plantations, part of the "tangle of survivals" that constitutes the island's culture. Inevitably, he talks of Vodou, the "mysterious, smoldering, shuddering" that is presented as an act of memory, a Haitian example of the "eternal human impulse to remember." The tourist is "bewildered" by the carnival's mix of historical remembrance and "modern things" like motor cars and "jazzy saxophones." Haiti is also modern in its government, the second independent legislature in the Americas, the narrator says.

The perspective switches from land to sea as the narrator talks about how the country is made up largely of two peninsulas and as such has an

---

[11] https://www.youtube.com/watch?v=y3aeW2jPwZo.

extraordinarily long coastline, and no less than fourteen seaports. It is from the sea that the narrator approaches Cap Haïtien, which he visits less for the city than to make the short journey to Milot, to see Sans-Souci. The view of the palace is from above, and from that perspective it looks rather less impressive than it does from ground level. Tourists are then shown mounting horses to make the two-and-a-half hours climb to Christophe's Citadelle, which is viewed necessarily from below at first and then filmed in more detail from inside the building. The narrator speaks of Christophe's great virtues as an administrator, in establishing schools, building roads, and encouraging agriculture. Remarkably, the narrator says that the Citadelle is a reminder of the "lasting debt" that all of North America has to Haiti, as it stands for the "great change" at the beginning of the nineteenth century in Europe's attitude toward the New World, the end of its "fond dreams of American conquest." Everything in Haiti he says, "symbolizes our own liberty." America's proud history might not have been what it was had Christophe and his fellows not prized their own freedom so highly.

The film's restrained presentation of Vodou contrasts with that in "Song of the Voodoo," by Walter O. Gutlohn.[12] The title of this short film immediately gives an idea of the tone of the content that will follow: the narrator evokes the times of piracy, and states that along Haiti's shores lies more treasure than anywhere else in the Spanish Main. Port-au-Prince was once the "Paris of the New World." To understand these people and their "strange beliefs," one must understand they are an African race, brought here as "human chattel" that nonetheless freed themselves from slavery and founded a free republic. A "voodoo priest" is encountered in the market, while a woman holds up a piece of cloth with an intricate design that is described as a "design of demon worship," and silversmiths work nearby, artisans with tools as old as those used "in the days of Babylon." A sculptor works on a life-size female statue called "The Awakening of Haiti," and the narrator remarks that these descendants of slaves are artisans equal to those of any country in the world. The people's progress is reflected in the beauty of their architecture, notably the Notre Dame Cathedral, which shimmers and glows in the bright sunshine. The narrator talks of the people's struggles, of Makandal, whose "superhuman strength" allowed him to escape from being burned at the stake. Toussaint Louverture is also mentioned, though rather more luridly as one who "drank the hot blood of sacrifice." The sacrifice was not in vain, the narrator says, as he describes approvingly some modest houses with thatched roofs, "exactly like in Africa." The people there are a "peculiar blend of the

---

[12] https://www.youtube.com/watch?v=Ikdz44PtwOI.

past and the present," accepting elements of "civilization," but also visiting the "witch doctor." When he hears drumming nearby, he can "hardly believe [his] ears," as he knew voodoo rites were forbidden by law, but as he penetrates deeper into the jungle he sees that which few white men ever see: the cult of the voodoo. Like a latter-day Moreau de Saint-Méry, he watches as the people "abandon themselves to the rhythm of the drums." The dance, he says, has nothing to do with religion or ceremony, for voodoo has "only to do with the mind." The narrator's tone of voice becomes more dramatic and menacing as he describes the dance and how once the drums start "he who is wise will never interfere." As he talks of the "uncanny power" of the drums, two men dressed as women move rather half-heartedly in circles, and the whole scene, far from being an insight into a secret world the white man never sees, seems staged and touristic. The drum, he says, has a metaphysical meaning, not just in Haiti, but in Africa, the American wilderness, and the deserts of Arabia. Some day in the future, he concludes, when the races of mankind better understand each other we will have found the secrets of the voodoo drums that "call from the hills of Haiti."

There is a tension in these films between showing and interpreting, the lurid and the mundane, the sensational and the everyday, information and titillation. Their particular orientation tends to reveal more about the filmmaker than about their subjects, the degree to which the viewer is interested in the exotic and mysterious aspects of Haiti, which almost always have to do with Vodou. As such, the films demonstrate the "need to assert atavistic impulses" that Michael Dash analyzes in relation to Haitian–American cultural relations in the mid-twentieth century (*Haiti and the United States* 65). In this regard, some of the more lurid tourist-traveler films of the 1950s have much in common with the interests of Maya Deren, who first visited Haiti in 1947, and whose fascination with Vodou is explored in her *Divine Horsemen: The Living Gods of Haiti* (1953). As Dash writes, Deren "saw herself as an artist, marginalized and displaced within 'modern industrial culture' [...] she approached Haiti as an 'artist-native' whose experience in the United States created a special bond with Haitians to whom she was 'not a foreigner at all, but a prodigal native daughter finally returned'" (*Haiti and the United States* 83). Unlike the tourist-traveler filmmakers, she did not come to Haiti to "observe but to be initiated" (84). Deren's engagement with Haiti was distinctly sensorial: "She felt that sensual experience was the only valid approach to Oriental and African cultures which were not based on the dualism of mind and body. [...] Deren's account of Haitian voodoo was a plunge into the world of cosmic myth, of which only the artist was capable" (84). In general, however, Deren's sensorial-mystical engagement was the exception in a period that saw the publication of key works in Haitianist ethnography, such as Alfred Métraux's landmark study, *Le Vaudou haïtien* (1958). The visual biases of Western ethnographers are suggested in Sidney Mintz's introduction to Métraux's study: a good ethnographer, Mintz says, "always recognizes that reality is, among other things, what people have learned to see" (qtd. in Dash, *Haiti and the United States* 84). There is therefore in this period something of a turn to the quotidian in Haitian–American cultural relations, where the emphasis is less on the lurid and mystical than on the "normal and everyday processes that lay behind these disorientating phenomena. For about two decades a new discourse held at bay images of primeval menace that prevailed previously" (Dash, *Haiti and the United States* 85).

This "new discourse" apparently extended to Canada–Haiti relations, at least in official representations of Haiti, such as the National Film Board documentaries released in 1957. In other regards, however, Canada–Haiti relations were different from those between Haiti and the United States. Specifically, relations between Quebec and Haiti were quite particular, especially in the postwar years, when the Quebec government sent a delegation to the Port-au-Prince bicentenary celebrations, held in 1949–50. A key figure in that delegation was Jean-Charles Magnan, a government agronomist who would return to Haiti and publish works based on his travels there. Quebec and Haiti were for Magnan bound not only by French language and civilization but also by "'identical interests and by values not based solely on either making money or on the priorities of a mercantile civilization'" (qtd. in Mills, *A Place in the Sun* 46). There was judged to be a natural connection between Haitians and French Canadians, and as Mills writes, the latter "were not like the tens of thousands of other tourists flocking to Haiti as an exotic destination for beaches or shopping but were instead on a pilgrimage to visit a long lost relative" (*A Place in the Sun* 46). Magnan moreover "ridiculed the ignorance of American tourists who saw themselves as superior to Haitians, clearly implying that Quebec had a different, deeper, and more meaningful connection" (Mills 46). At the same time, Magnan insisted on the importance of the work of Canadian missionaries in rooting out Haitian "superstition" and "had a vision of Haiti that remained locked in a binary, with Haitian peasants as uncivilized and needing French-Canadian missionaries to help teach sexual morality and Christian faith" (Mills 47). Nevertheless, Magnan did succeed in spurring closer cultural and economic exchanges between Haiti and Quebec. The 1957 National Film Board documentaries focus on French-Canadian missionaries, and the need for foreign capital in order to "develop" the country. As Mills writes, "The lines between religion, development, and capitalism seemed to be blurring" (48).

The Canadian film "Haiti" begins with music, voices, and drumming—we hear the place before we see it, and the first person we see is a drummer, shot from below against the blue sky.[13] The narrator speaks in English in the first person plural about "our nation" and "our emancipation." The sounds of the drum give way to those of language, the Creole that a peasant woman speaks and that is described as the "expression of our freedom and our zest for life." An older woman beats a stick while singing a song, and the narrator connects such songs to memory, to Africa and slavery. The peasant people bring their products—vegetables, coffee, charcoal—down the mountain to the market.

Somewhere along the way, the narrator says, there is bound to be a wedding, and a wedding party promptly appears to the sound of a flute. Music and dancing are not, he says, "interruptions in our work," and "there is always a drum calling somewhere." As a drum sounds, a group of peasant dancers perform an elegant dance, a parody of the French minuet, "which our French masters tried to teach us," and which gradually builds in intensity to the sound of drums, flutes, accordions and a voice that directs the dancers' movements.

A drum plays as Marie the peasant woman arrives in the city, and the narrator says that the people feel they belong in Port-au-Prince. "Surely," he says, "there is no suburb in the world prettier than the one in the hills" leading down to the capital city. Lines of motor cars and motorcycles fill the city streets, as an upbeat song plays. The market is the center of their lives, he says, and once the produce has been sold, the country traders go in search of their own goods: kettles, pots, or printed cloth. Craftspeople patiently carve and polish plates and bowls from mahogany wood. The markets are filled, he says, with the products of the land and the people's handicraft. Interestingly, in ways that recall Mills's argument that the film promotes an engagement with global capitalism, the narrator goes on to say that if they are to ever afford more of these things, they need to open their markets "to the world." A large ship in the bay offloads sacks of food, men work with the pulleys to land the goods on the shore, to the sound of a work song. The country is working hard, he says, to increase its foreign trade, and "Canada is a respected customer." Sisal, coffee, and handicraft are exchanged for flour, fish, and machinery. Growing cultural links between the "French-speaking" nations help in turn to develop trade relations. The sisal industry employs thousands of people, he says, "on vast plantations."

Progress, he says, "must go hand in hand with education," and to this end foreign missions and other agencies set up schools in Haiti, while many

[13] https://www.youtube.com/watch?v=WwwpcUE1KnA.

Haitians study abroad, notably in Canada. Tourism is another vital component to the progress the narrator promotes. Loud drumming accompanies a panning shot of urban scenes that accentuate "the elegant life of our elite": shots of hotels, swimming pools, and tourists. If people are at first attracted to the "primitive aspects" of Haiti, then they are also able to enjoy the modern hotels, the food, the modern comforts. In ten years, he says, they have built a tourist industry that welcomes sixty thousand people to the country.

Environmental concerns preoccupy the narrator: each year, he says, they try to cope with the effects of erosion and flooding. The boldest plan in this regard is a $40 million dam built in the Artibonite Valley, which will hold the water washed down the "naked slopes" of the mountains and then feed it into the valley, to be used for the crops. Water is no longer an enemy, he says, it is "obedient" and a crucial element in increasing agricultural production, which is necessary as the population is growing so quickly that "no one can keep count." Foreign aid is helping in this regard, and the greatest of the new crops is rice. Here, too, there is music, drumming, and dance, which is used to emphasize that cooperative work systems are nothing new to Haiti, and that the people have long worked together, "to the pulse of our drums and the beat of our dances." This is the *coumbite*, the traditional collaborative work system that is presented here as a natural means of sharing work and its fruits, of celebrating the cycle of planting, cultivation, and harvest.

The ancient sounds of the dance are followed quickly by that of dynamite exploding on a mountainside and the image of a foreigner drilling underground. As the narrator says, "new sounds are shattering the quiet pattern of our country's life." Haiti has welcomed the men, machines, and capital of "friendly nations" to help it uncover the hidden wealth of its mountains. A Canadian firm is developing a copper mine, the sounds of explosions and machinery fade into those of the people, the workers, who bring their songs and instruments to the worksite. The new sounds here are metallic—a man taps on a spade as others blow on the traditional bamboo and still others sing as a line of men strike their picks into the earth in perfect time.

The sound of a blown conch shell announces a scene from a play, which a peasant man and woman act out in front of a mixed foreign and local audience. Many writers and artists, he says, are rediscovering Haiti's folklore, and are even writing in Creole, "for only Creole can capture much that is intimate in our people." The writer Morisseau-Leroy is seen speaking to the actors, and is said to have turned to the people for inspiration, using Vodou as a key theme and structuring device. The play is about the right to celebrate carnival, and a rara band plays as part of the production. These scenes then shift to a dance hall, where the "modern tempos of the western world have become a part of our daily life." Light-skinned dancers move in their own ways to their own music and their own rituals of common culture, their own experience of time and place, which is presented as "Western," but is still distinctly Haitian, not completely separate from the popular rhythms that are the more predominant focus of the film. The dance hall scenes and sounds cut swiftly again to drums, to a *veve* being marked out in the earth as a Vodou ritual is presented. Interestingly, the narrator no longer speaks in the first person plural: these are not "our gods," but "their gods," as the narrator disowns or dissociates himself from the Vodou believers, in ways that underline the film's subtle "antisuperstitious" intent.

The film finally returns to the peasant woman, Marie, for whom life is as simple as eating, breathing, and dying, and who must wish, he says, that Haiti's development—the rice fields, the dams—will create a more abundant future for her children and Haiti will become the "magic isle of the Caribbean." In all, the film is part of the effort to promote the "patriotic tourism" that Mills writes of, the increase in French-Canadian cruise ship visits to Haiti in the late 1950s driven by the "rhetoric of the broad reach of French civilization in the Americas as well as by the connected paternalist and racially inflected language of French-Canadian missionaries" (*A Place in the Sun* 48, 49).

The Canadian film and the others discussed above may finally be contrasted with another, more lurid short piece made in the 1970s, but that presents the country just before Duvalier.[14] The film begins with lively music and images of pretty girls and the Port-au-Prince bicentenary monument, which switch rather abruptly to a scene of lighter-skinned people in suits and dresses enjoying a fancy dinner with a band playing in the background. The voice-over is equally abrupt in its swift and direct critique of this sector of society and its "thoughtless" contributions to society's "disaster." The bourgeoisie live in harmony with this "self-deceit" in the hall, which is "deliciously adorned with rosewater." The exploitation of a people "is often the way to hold onto one's privilege," the voice says, as a couple dances alone, and men in suits smoke cigars. "Popular malice," he says, expresses itself in the only means left to it: "the satirical carnival."

One of the first images of carnival is of a large man and woman, the man dressed in a dark suit, a kind of smiling "fat cat" with top hat swaggering along the road. The voice-over states that "social satire" is allowed in this nation that "suffers yet sings." Large carnival bands dance in time, joyously, in a marked

---

[14] https://www.youtube.com/watch?v=gaWlMbprLMk.

contrast to the almost empty dance floor in the opening scenes. Dance is, the narrator says, "the only escape" possible for the people; "to hell with austerity," as he says, and a float passes stating that there is "joy in austerity."

The carnival images cut abruptly to other parades, more militaristic and somber, with men in uniform. "Nothing has really changed," the narrator says, as if to comment on the effectiveness of social satire and carnival in bringing about social change. He cites headlines from 1977 editions of *Le Monde* that state that Haiti is a "land without bread" and a "veiled republic" and says he protests the father-to-son dictatorship of the Duvaliers. "Wake up, Haiti," he says, "wake up and burn your carnival mask." "Show us your true face," he says, "take a human and brotherly step forward." The voice-over quite deliberately directs the viewer to a certain interpretation of Haiti, insistently, so that it rather distracts from the images, and especially toward the end the correlation between the words and the images is not obvious. To throw off the mask is almost a coded way of saying to throw off the dictatorship in order to show its "true face."

This later film is ultimately useful in that it casts back to the 1950s, the time before Duvalier, only to move forward to the 1970s to critique Haiti's elite and its role in the downfall of the nation, the betrayal of the muted promise and hope expressed in the other films for stability in the country and in its relations with its North American neighbors. It is ultimately significant that the first film is titled "Come to Haiti" and that the implicit message of the final film is "do not come to Haiti," as the Duvalier dictatorship establishes itself, and lurid, fantastical accounts of Haiti replace the representations of the everyday, and the unexceptional nature of Haiti that attracted the ethnographers and indeed the tourists of the 1950s. The films, both unofficial, made by tourists, and official, made to encourage tourism and trade, are precious records of this period and suggest a more complex exchange of touristic sounds and images than that discussed by Thompson in regard to the British colonies. There is in particular a far lesser degree of "tropicalization" in the foreign representations of Haiti during this time—no beaches or swimming pools, only a residual interest in Vodou to suggest the otherness of Haiti and its people. More commonly, the films tend to "de-tropicalize," to attempt to undo many of the myths surrounding Haiti, and to focus on the everyday, the normality of quotidian life, and the ways in which Haitian history is connected to that of its North American neighbors. For sure, there are still latent paternalistic impulses, notably in the instances discussed by Mills of French-Canadian attempts to bring Haiti under its umbrella of Francophone nations. Even in those cases, however, there is only a muted sense in the films of the colonial regime of the eye that persists in Thompson's British examples. In the case of the film

"Come to Haiti," in particular, one senses the limitations of the colonial, outsider gaze, as the power dynamics are reversed and the viewer becomes the viewed, so that history appears not as a touristic relic of the past but as a living, seeing, and clamorous entity, a force that the tourist's camera, as in Morisseau-Leroy's poem, cannot contain.

4
Who Stole the Soul?
Rhythm and Race in the Digital Age

Tourists and other visitors to the Caribbean have long heard the place and the people as essentially rhythmic—more than a particular sound, visitors seek a rhythmic feeling, a sense that they apparently cannot experience in other places. As such, they tend to be drawn to music, drumming, and dance, which in the Canadian film analyzed in the previous chapter, are used to suggest that everything in Haiti, including work, is ruled by rhythm: the people have a long history, the narrator says, of working together, "to the pulse of our drums and the beat of our dances."

In the earliest days of European settlement in the Caribbean, Spanish and French settlers brought with them their rhythmic folk music, which in form, structure, and function bore comparison to the animist rhythms of the Africans, who arrived later and who made the colonies a place of rhythmic encounter and conflict. This provoked in turn what Jacqueline Rosemain terms an "anti-rhythmic crusade" on behalf of colonists and planters, ever wary of the close connection between rhythm and revolt. Gradually, and with the mass expansion of the slave trade, the putative dangers of rhythm and dance were attributed to uniquely African sources (*La Danse* 34). Rhythm thus became a racialized concept, attached to notions of blackness, and an important element in racist, white ideas of black inferiority.

In the twentieth century, many of the diverse anticolonial, pan-African cultural movements reappropriated rhythm in their attempts to revalorize blackness and overturn centuries of negative racist stereotyping. In the poems, novels, essays, and songs of Haitian Indigenism, Négritude, the Harlem Renaissance, Afrocubanismo, and the U.S. civil rights movement, rhythm became a marker of black resistance and identity, still associated with blackness but now in an apparently positive, liberating, politicized way.

This chapter asks the following basic questions: What happens to the relationship between rhythm and race in the digital age? What happens when mastery of rhythm is no longer necessarily tied to work, to ritual, to manual drumming, and to the physical, bodily re-creation of rhythm? When electronic and digital media allow virtually anyone the ability to "drum" and to create rhythmic music, what happens to the long-standing association between blackness and rhythm? Referring to David Scott's arguments on a stalled, tragic time in the Caribbean in particular, I draw connections between the apparent redundancy of revolutionary, anticolonial thinking in the present and the perhaps less apparent decoupling of rhythm and race in contemporary musical styles. If, as Scott says, the teleologies of anticolonial politics no longer hold true, has rhythm as a marker of time, and an integral element in the poetics of resistance, lost its association with radical blackness, and become a deracialized, dehistoricized commodity?

The chapter's title refers of course to the 1989 Public Enemy track that rails against the musical industry's exploitation of black artists, from Wilson Pickett to James Brown and Otis Redding. Stealing the soul in this case relates to both financial misdeeds and the appropriation of "soul" itself by the system, which plays the role of the "pimp." Although there appears to be no direct connection between the two, I had always related this track to Nelson George's *The Death of Rhythm and Blues*, which was published one year previously, and which similarly critiques the ways in which the music business has progressively eroded and appropriated the concept of soul. It is George's text that I will draw on first in order to lay out some of the rhythm related issues that interest me here, in the U.S. and the Caribbean.

Specifically, I refer most directly to George's sixth chapter, titled "Crossover: The Death of Rhythm and Blues (1975–79)." "Crossover" is the key term here, as it denotes a process of cultural and social transference, a movement for some across the "barricades" around which, George says, rhythm and blues music had been formed (147). Socially, by the mid-seventies, a degree of integration and upward mobility had become possible through civil-service jobs, low- and middle-level management positions and increased college attendance (156). These factors, George says, "affected the pocketbooks and tastes of black America" (156). George laments this process, arguing that "much of what had made the R&B world work was lost, perhaps some of it forever" (147). "Sadly," George writes, "R&B as a metaphor and a music, looked like a terminal case; the world that had supported it no longer existed. The connections between blacks of all classes were loosening, as various forms of material success (or the illusion of such success) seduced many into the crossover mentality" (156).

Musically, it was disco and what George terms its "rigid rhythms" that characterized crossover and announced the apparent death of R&B. These rhythms came not from the R&B tradition that George venerates, but from Eurodisco, whose "metronomelike beat" he derides as being "perfect for folks with no sense of rhythm" (154). Crossover artists such as Billy Paul and the Stylistics made what George terms "glossy, upwardly mobile corporate black music," which tended to underplay the rootsy, rhythmic elements of R&B and "to be sweet, highly melodic, and unthreatening" (155). This is crucial, in that George relates the advent of Eurodisco's machine-produced rhythms to the coming to prominence of melody in crossover music, and the loss of the apparently unshakable bond between blackness and rhythm. In effect, the history of Eurodisco is intimately connected to that of the drum machine, and the automated beats and mechanical rhythms that George sees as the major causes of the death of R&B (Shapiro, *Turn the Beat Around* 98). My point at this stage is not so much to endorse or refute George's views, but to use them as an instance in which the rhythms of electronic music seem to both instantiate and echo a crisis in black identity, understood at least in part in terms of its long relationship to rhythm.

The musicologist Anne Danielsen raises a question similar to those posed by this chapter when she asks: "what happened to the sound and rhythm of African-American derived, groove-directed popular music styles when these grooves began to be produced and played by machines?" ("Introduction" 1). She challenges the assumptions that "groove depends on human performativity to be aesthetically satisfying" and that "machine-generated music must be necessarily devoid of groove qualities, because it typically lacks the microtemporal variation added by people in performance" (1). She cites two trends in "computer-based rhythmic music" that challenge these assumptions: first, the increasing experimentation and manipulation of the microtiming of "rhythmic events" in digital music, a development she sees particularly in "African-American dominated genres such as rap, neo-soul, and contemporary r&b, where the use of digital equipment for music production was quickly accepted and cleverly applied" (1). The second trend constitutes a challenge to the idea that a successful "groove" requires microtemporal deviations in order to succeed. In apparently rigid digital electronica-related styles, she finds still that the music is danceable and that it has "unmistakable groove qualities" (2). Digital music, she says, poses a challenge to the rhythm researcher in explaining the rhythmic qualities of music "whose rhythmic events lie rigidly on a metric grid" (3). Importantly, she argues that this challenge applies not only to "the hyperquantized grooves of our digital age" but also to earlier forms that are characterized by a "strictly metronomic organization of rhythmic events, such as disco" (3). Her analyses are related more to the technical qualities of music than the discourse around rhythm and race that is this chapter's primary interest, but her conclusions do echo those that this chapter will ultimately arrive at, in that as she argues, implicitly critiquing

George's position, the common assumptions regarding the diminished "soul" of black music in the digital era do not hold firm. As she puts it, "The grooviness and expressivity of African-American-derived musical styles did not die with the new technology. Rather, they were reproduced and transformed" (4).

* * *

In the Caribbean, the relationship between blackness and rhythm dates to the early plantation period, when, with the arrival of African slaves, the colonies became places of encounter between what Jacqueline Rosemain calls the ancient "cosmogonic rhythms" of Europe and Africa—between the pagan rhythms that were appropriated by European Christianity and the animist rhythms of the Africans (*La Danse* 34). On the plantation there was something of a "crusade against rhythm" (37). All rhythms, of European or African origin, were subject to antirhythmic legislation: because they were seen as savage and dangerous, and because they accompanied the dances of cults not recognized by the official religion, they were prohibited. These prohibitions applied equally to European folk, pagan rhythms as to the rhythms of African rituals.

With the mass influx of African slaves to the circum-Caribbean, rhythm became on the one hand a marker of racial difference and cultural inferiority, and on the other a sign of resistance and impenetrable black subjectivity.[1] As slave ships left the coast of West Africa, many distressed slaves would throw themselves overboard, beat their heads off the walls, or else try to suffocate and starve themselves to death. Once Africa was out of sight, however, as one slave trader reported, the slaves' spirits could be raised through the playing of music.[2] In this sense, music was also a source of comfort, and a means of making the experience of slavery to some extent bearable. For newly arrived slaves, music and rhythm soon became some of the strongest markers of identity; even if the sounds of their songs initially seemed "absurdly out of place" in the New World, gradually the "reassuring texture of their own words" and

---

[1] The historical contexualization of rhythm and race here is adapted from my previous work in *Different Drummers*. The reference to the circum-Caribbean indicates that I am working with a fluid, transnational context, one that takes the plantation, as Glissant does, as the basis for a common regional, and I would say rhythmic, culture. In Glissant's terms, "The configuration of the Plantation was the same everywhere, from Northeastern Brazil to the Caribbean to the Southern United States: *casa grande e senzala*, the Big House and the slave hut, masters and slaves" (*Faulkner, Mississippi*, 10). This is not to say that every Caribbean territory was the same, nor that the plantation was the dominant model across the region. Also, while the divergent histories of the United States and the Caribbean complicate any direct conflation of the history of rhythm and race across the plantation world, it is potentially instructive to discuss them together, as rhythm is one of the oldest, most long-standing, ingrained, yet evolving and dynamic markers of race in the Americas, one that has endured virtually since the first Africans crossed the Atlantic to the present time.

[2] See Christopher L. Miller, *The French Atlantic* 48–49.

the "resonance of the music's pulse," in other words its rhythm, "transported them to a place where something other than their appalling conditions mattered" (White and White, *Sounds of Slavery* xi). In terms of musical modes, the diverse African peoples brought to the New World the apart-playing, polyrhythms, cross-rhythms, time-line, elisions, hockets, ululations, tremolos, vocables, grunts, hums, shouts, and melismatic phrasings of their homelands (Floyd 38). In other ways too, just as drums communicated messages, or "talked" by imitating the rhythms and tonality of speech, so too some of the wordless calls, howls, and hollers of slaves functioned as an "alternative communication system," which conveyed information through sounds in ways that whites "could neither confidently understand nor easily jam" (White and White, *Sounds of Slavery* 20). While African music and dance were often viewed with suspicion and suppressed by whites, slave masters soon learned that their slaves worked more effectively when they sang, and appointed a lead singer for each group of working slaves. Indeed, when slaves were auctioned, singers with the strongest voices attracted the highest prices (Kebede 130). In work songs, pronounced, regular rhythms at once echoed the repetitive nature of much of the work, and helped slaves endure its monotony. Thus, one contemporary observer of plantation life in prerevolution Saint-Domingue wrote of the "adundance" and "peace" of the place, and of "The dutiful Africans working in cadence" (Popkin, *Facing Racial Revolution* 70). Game and social songs were also marked by regular meter, and consisted of simple additive rhythms and repetitive pentatonic melodic constructions, with accents on the offbeat (Floyd 51).[3]

In the mechanized world of the plantation, slave dances were rare moments of escape and, moreover, seminal episodes in the creation of Caribbean social relations and aesthetics. For it was through dance and rhythm—chiefly the language of the drum—that slaves began to (re)form an idea of themselves, an identity other than, if not entirely different from that of the deadening machine of the plantation. As Gérard Barthélemy states "music through dancing and especially rhythmic motions were to constitute [. . .] the only means of socialization since rhythm allows the emergence of collective expression while foregoing any pre-established structure" (qtd. in Lahens, "Afterword" 159). Dances both erased and replenished memory; as one contemporary observer noted in colonial Saint-Domingue, dances such as the chica were the slaves' "only way of forgetting and of remembering" (Popkin, *Facing Racial Revolution* 334). In a sense therefore, the slave dances effectively

---

[3] See also Tolstoy's remark to Gorki that "Where you want to have slaves, there you should have as much music as possible" (qtd. in Schafer, "Open Ears" 30).

helped perpetuate the plantation system, as they were means of releasing some of the tensions that forced labor inevitably created. Indeed, despite their reservations about the potential rebelliousness that music and dance might lead to, most slave owners permitted their slaves to hold their dances and to sing while working, "mov[ing] their bodies rhythmically to the beat of their songs" (White and White, *Sounds of Slavery* 55). Moreover, both on the plantation and at the dance, rhythm leveled individual identity and demanded the submission of the individual to a wider entity, be it the machine of the plantation or the rhythmic collectivity that Barthélémy suggests.[4] In short, this early Caribbean rhythmicity seems to have been more than a straightforward cultural memory of Africa, in that it mirrored, echoed, and partially purged the alienating everyday reality of slave existence.[5]

It was with the arrival en masse of millions of Africans (speaking many different languages, and with their own diverse cultural traditions) that the notion of a distinct black and white culture began to solidify into the dualistic models that we are still living with today. This process of racial and cultural differentiation, shaped and supported by the racial thinking of European philosophers such as Hegel and de Gobineau, came to attribute rhythmic music and dance exclusively to Africans and to the state of savage, premodern humanity that the Africans were supposed to exemplify. The Africans had brought with them a particular affinity to rhythm, which was never biologically inherited, but was an acquired aspect of music and everyday life, social interaction, speech, recreation, and work.[6] These rhythms clashed with the industrial rhythms of the

---

[4] This submission of individual identity is still apparent in modern day Carnival, which relies less on expressions of individuality than on the yielding of discrete subjectivity to the broader body of collective masqueraders, dancing more or less uniformly to fixed, repetitive rhythms.

[5] This interpretation of early Caribbean rhythms seems to echo Allesandro Falassi's theory of festival representation, which argues that carnivalesque social commentary cannot be properly achieved by simple role reversals, but only by "the simultaneous presence in the same festival of all the basic behavioral modalities of daily social life, all modified—by distortion, inversion, stylization, or disguise [...]. In sum, festival presents a complete range of behavioral modalities, *each one related to the modalities of normal daily life*" (*Time out of Time* 3, emphasis added). See also Gordon Rohlehr's argument that slave dances "provided therapy for the enslaved trapped in the tedious ménage of plantation labour" (*Calypso and Society in Pre-Independence Trinidad* 3)

[6] Barthélemy agrees that "there is nothing in rhythm that is due to a particular morphology, and even less to race; genetics clearly have nothing to do with it. Everything is on the contrary the result of automatisms, themselves due to a long apprenticeship in the course of growing up" (*Créoles-Bossales* 173). For example, in his seminal study *African Rhythm and African Sensibility* John Miller Chernoff talks of the functional importance of rhythm at all levels and all ages in African existence:

> African children play games and sing songs displaying a rhythmic character [...] learn to speak languages in which proper rhythmic accentuation and phrasing is essential to meaning. [...] Facility with rhythms is something people learn as they grow up in an African culture, one of the many cultural acquisitions that make someone seem familiar to people who have also learned the same things. Rhythms are built into the way people relate to each other." (94).

Miller's project examines the sociocultural significance of African rhythm and music, and its deep "integration into the various patterns of social, economic, and political life" (35).

plantation system, the unnatural, dehumanizing, profit-driven cycles of work that radically interrupted natural rhythms of life, birth, and death. African rhythms adapted themselves to this alienating environment, in the antiphonal work songs that accompanied field labor and in the slave dances that were sometimes sacred, sometimes secular gatherings that purged to some extent the suffering endured in working to the machine-like rhythms of the plantation. Across the Caribbean, too, vernacular culture—dances, music, religion, storytelling, language—acted as a repository of rhythm, and as the three-tiered social structure typical of Creole societies developed, the brown-skinned middle class often as much as the white elite distanced itself from rhythm and "black culture" in general. Even in revolutionary Saint-Domingue and independent Haiti, the rhythmic culture of the masses was viewed with suspicion by the leaders of the revolution. In 1800 Toussaint Louverture issued a decree prohibiting nocturnal assemblies and gatherings, and particularly "Vaudoux" dances, an act that suggested that the political impulse to control and regulate could not exist alongside the cultural and religious freedom that had played a significant role in fomenting and ensuring the success of the slave revolt. Unlike the later case of Congo Square in New Orleans, whereby rhythm and music were to become secularized, in Haiti music, rhythm, and dance remained closely associated with religious practice, and hence with a metaphysical, political, and cultural alterity that was the antithesis of the modern, essentially capitalist state envisioned by Haiti's first leaders. In short, Toussaint's revolution envisioned full "participation in the mainstream of world history rather than away from it" (Genovese, *From Rebellion to Revolution* 92). Vodou and its rhythmic dance and music were, it seems, too closely associated with Africa and antimodernism to be incorporated into the reason of state of the Haitian nation, which resisted "atavistic longings for a racial past," and whose impulses were "toward the future and not dwelling in mythical origins" (Dash, *The Other America* 44–45). For Dessalines, Christophe, and the other ultimately failed rulers that were to succeed them in the nineteenth century, popular dance, music, and religion would be considered obstacles to Haiti's development, even if, like Toussaint before them, their personal relationships to Vodou were quite complex and contradictory.

Rhythm therefore became associated not only with a certain "race" of people but also with the lower class and with notions of cultural backwardness. As such, especially in the Caribbean, middle-class intellectuals of color often aligned themselves with the putatively superior, arrhythmic literary and musical culture of Europe. In the nineteenth century, with a few exceptions, rhythm remained for many mulatto intellectuals a marker of Africa, and thus of social and cultural inferiority. The poetry and art music of this period rarely evoked rhythmic, vernacular culture in anything but derogatory, disdainful terms. At the same time, rhythm has been a primary means through which lower-class Caribbean and New World black peoples have asserted and enacted their historical and political agency.

As the twentieth century began, and as various pan-African movements gathered momentum, rhythm was slowly recuperated into the emerging middle-class, nationalist consciousness as a potent sign of racial difference and a primary element of the lost, devalorized parts of national culture. The terms in which rhythm was now evoked—as something irrevocably premodern, primitive, and antirational—were virtually the same as before, but now these qualities were seen positively as means of uniting separated diasporic peoples and of further solidifying the notion of black culture as radically, incontrovertibly different from white culture. Rhythm now flooded into all areas of middle-class, mulatto culture, and became for the first time a prominent, distinguishing feature of poetry, art music, and choreography. "Primitive sources" were now raided in the quest to recast national culture in primordial, anti-European (and often anticolonial) terms. The putatively authentic culture of the previously neglected masses was now seen as the single most important marker of national difference, a great, supposedly uncorrupted resource to be plundered and appropriated as the middle classes slowly shed mimetic impulses and embraced cultural nationalism. In the great political, cultural, and social maelstroms of the New World in the twentieth century, rhythm was thrown center-stage, and played a dynamic role in, for instance, Haitian Indigenism, Negritude, and Black Power, movements that harnessed rhythm to their notions of black culture and black difference. In a 1961 interview, Aimé Césaire was asked about the importance of language in his work, and replied that words are less important to him than rhythm, for rhythm, he said, "is an essential element of the black man" (Sieger, "Entretien" 152). Much later, Antonio Benítez-Rojo writing of the rhythmic culture of the Caribbean, albeit in less essentialist terms, cites the importance of African rhythms to the region's cultures: "Black Africa has an even greater dependence on rhythm [than India]. [. . .] In reality, it can be said that African culture's genes have been codified according to the possibilities of percussion. African culture is, above all, a thicket of systems of percussive signifiers, to whose rhythms and registers one lives both socially and inwardly" (*The Repeating Island* 169).

The Negritude movement allowed for—indeed largely relied on—the elaboration of dualistic, racialized notions of culture, in which rhythm was recuperated as a marker of pan-African blackness. In the 1960s United States, although black nationalists such as Amiri Baraka sought to racialize James Brown's rhythms and limit their possible meanings, the rhythms of seminal tracks such as "Cold Sweat" and "The Payback" escaped this potential prison and spread across the globe, to Africa, where they were enthusiastically greeted as new creations, and to Europe, where everyday Europeans began to rediscover the exhilaration of finding the beat, and getting with "the One." This process of rhythmic globalization had actually begun in the 1920s with the spread of swing, boogie woogie, and other forms of African American music. The global proliferation of rhythm—so often viewed as a marker of cultural primitivism—has paradoxically coincided with the expansion of modernity, urbanization, and industrial development.[7] In a sense, too, the history of popular music from the 1960s to the present has seen the partial deracialization of rhythm, particularly since the late 1980s and the emergence of hybrid forms of dance music such as Chicago house and its various offshoots.[8]

In the classic colonial situation of twentieth-century Trinidad, rhythmic popular culture was under constant attack from the white establishment, particularly the Protestant British. Carnival became the focus of dualistic debates over culture and rhythm, and throughout the nineteenth century the colonial authorities systematically repressed the rhythmic music of the masses. Slowly evolving from a mainly white celebration, Carnival was gradually appropriated by the black lower classes, who translated their rhythmic culture and music into the secularized space of the festival, spreading fear among the whites who saw (and heard) constantly in black expressive culture intimations of revolt. The many ordinances banning drum playing only further strengthened the connection between black identity and rhythm. At every point, rhythm did not disappear, but returned in new forms, by means of new instruments. Something like in Haiti, but in a more muted way, in the early-to-mid twentieth century Trinidad's rising class of largely nonwhite intellectuals turned to popular culture as an untainted repository of authentic, rhythmic black culture. As the proindependence movement gathered momentum in Trinidad, rhythmic music was slowly rehabilitated into nationalist discourse. The decisive step in this evolution was the promotion of the steelpan, which had emerged from the long-neglected culture of the urban poor, as the national instrument of independent Trinidad.

Ultimately, Trinidad's history, sounded out, shaped, and prophesied by the various changes in rhythmic music and developments in percussive

---

[7] Lefebvre writes of how modern (Western) music has been shaped by a "massive irruption of exotic rhythms" (Éléments 58).

[8] See also Paul Gilroy's argument that purpose-built reggae sound systems in English inner cities "disperse and suspend the temporal order of the dominant culture." As the sound system wires are strung up and the lights go down," Gilroy says, "dancers could be transported anywhere in the diaspora without altering the quality of their pleasures" (*There Ain't No Black in the Union Jack* 284). See also Bull and Back, "Introduction" (13), and Hesmondhalgh and Negus, *Popular Music Studies* 8.

instrumentation, is a history of popular improvisation. The apparently chaotic, unplanned shifts from one style of music, one kind of percussive instrument to another mask a deeper, irresistible purpose. While improvisation is usually understood as an act without foresight, prescriptive vision, or deep motivation, in practice it is often a knowing, future-oriented performance that operates as a "kind of foreshadowing, if not prophetic, description," which carries "the prescription and extemporaneous formation and reformation of rules, rather than the following of them" (Moten, *In the Break* 63). In the history of Trinidad, music and other kinds of performative improvisations, are far from simple, naive, ahistorical acts; instead they foresee and embody what Moten calls "the very essence of the visionary, the spirit of the new, an organizational planning of and in free association that transforms the material" (64). Improvisation is always also a matter of time and sight, a glance to the future, and in Trinidad's case, the occasion to see the shape of that future, in a way that echoes what James Brown says of his own rhythmic innovations in the 1960s. "It's—it's—it's just *out there*," Brown says, "I'm actually fightin' the future" (qtd. in White and Weinger 27, emphasis in original). In the mid-sixties, Brown says, he was not seeking to reproduce "some known sound," but was "aimin' for what I could *hear*. 'James Brown Anticipation' I'd call it. You see, the thing was *ahead*" (Rose, *Living in America* 59). As Dave Marsh says, in 1965, James Brown "invented the rhythmic future in which we live today" (*The Heart of Rock and Soul* 5).[9] In Trinidad, a similar future-oriented vision has also been communicated primarily through sound, rhythm, and the music without which the great transformations in Trinidadian society from the colonial era to today could never have taken place.[10]

The case of Trinidad, and of the history of the steelpan in particular is important, as it offers an implicit critique of the idea put forward by Nelson George that modern, technological innovation inevitably diminishes the "blackness" of the music. Fashioned literally from the wreckage of industrial society—bits of old cars, paint pots, dustbins, and cement and oil drums—the steelpan is a quintessentially modern invention, and yet its modernity apparently does not loosen its association with black identity. On the contrary, its history suggests that it is rhythmic innovation and technological invention that are some of the defining aspects of black identity in the Americas.

This is a line of thought expressed in Alexander G. Weheliye's *Phonographies: Grooves in Sonic Afro-Modernity*. In this work, Weheliye

---

[9] Craig Werner similarly argues that "'Papa's Got a Brand New Bag' unleashed a polyrhythmic ferocity that eventually reconfigured every corner of the American soundscape" (*A Change is Gonna Come* 138).
[10] For more on the history of rhythm in Trinidad see Munro, *Different Drummers*, chapter 2.

questions the idea that the human and the technological can be definitively separated, and proposes that "one is hardly conceivable without the other" (2). More specifically, he critiques the common placement of black culture and being beyond the realm of the technological, the notion that "Afro-diasporic populations are inherently Luddite and therefore situated outside the bounds of modernity" (2). Similarly, he questions the neglect in most academic work on technology of what he calls the "sonic topographies of popular music," which he says has long been one of the most fertile areas for the "dissemination and enculturation of digital and analog technologies" (2–3). Popular music is also the primary domain, he says, in which black subjects have engaged with technology, so that "any consideration of digital space might do well to include the sonic in order to comprehend different modalities of digitalness, but also not to endlessly circulate and solidify the presumed 'digital divide' with all its attendant baggage" (3).

Weheliye's book proceeds to examine some of the many ways in which twentieth-century black cultural production intersected and engaged with sound technologies, from the phonograph to the Walkman. Throughout, he regards the technologization of black music and culture not as moments of inauthenticity, but "as a condition of (im)possibility for modern black cultural production" (*Phonographies* 12). In general, he makes a compelling case for the reconsideration of the idea that black cultures are pre- or antitechnological, and for the study of sound recording and reproduction in relation to black cultural production as a means of identifying the "singular mode of (black) modernity" (3). As he puts it later in the work, there is "no Western modernity without (sonic) blackness and no blackness in the absence of modernity" (174).

This is an idea he restates in the *Small Axe* discussion of both his book and Julian Henriques's *Sonic Bodies*, another work that considers blackness to be integral to sonic technological innovation and vice versa, in its analysis of the sound system. In his response to the discussion, Henriques echoes to some degree Weheliye's argument on the importance of blackness to modernity, saying that "those human beings whom slavery attempted to reduce to machines are precisely the ones who gave the modern world its musical humanity" and that "there is little disjuncture between African sensibilities and technologies" ("Dread Bodies" 200). Henriques's book shows how Dancehall "riddims" draw on Kumina rhythms and that as such "ancient old-world African traditions 'come up to the time' [. . .] with the latest digital technologies" (*Sonic Bodies* 12). His analysis of the figure of the MC further demonstrates the dynamic fusion of traditional performance motifs and ultracontemporary technological innovation to create a form that constantly renews itself. Henriques talks of how under the MC's direction "Rhythmic energies flood the show," and of how these energies range from the "electromagnetic flows within the set, such as the forces of electrical currents [...] to the audio-cultural flows of the music, the musical flow of the selector's segueing from one track to the next, the corporeal and kinetic flow of the crowd, and the socio-cultural flow of the MC's lyrics themselves" (191–92). Rhythm in this context is "energy, force, or flow" and is related to time through the "ultra-fast turnover" of styles, sounds, and fashions that characterizes Dancehall (192). This is rhythm much as James Brown saw it—as a force of change and renewal, the embodiment of the imminent future.

Similarly, in Weheliye's contribution to the *Small Axe* discussion, he states that in his book, "instead of imagining Afro-diasporic cultures as disconnected from the heart of modernity's whiteness, I demonstrate how black cultures have contributed to the very creation and imagination of the modern, interrogating the facticity of blackness, that is, how certain groups of humans became black through a multitude of material and discursive powers" ("Engendering Phonographies" 181). This recognition that blackness is an integral element of technological modernity has for Weheliye a potential political value in that if blackness is commonly judged to exist beyond what he calls the "iron grip of the West and modern technologies," despite it being a product of these forces, such a recognition offers a way of dismantling "the coloniality of being in Western modernity," that is the sense of separation, almost of exile from modernity that informs certain understandings of blackness, across the Americas, and since at least the Negritude movement (181). By insisting on the fundamental importance of black people and cultures to the "territory" as he puts it of Western modernity, its unique association with whiteness and alienation is diminished (181). It is telling that he uses metaphors of space in his imagining of the political potential of recognizing blackness as an integral part of modernity, as they suggest a sense of belonging physically and culturally to a place, and a possible way out of the feeling of alienation and exile that are found, again, in classic formulations of blackness from Negritude to Indigenism, and exist still in residual form in Nelson George's critique of disco. Crucially, too, such a recognition does not imply the loss of the specificity of "black life" itself, rather it calls into question the nature of modernity, and blackness is reconsidered as a dynamic, evolving, unpredictable phenomenon, which is not (only) to be recovered from the past but (also) is something that is in constant, irregular, future-oriented creation.

Although he does not refer extensively to rhythm, it follows from Weheliye's argument that blackness is an effect of modernity, that the blackness–rhythm equation that Nelson George invokes is similarly related to and dependent on the binary construction of whiteness and blackness whereby the former is related to technology and machinery, and the latter to earthiness and untainted humanity.

A similar argument is proposed by Peter Shapiro in his 2006 work *Turn the Beat Around*, which is a more straightforward history of disco music, and which suggests that the "standardized meter and mechanical beats of disco can be traced back to the very birth of African-American music" (90). In his third chapter, subtitled "Automating the Beat," he pays particular attention to rhythm and traces the history of regular, repetitive beats to Congo Square, and the "regimentation and rigidity" of marching band music (90). Shapiro also hears in the rhythms of Bo Diddley and Kraftwerk echoes of the regular, mechanical sounds of the railroads, and in the latter's machine-produced beats he hears something that he says exists in all music: the "trance ritual," the "eternal rhythm loop that could transport you across its waves of sound" (93). Given what he calls the "strong presence of automated beats and mechanical rhythms throughout the history of African-American music," Shapiro argues that critics of disco's "machinelike" qualities such as Nelson George tend to ignore the regular, repetitive rhythms of much black American music of the twentieth century and to rely on a nonexistent contradiction between blackness and technological modernity (97). George is right to the extent that there is a long and complex relationship between rhythm and notions of blackness in the Americas, but he seems not to recognize fully the historical conditions in which that association was formed, and that the relationship was always dynamic and evolving, a product of and not an uncorrupted counter to technological modernity.

* * *

The case of Jamaican music further exemplifies this relationship between rhythm, race, technology, and nation. Early pre-echoes of the fusion of these elements are found in a striking passage from the anonymous 1828 novel *Marly, Or a Planter's Life in Jamaica*, in which the eponymous protagonist is constantly unsettled by the sounds of the plantation, both of the people and the machines. The passage recounts how when Marly tries to sleep, and though he is "considerably fatigued," he finds he is kept awake by the sounds of the plantation: "The almost incessant cries of the boilerman for more fire, or up and down with the cooler, bawled in a stentorian voice through a long bamboo tube to the fireman, [which] was enough of itself to prevent sleep to one unaccustomed to such sounds" (39). Marly's wish for rest and peace is thus disrupted by the sounds of the plantation, not so much that of the machinery, but of the people, the noise of the workers, who somewhat ingeniously adapt the bamboo tube as a means of communication, and of amplifying the booming voice of the boilerman so that the sounds become a form of music that is attuned to the workings of the sugar plantation but which disrupts the white man's desire for peace and quiet. That this is a form of human-industrial music, deliberately created by the workers, is emphasized by the narrator's observations about the other sounds that tended to "murder sleep," those of a dozen girls and boys seated "on the shafts of the gin, forcing on the mules that turned the mill" (89). The children "partly for their own amusement, and partly to increase the speed of the beasts," the narrator says, "joined in a genteel chorus, which, according to their natural ideas of melody, they kept up at the height of their voices, and though it was then rather grating to Marly's ear, it pleased themselves, and what was of more consequence, it pleased the mules, and made them perform more work than whipping in all probability would have done" (39). This is a fascinating description of the ways in which sounds become part of the soundscape of work on the plantation, and how the "natural" musicianship and melody of the people are harnessed to the processes of work. It is in essence an early industrial music, in which the human sounds add melody to the rhythms of work so that the music plays a dual and somewhat ambivalent role: it at once soothes the workers, and increases the efficiency of the industrial process. Music is more than an accompaniment to the work: it drives it and is part of it. The scene also underlines the ways in which sounds are heard differently by different listeners: to Marly the sounds are "grating," "roared," and have no "rhyme, reason, or melody," but to the people they form part of a sense of working together in harmony, of sharing the load, and no doubt of expressing the experience of being enslaved, being tied to machines and animals and having to recuperate from that a sense of humanity, which is expressed in the high pitch of the voices, the human sound being heard above the others as an auditory marker of identity and being. Clearly, too, the music is meant also to unsettle the whites, and it succeeds in disrupting Marly's rest, his desire for sleep, of which he says, "there was none" (39).[11]

The early scene of music and sound being produced through the fusion of machines, technology, rhythms, and human voices effectively anticipates later developments in Jamaican music, and to make machines very much part of the production of rhythms and music. Lloyd Bradley writes, for example, of the nascent recording industry in postwar Jamaica, and how by the beginning of the 1950s technological modernization had begun to make music production

---

[11] Parts of this material on Jamaican music appear in my *Listening to the Caribbean*.

a viable enterprise, even if due to the lack of mastering facilities, most of the records sold were still licensed American works. It was with the "second wave of sound men"—principally, Duke Reid, Clement Dodd, and Prince Buster— that the local phenomenon of the sound system began to be considered a "both a social and commercial event" (*Bass Culture* 27). A trained carpenter, Dodd built speaker cabinets for the sound men, and when he worked on short-term cane-cutting jobs in Florida, the same men would ask him to bring back pieces of equipment, as they "trust[ed] his ears" (28). Presenting new records as a "visual as well as an aural experience," Dodd and his partner would devise new dance steps to go along with the new sounds, so that crowds anticipated the new dance as much as the new sounds (28). Sensitivity to sound was, however, Dodd's defining characteristic: he was "the undisputed boss when it came to tonal range and sheer power" in his selection of new tracks (28). Duke Reid was similarly said to "have ears," and to be in touch with what the people wanted. He was astute enough to sponsor and present the R&B radio show, *Treasure Isle Time*, which led in turn to the creation of his own redoubtable sound system (29). Buster also had an "acute ear" that he would use to identify the tracks being played at other sounds' dances (32). Sound clashes were decided on "devastating volume," thus the best equipment and latest technology were essential to a system's success (30), and the "scope and quality of equipment seemed to advance on a weekly basis" (36). The "only place" for a sound man to shop was Wonard's Radio Engineering, which was run by the Wongs, a Chinese-Jamaican family who imported speakers, amplifiers, and other equipment from the United States and England (36). The sound men quite naturally progressed to producing records made by Jamaican artists, originally for their own sound systems, with little thought of selling the records to a broader public, an idea that was taken up initially by Chris Blackwell and Edward Seaga, elite figures whose ears were attuned to the popular music and founded their own labels: R&B, and West India Records Limited, respectively. The budding politician Seaga had studied indigenous Jamaican music in his graduate work at Harvard, and realized that music and politics were closely intertwined. As Bradley says, "the best way to reach the people was with the right beat," and as such there was a synergy between politics and rhythm: politics were rhythmical, and rhythm was political (43).[12]

The growing commercial success of the sound men, and of indigenous Jamaican music was further facilitated by the availability of radiograms and other record players toward the end of the 1950s. Relative prosperity was part

---

[12] Seaga reaped the benefits of his close relationship with the music and rhythms of the people when he became leader of the Jamaica Labour Party in 1970 and Jamaican prime minister in 1980.

of a growing spirit of optimism, and "all the talk," as Bradley writes, "was of independence within the next few years" (*Bass Culture* 47). The close relationship between sound and politics is further indicated in Bradley's statement that the people were searching for music "that reflected the creeping national euphoria. [. . .] Music that acknowledged the myriad influences stamped on Jamaican culture. But, most of all, music that beat with the very soul of downtown Kingston. Sufferahs' music. A true expression of Jamaican blackness" (47). Remarkably, this national feeling manifested itself most immediately, and enduringly, in rhythm: as Jamaica became self-governing in 1959 before final independence in 1962, "what finally emerged was a new rhythm to match the new mood of a very upbeat Jamaica" (51). The new rhythm was part of a more recognizably national sound, which the people demanded, as they heard their own voices and accents on records, and to a beat that in effect kept the R&B shuffle beat, but with the stress on the afterbeat, the second and fourth beats, "to such a degree that it turned the arrangement around," so that early ska was often referred to as "upside down R&B" and with the guitar adding stress to the off-beat, it "became the focus of all Jamaican music that followed on after it" (53).

It is striking that the new rhythm is generally considered to be a national as opposed to a racial or social class expression, but in truth the three categories were inseparable, and Prince Buster in particular pushed the music further away from its R&B influences, believing that "what was required was a music that celebrated its blackness through its African roots and reflected what downtown folk actually took seriously" (Bradley, *Bass Culture* 56). In other words, the music needed to speak for the black, working-class majority of the island. Rhythm was for Buster the defining aspect of the new sound, as he sought to bring in the sound of the marching drum, which he had heard in "lodge processions, funerals, military parades, anything with that marching drum" (57). Although, he says, he didn't know it then, "this was ska. The belly of the ska sound is that marching drum" (58). The rhythmic heart of the music was only further enhanced when Buster invited the master drummer Count Ossie and his troupe to record with his band. Ossie was widely respected in the ghettoes, as Rastafari's influence spread and was seen as "black Jamaica's strongest remaining bond to its African roots" (59). The 1961 session produced, most notably, a version of "Oh Carolina" with a shuffling, slow, looping beat that Buster knew was original, "something special" that included Count Ossie's drums and which was, he says, "for the first time ever [. . .] was the sound of Rasta searching for some kind of identity" (60). It was of course also the sound of Jamaican music searching for its own identity, and that identity was in the rhythm, as the people flocked to Buster's dances, "running to those drums" (60).

Significantly, virtually all of these technological advancements—in recording equipment, speakers, amplifiers, record players—had to do with listening and sound. This coming to prominence of sound may be compared to the prevalence of sight and seeing that scholars have identified as the source of colonial control. Nicholas Mirzoeff, again, writes of the ways in which "modern visual culture" begins with the major shift in the mid-seventeenth century in the "European division of the sensible." The new sensorial order of things was, Mirzoeff argues, produced by the needs of European expansion and encounter, "above all in the plantation colonies" (*The Right to Look* 49). The primary "thing" to be determined in visual terms was the "slave," constituted as a new subject by, for instance the French Code Noir and the Barbados slave code (1661).

For Mirzoeff, again, the age of revolutions in the Caribbean marked a moment of crisis for the "plantation complex of visuality," which was challenged first by the enslaved and then by the plantocracy. He analyzes Makandal's Revolt in Saint-Domingue as the beginning of the "crisis of visuality." Oversight, he writes, had sought to affirm its authority by means of the surveillance of the overseer, but by the late eighteenth century, "this localized practice was challenged from within and without by Maroons, abolitionists, rebel slaves, and finally even the planters themselves" (*The Right to Look* 76). In the case of Makandal, European oversight came into contestation with the maroon's invocation of second sight, a power the rebel made available to each of his followers (68). Mirzoeff's insistence on the countervisual strategy of the enslaved pays no attention to sound, however, even as he quotes Boukman's famous address at Bois Caiman in 1791: "Listen to the voice of liberty, which speaks in the heart of us all," (69), which clearly suggests that the challenge to visuality and oversight came largely through the noisy resistance of the enslaved and others, the sounds and voices that the colonist's visualism had never truly silenced.

Oversight was, again, a completely successful enterprise, largely because of the resistance of the enslaved, and their creation of what Mirzoeff calls a "counter-theater" to the system of surveillance and discipline. This "counter-theater" was, by contrast to the visually controlled world of oversight, full of noise—the voices and sounds that were never silenced and that ever challenged the regime of the eye. As the example from the novel *Marly* shows, these voices and sounds were often attuned to the machinery of the plantation, and evolved as technology itself developed. The sound men of the 1950s and 1960s adapted in their own ways to the new recording and related technology, and in this their efforts were enhanced by the timely arrival in 1959 of the new radio station of the Jamaican Broadcasting Corporation (JBC).

The JBC's arrival constituted a challenge to the existing dominance of the British-owned Real Jamaican Radio (RJR), and the American stations in Miami, Nashville, and New Orleans. The new station's brief was to "promote the indigenous arts and to reflect local taste accurately," and it quickly ensured that for the first time, the Jamaican Top 30 was composed uniquely of Jamaican artists, which, in tandem with the burgeoning domestic recording industry, meant that the sound men began to be consulted by the radio show programmers (Bradley, *Bass Culture* 88–90). In addition, with the increasing availability of record players and radio sets—by 1960, 90 percent of Jamaican households had a radio—the demand for local recordings grew (Bradley 92).[13]

With independence in 1962 came along with the new technologies a new rhythm, driven by a younger generation, the most prominent of whom would provide the beat for the Skatalites, and would determine the new beat, as it is described by Bradley:

> Rimshots on the downbeat heralded the change of style as a new beat that practically cut itself in half from what had established the style. While it kept that 4/4 time, with the bass drum accenting the second and fourth beats in that marching-drum style, the off-beat emphasis increased by presenting itself as a single stroke. [. . .] A punching brass section added to the emphases already going on inside the structure, while a creeping-type-bass-line underpinned the whole thing. (*Bass Culture* 94)

The rhythm was the music's signature, its identity, unchanging but adaptable, as Jimmy Cliff suggests in his recollection that "The best bands could play any tune, in any style, in any arrangement, in any key, but with a good strong ska beat" (qtd. in Bradley 97). The music, including the rhythm, was moreover closely aligned with the national feeling at particular moments in time, as Bradley writes: "The best ska or rocksteady or dub or dancehall or whatever form it was taking that year, has always had enormous spiritual and populist elements evolving in relation to Jamaica's black nation's mood swings" (100). It is no doubt too simplistic to equate changing rhythms with evolving social and political times, but it is true that by the mid-1960s, the relative prosperity of the 1950s had faded and the early wave of postindependence optimism had begun to evolve into something else—an awakening to the difficulties of postcolonial nationhood—and by that time ska itself had lost its luster in the ghettoes, where "cooler, more restrained rhythms [. . .] had been battering down Trench Town" (Bradley 110). In the words of Jimmy Cliff, the people

---

[13] For an analysis of the regional impact of radio, see Bronfman, *Isles of Noise*.

soon knew the reality of 1960s Jamaica "wasn't independence at all [. . .] and as the music start to slow down—like the party *finish*—people start observing what was happening [. . .] and the figured they better start looking out for themselves" (qtd. in Bradley 155).

This was also a traveling culture, not just across Jamaica and the Caribbean, but to England, where the sound men were similarly aware of the importance of proper technology to be taken seriously. They had to get their own amplifiers, as the English equipment could not deliver the bass the people wanted, "the beat of the bass" that would get the people dancing (118). The whole system had to be built to their precise specifications, and to the requirements of the rhythms—"because of how we dance it have to sound different": English people would shake their heads as they danced, while West Indians would dance with their waist and hips, and so, "we need the bass" (118).

The music also traveled to the United States, and to the New York World's Fair of 1964, just two years after independence—a sign of the ways in which the new music and its beat were attuned to the spirit of the new nation. Stalwarts such as Jimmy Cliff, the Blues Busters, Millie Small, Monty Morris, and Prince Buster would perform ska hits at the Jamaica marquee, though the choice of Byron Lee's Dragonnaires as the house band was controversial, for reasons of rhythm and feeling, as that band was seen by Cliff as "just a calypso band really, playing dance music for people in the hotels" (Bradley, *Bass Culture* 134). The result was, according to Cliff, that the tour was unsuccessful as the music did not sound as it was meant to, "natural—the music just didn't get across" (135). Somewhat counter to Cliff, Bradley argues that the point of the Fair was never to promote the music, but to encourage tourism, and to harness sound to the visual images of Jamaica: ska was but one facet of "an overall canvas of 'Jamaicanness'" that included Dunn's River Falls, sunshine, and Blue Mountain Coffee (136). As such, the ska dance was as important as the ska music, and dancers demonstrated their steps at the Fair in a fusion of movement and sound that presented Jamaica as rhythmic, moving literally to its own beat, in a nonthreatening way that the tourist board hoped they could profit from, in an early form of what now is termed "sonic tourism," the trend to present the Caribbean in terms of sounds, strictly curated and harmonious, and with none of the discordant noise that was always there in the music.

Travel and mobility pushed further innovations and led to the introduction of new instruments. Byron Lee's band was the first, he says, to "come up with the idea of touring," and to make that happen he went to the United States to get the first Fender bass and Fender bass amplifier in the Caribbean, as well as an electronic organ (Bradley, *Bass Culture* 157). The bass and the organ gave the sound "more punch," he says, and the people wanted to "*feel* the music coming off the stage" (157). The sound was therefore about more than the ears, more than listening—it had to be felt, to vibrate into the body like the rhythm always had done, but the Fender bass as Bradley says, "rewrote the rules of rhythm" and had a profound effect on Jamaican music. The new technology fired the spirit of experimentation—the electric bass allowed players to rebalance arrangements and to slow the playing down. The more rigid, driving beat of ska was now complicated by the ways in which innovative bass players would not follow the drumbeat, but mark out a "precise, syncopated rhythm [. . .] to create time and space for other players to insert counter rhythms, which meant they were able to carry the tune's swing and so give the bass player the opportunity to let his musical hair down and show off a bit inside what were essentially his own patterns" (158). The bass "as a lead instrument" was to become a "cornerstone" of the music for the next twenty years (158). Again, the musical slowdown was related to the national mood, as the "frenzied, galloping quality" of ska that was driven by the "radio-promoted, government-sponsored optimism" of the early '60s gave way to the more complicated, measured, and experimental rhythms driven by the electric bass and the way it seemed to expand and contract time within the structure of the song (163). The rhythmic slowdown is also attributed to the increase in gang violence and tension in the dancehalls: the "rude boy" era literally slowed everything down as dancers remained on their guard, and stayed rooted to spot, moving their hips and shoulders, while looking around, ever wary (164).

Such an image of detachment and control in the middle of sound and potential disorder seems to relate to a sense of balance, such as it is theorized by the anthropologist Kathryn Guerts, who writes of how "*sensing* [. . .] is profoundly involved with a society's epistemology, the development of its cultural identity, and its forms of being-in-the-world" (*Culture and the Senses* 3). Guerts is particularly interested in balance, which is not normally thought of as a sense in the West. Balance is of course related to hearing, or at least to the ear, as the vestibular organ is located in the inner ear, and is essential for maintaining equilibrium, and for sight, too, as it coordinates the position of the head and the movement of the eyes. Guerts finds that in contrast to Western notions of the five senses, which she calls a "folk ideology" (8) and "culturally embedded" (9), in Anlo-land in West Africa (southern Togo and the southeastern corner of Ghana) there is no clearly defined taxonomy of the senses and balance is considered to be an essential sense: "Anlo-Ewe people considered balancing (in a physical and psychological sense, as well as in literal and in metaphorical ways) to be an essential component of what it means to be human" (4). This matters as it indicates the importance of a culture's sensory order (or sensorium) in learning how to perceive and experience the world, and ultimately to one's identity, as this order is "fundamental to an expectation of what it is to be a person in a given time and place" (5). If balance is included in the sensorium of the West African people that Guerts writes of, this has profound consequences for the ways in which everyday events are experienced and committed to memory, and this is perhaps especially true in largely oral cultures, in which the sensorium serves as a code for processing and transmitting memory. Such embodied experiences of the senses, time, and memory are also means of forming notions of identity, in which Guerts says "are subsumed [. . .] ideas of well-being and [. . .] conceptions of person and the self" (10). In the image of the Jamaican dancer of the mid-1960s, moving yet immobile, we can sense the importance of a similar sense of balance, and how it is related to the ear, to listening—the slower music allowed the attainment of this more detached, balanced condition, which in turn was a rhythmic reaction to the more general conditions of the society, the growing insecurity and the resultant wariness that replaced the initial, forward-driven notions of time, rhythm, and history.

Shifts in society seemed to lead inevitably to changes in the way the music sounded, and in this case the horns were de-emphasized in favor of the rhythm section "that had now stepped forward to drive the style. The bass player in particular" (Bradley, *Bass Culture* 165). New technology bolstered the rhythm section, with the electric organ underscoring the new rhythmic structures, and the electric guitar being used to augment the work of the bass (166). The increasing influence of Rastafarian philosophy was in turn a key factor in the movement from rocksteady to reggae, around the end of 1968, which marked the "coming of age" of Jamaican music, and a new stylistic freedom that would propel it into the new decade and beyond (199).

Bradley identifies Lee Perry's "People Funny Boy" as one of the earliest examples of the new reggae sound, with its prominent electric bass and several guitars used "rhythmically rather than merely melodically" in ways that recall the banjo strumming of mento music and which leave gaps that are filled with "Burru- and Kumina-style rhythmic statements" that in turn indicate an underlying "Jamaicanness so intrinsic that it doesn't need to worry about the here and the now as it draws a line—a thick black line—straight back to Africa" (*Bass Culture* 198). In this sense, just as the music becomes fluid and flexible, creating gaps that could be filled in various ways, or left empty, so its temporal and geographical frames seemed to expand: this was Jamaica in the late 1960s, but the sound carried echoes and silences of other places and of the long past, and indeed the future. Again, the new "organic" sound did not involve a turning away from technology; rather, the technology was harnessed to the sound, enhancing it, so that "electronic advancements served to make what was created sound more rather than less human" (200). The early fusion of technology, history, and emerging nationhood meant that there was little or no contradiction between advances in sound technology and the artistic or spiritual content of the music; indeed, the music relied on innovation even as it drew on its roots, and those roots were themselves but earlier versions of such a spirit of adaptation and renewal.

Again, the musical shift occurs against a backdrop of political, social, and cultural change, not only in Jamaica, but across the Caribbean. Haiti in 1968 was firmly in the grip of the dictatorship of François "Papa Doc" Duvalier, and therefore comparatively less free to participate in the global upsurge in liberatory political protest. Nevertheless, 1968 saw the publication of one of the most incendiary works of Haitian and broader Caribbean literature: Marie Chauvet's *Amour, colère, folie*, a remarkable, courageous work published by Gallimard in Paris, with the encouragement of Simone de Beauvoir. The spirit of revolt that courses through the work was directed principally toward the dictatorship and the racial ideology that underpinned it: it was a very local revolt that nonetheless resonates still in all who read it of whatever nationality in its reminder of the necessarily connected nature of the personal and the political.

Across the rest of the Caribbean, the global events of May 1968 did not so much spark new revolts as reinvigorate long-standing anticolonial movements that had evolved over the twentieth century in various forms. In Puerto Rico, anticolonial sentiment coalesced around the anti-draft movement that saw more than one hundred Puerto Ricans indicted by U.S. federal prosecutors. The subsequent legal convictions led to students at the University of Puerto Rico in Rio Piedras setting fire to the campus ROTC building and to 10,000 Puerto Ricans marching through San Juan to protest the call-up and the Vietnam War more generally. Similarly, in Guadeloupe, protests preceded those in Paris by a year: the major unrest on the island that followed the police shooting at a crowd of striking workers is known locally as "May '67." The claimed number of people murdered ranges between eight and two hundred. The French government blamed and arrested members of the clandestine independence movement, the National Organization Group of Guadeloupe (GONG). The activists were supported during their trial by students protesting in Paris and by public figures such as Jean-Paul Sartre and Aimé Césaire, who stated that Guadeloupe and other French Caribbean departments were de facto colonies.

The newly independent nations of the Anglophone Caribbean were no less affected by the general spirit of revolt, most notably perhaps in Jamaica, where the gifted Guyanese scholar Walter Rodney was refused re-entry following his attendance at the Congress of Black Writers in Montreal. Students at the University of the West Indies campus at Mona staged a peaceful protest that ended in violent confrontations and a subsequent ten-day siege of the university that would radicalize many of the students in their subsequent activities throughout the 1970s. In Trinidad in February 1970, there was a black power insurrection that almost overthrew the government of Eric Williams. This Caribbean revolutionary spirit arguably lasted until the Grenada Revolution collapsed under the American invasion of 1983, and the music of the region continued to evolve in relation to social, political, cultural, and technological change.

Much of that technological change was driven by the Jamaican artists, DJs, producers, and soundmen themselves—the idea would propel the technical evolution, as when King Tubby, a talented electrical engineer and disc cutter who worked for the producer and label owner Duke Reid, and thus had access to the Treasure Isle label's master tapes, from which he would cut discs that he would tailor to use with the vocals of U-Roy, the "founding father of modern deejay style, due largely to his ability to ride a rhythm—going with the tune, working inside and around it to embellish spectacularly what was there already" (Bradley, *Bass Culture* 295). Tubby and U-Roy would start a dance as normal, then play the beginning of a tune, before swopping discs to play the same tune's dub version, "and after a couple of lines of the original all the crowd could hear was pure riddim, then U-Roy came in toasting, *and they went nuts*. He had four dub plates, and for the rest of the night it must have been just them he play (Dennis Alcapone, qtd. in Bradley 296–97).

The need for sound innovations—to make the technology do what he wanted it to do—continued to drive Tubby's work. He was likely the first to use high-frequency horn tweeters, and used early transistor technology to split frequencies between two different amplifiers—a valve amp for the bass ("weight") and a transistor for the treble ("treble"); he also introduced echo, reverb, and sound effects through using his own modified or custom-built equipment (Bradley, *Bass Culture* 314). As his protégé, Mikey Dread, said of him, Tubby read constantly on new innovations in sound technology, and gave the impression that "He is one of the most brilliant person I've ever met. *Intellectually* as well as technically. It's because he truly understood sound, inna *scientific* sense, that he was able to do what he did. He knew all the theories of how sound work, as well as understanding how all the circuits worked and what electronics did what" (qtd. in Bradley 319). In all, Tubby had a "professorial expertise in electronic theory" that would not only drive his own system's continued evolution in line with technological innovation but also set the standard for other sound men (Bradley 317).

It is one thing to customize equipment according to how the sound men wanted the music to evolve, but what happens when that technology arrives ready-made, from the outside, and can be programmed by virtually anyone, anywhere, whether they are a musician or not, Jamaican or not? Made from a beat on the Casio MT40 keyboard, Wayne Smith's 1985 track "Under Mi Sleng Teng" is considered a revolutionary work that ushered in the dancehall era and was the first reggae record to have no bassline.[14] Bradley seems to regret this change, not so much in the music, as in the "attitudes" of the new performers. "The spirit of one of the world's most powerful folk musics was diluted," he says, in a time marked by the "globalization of popular music" and the Americanization of the sound—"computerization allowed usage of the same samples as hip-hop," and, for Bradley, in the "recalibrating" of its "fundamental values [...] modern reggae deliberately detached itself from its own history," and thereby lost much of its distinctiveness (*Bass Culture* 519).

Others, however, consider the release of "Under Mi Sleng Teng" in positive terms as a striking and decisive step forward that opened up the music in ways not possible in the analog era.[15] Even in Bradley's account, the way the record was put together is not so different from the ways in which the first ska records were made twenty-five years previously. The engineer for the recording was Bobby "Digital" Dixon," who tells of how Noel Davey and Wayne Smith came to him with the Casio keyboard: "most of them come with built-in drum beats," Dixon says of the machines, "but they are not reggae beats, they are like rock beats [...]. But because the sounds sound interesting, what was really done was we took down the speeds of what they had in the machines originally to what was close to a reggae tempo, *then* we could start constructing something from it." The rhythm, he says, was a "manufactured beat—it was

---

[14] For a comprehensive, informative introduction to the keyboard and the history of the sleng teng riddim, see this online review by "Keen on Keys": https://youtu.be/4zpjGXH4umQ. Accessed February 22, 2021.

[15] Consider this informed comment from a YouTube subscriber:

> Under Me Sleng Teng marked a paramount point in history for the production of riddims. The Sleng Teng riddim is now one of the most rerecorded Jamaican riddims of all time, which is incredible given its experimental nature; it was one of the first entirely digitally produced riddims. Sleng Teng was created using digital keyboards. This created musical accessibility amongst Jamaican musicians, who previously could not record without access to studio musicians or studio time. Now, anybody with access to digital instruments had an avenue to produce music, leading to a new era of riddims and the proliferation of new and creative Jamaican music from a variety of artists that previously could not record. It created an avenue that amplified what the riddim method represents: the ability for any Jamaican artist to establish themselves in the music industry, regardless of music label backing or prestige in the music industry. As the hundreds of DJs that have used the Sleng Teng riddim in their own recordings would agree, Under Me Sleng Teng was an incredibly important and seminal work of music that marked a drastic change in the landscape of Jamaican Dancehall and helped feed the Jamaican World Music sensation around the world. (https://www.youtube.com/watch?v=Wjw7m-BKmQ8, accessed April 14, 2023)

already in the system—and we had to take the beat and add the chords to make it what it was" (qtd. in Bradley, *Bass Culture* 522–23). Somewhat in contrast to Bradley, and apparently in accordance with Dixon, the move to digitally produced riddims is considered by Chang and Cheng as evidence not of a reduced or diminished reggae aesthetic, but as a new example of the music's "unsurpassed capacity to absorb new technology without compromising its roots" (*Reggae Routes* 77). "Sleng Teng," as they point out, was "only the beginning. Computer driven riddims were the wave of the future" (77). The wave was certainly resisted or feared by some, but others, including established artists like Gregory Isaacs, Dennis Brown, and Sly Dunbar adapted and thrived in the digital era. In an interview, Dunbar discusses how the digital technology was received by musicians, saying that certain drummers were wary of the technology but that he worked with it, and that rather than be controlled by the machine, he controlled it.[16] In another interview, he discusses the new drum machine technology, and how the creation of new rhythms requires still requires the delivery of "a good groove," that is it requires the kind of sound- and rhythm-based knowledge that he acquired as a young drummer, and that in turn came to him from his predecessors, who themselves were ever attuned and open to the possibilities that technology offered them.[17] There is not for Dunbar, or indeed for any of the figures mentioned in this short survey, any profound anxiety over the ways in which technology might contaminate the sound, especially the rhythms, which remain distinctively Jamaican, for even the machine must adapt to the sound, which relies on renewal and innovation, and in which one can hear still echoes of that industrial sound heard by the fictional figure Marly in the novel set in days of slavery, and which resounds with the same spirit that animates the music to this day: defiance, survival, and a refusal to live or move to anybody else's rhythm.

* * *

If the ideas of Weheliye, Shapiro, and Henriques, and indeed the evolution of Jamaican music, counter and negate George's argument that electronic rhythms effectively "steal the soul" of black music, there remains a further issue that the scholars do not engage with, but which is crucial to the history of rhythm in circum-Caribbean societies. At many moments in the history of social and political change in the region—indigenism in Haiti, Negritude in Martinique, negrismo in the hispanophone Caribbean, the civil rights era

---

[16] "Palm." https://youtu.be/-gfLqzf5piM from 49.00. Accessed February 22, 2021.
[17] https://youtu.be/xxswmIjqhLU, from 48.00. Accessed February 22, 2021.

in North America—rhythm has been allied to radical political movements as a marker of racial and cultural distinctiveness, and in music and literature rhythm has been an integral part of anticolonial, radical expression. In the contemporary period, the relation between rhythm and radical political ideas is less apparent; indeed, one might say that rhythm is no longer an integral element in any poetics of resistance, has lost its association with radical blackness, and become something of a deracialized, dehistoricized commodity.

Perhaps this apparent decoupling of radical politics and rhythm may be explained in part by the rather loose, unquestioning definition of what constitutes the "radical" in the discourses of blackness that have been mentioned thus far: chiefly Negritude, Haitian Indigenism, and Black Power. These movements would no doubt be included in Anthony Bogues's definition of the "black radical tradition" as a "distinct political and intellectual tradition in which the markers are African and African Diaspora elaborations of ideas, practices, cultural and literary forms, as well as religious formations and political philosophy" ("Black Radical Tradition" 484). In each case, though in different ways and in different circumstances, rhythm was harnessed to a certain idea of blackness that presented itself as radical but that was also in some senses quite conservative, even reactionary in certain regards. Negritude's essentialist idea of blackness has been critiqued by Fanon, Ménil, and Glissant in the ways I indicate above, while Haitian Indigenism mutated over time into the Noiriste ideology that underpinned the Duvalier dictatorships, and Black Power's radical edge was perhaps blunted by the masculinism exemplified by Amiri Baraka. Likewise, one might say that the idea of rhythm in many of these cases was quite traditional and conservative—the relatively straightforward, repetitive beats of "African rhythm" that could be incorporated into poetry and music to create a simulacrum of radical aesthetics and thought, but that retained a conservative edge that may have limited its political impact and allowed it to be appropriated and diluted in the ways that Nelson George decries.

The truly radical rhythms, and perhaps also the most searching explorations of modern blackness of the mid-twentieth century were found in styles such as free jazz. As Ekkehard Jost put it, "Without question, free jazz, with its retreat from the laws of functional harmony and tonality, the fundamental rhythm that went throughout, and the traditional form schemes, posed the most radical break in the stylistic development of jazz" (qtd in Lewis, *A Power Stronger than Itself* 41). George Lewis draws a distinction between "nonrepresentational" experimental "white" art of the period and the improvised, formally daring music of contemporary black artists who, he says, insist "music has to be 'saying something'" (41). Every effort, Lewis says, was made by black musicians "to recover rather than disrupt historical consciousness" and "the new black musicians felt that music could effectuate the recovery of history itself" (42). The rhythms of free jazz expressed in a sense an idea of blackness, or of being tout court, that was always on the edge, unpredictable, opaque, and unknowable in ways that reflect in turn the more radical expressions of postplantation identity that one finds in, for example, Edouard Glissant—the sense of a history and an identity that shimmers as it were, or quivers rhythmically in a way, rather than ever coming into full, knowable being. It is therefore no surprise that in one of his relatively rare references to jazz music, Glissant states, "My writing style is the jazz style of Miles Davis". (Tamby, "The Sorcerer" 148). When asked how the two styles could be linked, Glissant answers "through rhythm" (Tamby 148), and following a searching comparative analysis of the two artists' work, Jean-Luc Tamby concludes that "Through breathing, through *la mesure* and *la démesure*, and in the figure of the spiral, we can see that the work of these two creators, each in its own way, is centred on rhythm" (161). Glissant's (and Davis's) nontraditional rhythms bear comparison to Glissant's idea of the detour, a form of indirect resistance that is the "parallactic displacement" of the search for the source of domination (*Caribbean Discourse* 19–20). In Glissant's definition of a successful detour, the figure of Return [*Retour*] is an essential auxiliary component. Glissant's ideal return is not to a time or place of cultural and identitary oneness, but to the "point of entanglement," the point from where new configurations are possible, and these new configurations do carry with them residues of previous models, but constantly rework them, go *beyond* them in a process which should not, and cannot stop, as to do so would be to "perish" (26). As Glissant says, rhythm is more than a feature of aesthetic style; it is "a lever of awareness" (*L'intention poétique* 216), which "opens up space," liberating not just style but the imagination and existence itself, carrying with it "foreknowledge" of a "complex and unexpected new region of the world" (Tamby, "The Sorcerer" 162).

What is ultimately at stake in this discussion of rhythm and race in the "digital age," and in what sense might rhythm function still as a "lever of awareness"? In partial answer to that question, and to consider the issue of rhythm and race from a slightly different, though I think complementary perspective, I close by referring to David Scott's recent argument that this is a stalled, tragic time in the Caribbean, and draw connections between the apparent redundancy of revolutionary, anticolonial thinking in the present and the perhaps less apparent decoupling of rhythm and race in contemporary musical styles. This disengagement may be related to Scott's idea of a distinct separation of time and history in the Caribbean. In Scott's terms, the once self-evident notion of the natural convergence between time and history requires radical revision, for history itself has in a sense stalled, in the Caribbean and in the broader world. For Scott, history no longer unfolds in a process of "discrete but continuous, modular change," or as a "linear, diachronically stretched-out *succession* of cumulative instants" (*Omens* 5). The future no longer overcomes the past, and the present is not experienced as a "state of expectation and waiting for the fulfillment of the promise of social and political improvement" (5). The primary causes of the sense of historical blockage are the end of the era, again in the Caribbean and elsewhere, of "revolutionary socialist possibility" and the coming to prominence of "the new utopia of liberal democracy, its dogma of human rights, and the disciplining and governmental technologies to urge and enforce its realization" (4). As Scott writes, in the moment where history has appeared so resistant to change, "time has suddenly become more discernible, more conspicuous, more at odds, more palpably *in question*" (12, Scott's emphasis). The apparent end of the prospect of a discernibly different and improved political and social future in the Caribbean had led Scott to write previously that "we live in tragic times" (*Conscripts* 2). The narrative of Caribbean history, and therefore of time, has shifted from the Romantic anticolonial model of change and overcoming to one of tragedy, which Scott prefers as a mode of interpreting the stalled present (8). In terms of time, to read Caribbean history as tragedy is to question whether the past can be truly disentangled from the present. In place of what Scott calls the "seemingly progressive *rhythm*" of time, tragedy presents "a broken series of paradoxes and reversals," unpredictable, nonlinear movements in time and history that confuse any sense of the distinctiveness of past, present, and future (13). It is finally telling that Scott invokes rhythm to refer to the apparently lost sense of moving forward in time and history, for it was rhythm that has historically opened colonial and postcolonial societies in the Americas, however imperfectly and fleetingly, through cultural performances such as Carnival and Canboulay, and which, always turned toward the future, was one of the most persistent means by which social hierarchies were destabilized, and finally overturned. Historically, rhythmic performances in the Caribbean and the broader Americas have been future-oriented means of imagining a different, better time to come, and if we see in the present a decoupling of rhythm and race, it is perhaps at least in part because history itself has lost its own forward momentum, its own rhythm of change and renewal. If however we start to look beyond the apparently stalled present, and consider the dynamic, often unforeseen, ways in which rhythm has shaped black (and white) being in the Americas, we are left with a final, tantalizing question: could it be that the decoupling of rhythm and race is temporary, or that rhythm is already, as it has always been, in and of the future, a form of foreknowledge levering awareness as Glissant says, and that its presence in new digital arenas of black (and nonblack) production and performance constitutes already the pre-echo of a reconfigured, newly politicized notion of blackness (and perhaps race more broadly) to come?[18]

---

[18] On the continued importance of rhythm to notions of race and nation in the Caribbean, see the inscription of reggae music on the UNESCO Representative List of the Intangible Cultural Heritage of Humanity, and the efforts to have the compas rhythms of Haiti similarly recognized: https://ich.unesco.org/en/RL/reggae-music-of-jamaica-01398; https://lenouvelliste.com/article/227779/linscription-du-rythme-compas-comme-patrimoine-immateriel-mondial-une-occasion-de-briller-a-linternational. Both accessed April 8, 2021.

Coda: The Music of the Future

> Peter, I am glad you asked me along,
> but here is the question everyone will ask.
> Will your brush pick up an accent, and singsong
> infect your melody concealed in a canvas,
> picking the place where you really belong
> in Trinidad and all the bullshit that goes with it?
> What bullshit? Everything is wrong
> as all forms miss perfection, hence the mask
> in which this whole society is based:
> all its endeavor is composed in song
> because I love the place in spite of it
> for its immense variety of racial choice,
> and wished I knew all of its languages
> and observed all its customs with one voice;
> this craziness is just where we belong—
> where else have you heard such music, such great noise?
> —Derek Walcott, "Peter, I'm Glad You Asked
> Me Along" (*Morning, Paramin* 85)[1]

Published in 2016, Derek Walcott's final poetry collection was produced in collaboration with the Scottish painter Peter Doig, who has lived in Trinidad for significant parts of his life. *Morning, Paramin* is a singular work, pairing Walcott's poems with fifty-one of Doig's paintings. As such it brings together in remarkable and striking ways the visual and the verbal, sound and image, and stages in effect a contemporary meeting of the European and the Caribbean that echoes and updates many previous such meetings, those discussed in the rest of this book, and others that date to the earliest encounters of Europeans and non-Europeans in the region. In what ways does this work replicate or revise those previous encounters? Do the two men, great masters in their respective arts, manage to transcend the sonic-visual barrier that they are all too aware of and that is the legacy of history and the way that history casts them on either side of that barrier?

---

[1] All poetry quotations in this chapter are from Derek Walcott and Peter Doig, *Morning, Paramin*.

It is Trinidad that connects the two men, the island where both spent considerable parts of their lives and that draws them back in ways suggested by Walcott's poem above. According to the poem, it was Doig who instigated the collaboration, who asked Walcott to join in this experimental meeting of the visual and the verbal, the European and the Caribbean, poetry and painting. Indeed, Walcott's question relates to ways in which the verbal may be transformed, translated, or otherwise represented in painting: will Doig's work take on an accent, the "singsong" tones of Trinidadian language and thereby "infect" the "melody" of the art? Importantly, this question of adopting, even unconsciously, the accent of the place is related to that of the artist's sense of belonging, and suggests that it is accent and sound that attach a person to a place—the visual in this sense may be a means of keeping one's distance, of remaining in silence, but Walcott suggests, and no doubt knows from his own experience, that such distancing is difficult to maintain in a place like Trinidad, which for the poet evokes above all sound and noise. In Walcott's words, the visual, in the form of the mask, is a form of concealment, a means of hiding from the "bullshit" in the society. The visual is therefore unreliable in this sense, the society an ongoing play of masks. It is by contrast in sound that the "endeavor" of the country may be heard, in its multiplicity of songs and languages, and which ultimately brings the two men together: "this craziness is just where we belong," Walcott writes, the "great noise" in and from which the society is composed, and which he feels will inevitably find its way into Doig's work.

Interestingly, then, the painting that is "paired" with the poem appears at first sight to be typically resistant to, or detached from the great noise of Trinidad, the cacophonous society, and to bear little of the local "accent" that Walcott suggests must "infect" the work on some level. The painting's title, *House of Flowers (See You There)*, further suggests the primarily visual nature of Doig's encounter with the place—seeing is what orients the work, the place, and that brings the people together. The painting presents an indistinct male human figure, alone, almost translucent, facing sideways, so that we see he has a slightly stooped posture, and his hand rests on his side, as if he were carrying an invisible weight of some kind. Clothed only in checked shorts, he appears lost, homeless, placeless, and forgotten, liable to disappear completely at any point.[2] The man's physical, visual presence is uncertain in some way—we can almost see through him—and he is covered in petals that fall from what looks like a flamboyant or immortelle tree, on the branches of which stand two black birds. The blackness of the birds and the tree is set against the Von Gogh–blue

---

[2] Catherine Lampert writes, "The Man is suggestive of someone who used to stand at an intersection Doig passed on the way to the studio, until one day the man was gone" ("Peter Doig" 400).

Figure 1. *House of Flowers (See You There)* (2007–09). Oil on canvas. 118 × 78 3/4" (299.7 × 200 cm). © Peter Doig. All Rights Reserved, DACS/Artimage 2023

of the night sky, and the falling petals appear like stars against the blueness. In contrast to the man's uncertain presence, the physical objects, including the tree, but more especially the geometric shapes of the yellow wall and the black boxes piled neatly on top of each other, are more solidly *there*: they have a presence that the man does not have. The black boxes could be speakers piled high for a fête or some other party, but the man seems impervious to sound, and to exist in silence—his mouth is not painted at all—which is the sonic corollary of his shimmering, translucent physical presence. As such, he seems not to hear the "great noise" that Walcott writes of, or at least to have shut himself away from it, as if permanent noise can have the effect of erasing the man's being and of weighing him down, invisibly, so that the painting suggests that behind, or beyond the great noise are forms of silence, and this is what the man hears.

It is in fact the silence beyond, before, or behind the noise that seems to interest Doig the most, in, for example, his work *Lapeyrouse Wall* (2004), which presents another solitary man, alone on a Port of Spain street that would in reality be bustling with the noise and clamor of the city, but which here appears

Figure 2. *Lapeyrouse Wall* (2004). Oil on canvas. 6' 6 3/4" × 8' 2 1/2" (200 × 250.5 cm). © Peter Doig. All Rights Reserved, DACS/Artimage 2023

soundless, as if you could hear the soft footsteps of the man, his breathing even, as he passes the cemetery wall. It is the afternoon—the sun casts his shadow from the west, yet it is not the long shadow of later in the day—and the sun beats on his back as he walks close to the wall, as if he is trying to step in its shadow to avoid the sunrays. He shades himself further with a pink, patterned umbrella that appears a little battered and misshapen. It seems to be a woman's umbrella, and it contrasts with the rest of his outfit, the plain white shirt, the black pants and cap. It is interesting that he is wearing spectacles, too, as this draws the attention subtly to questions of seeing, sight, and the imperfections of human observation. His gaze is moreover fixed—he looks straight ahead, as he climbs the hill, as if he is following a path he knows well, and that is part of his regular routine, so that the walk may also be a form of ritual, which perhaps has to do with mourning. The cemetery remains hidden behind the wall, which is painted yet flaking and patchy, worn and scorched by the hot sun and the workings of time. And yet, it has a permanence and solidity that, again, the human figure does not: one senses he will carry out this ritual for as long as he can, and that one day he will stop, and disappear, something like the man in *House of Flowers (See You There)*. The man thus moves through different forms of silence, which is also a kind of wordlessness—there are no signs or posters or other visual-verbal markers. Therefore, just as he exists outside, before or beyond the great noise of the city, so his being has a similar relationship to language, and indeed to time, which is marked out only by his steps, which lead him up the hill, ever closer to the cemetery gates.

Walcott's response to the painting, "Lapeyrouse Wall," picks up on the importance of the umbrella, and suggests it is "both parasol and parachute" (29). Referring again to questions of the "language" of the painting, Walcott states that "the painting is in dialect," that it has something of the local accent that he feels will inevitably infuse Doig's work. He also evokes notions of time and routine, as he finds in the solid lines of the wall "both infinity and patience," qualities that he transfers to the man, who, he feels, "passes the same street / every day, repetitive as the painting of himself" (29). Indeed, for all that he invites Doig to be part of the "great noise" of Trinidad, Walcott is no less sensitive to the presence and importance of silences and other sounds in representing the Caribbean. In an article on the collection, Maria Cristina Fumagalli writes:

> Walcott has always considered as fundamental the act of creating this inner silence in order to properly attend to Caribbean soundscapes: in "The Castaway," he declares that to be able to "hear the polyp build" or the "silence thwanged by two waves of the sea" are important stepping stones for revolutionizing thinking and abandoning disabling "dead metaphors" [...]. In *Another Life*, the child who puts a shell to his ear "hears everything / that the historian," distracted by imperial rhetoric and other dominant discourses, "cannot hear, the howls / of all the races that crossed the water." ("Morning, Paramin" 261)

The poem "Baked" refers to the regularity of the Trinidadian sunset, and how it marks the rhythm of the days, so that Doig must live and work to that rhythm, "must soften / like us into some serenity at dusk / and mutter gratitude to the green hype [...] The frog dictates, the cricket starts to type" (37). The sounds of the night therefore are forms of meaning that are created once the sun sets, and that one must listen to and get to know to find the "serenity" Walcott talks of at the end of a hot day.

Hearing is also the concern of the poem "Abstraction," which places Doig's sounds in relation to those of other artists favored by Walcott:

> We imagine that we can hear what certain painters
> heard as they worked: Pollock the cacophony of traffic,

> O'Keefe the engines of certain lilies, Bearden
> cornets muffled in velvet, Peter Doig the
> brooding, breeding silence of deep bush,
> the chuckle of a lagoon, the soundless
> coupling of butterflies, the green thickness
> that is there in Conrad and Marryat
> or the rusty hinge of a century turning—
> sounds that surround the work of Peter Doig. (77)

Walcott is thus well aware of the importance of sound to painters, including Doig, though the sounds he associates with Doig are muffled, soundless, the silence that Doig himself seeks at the heart of the great cacophony of Trinidad. The silence exists in nature, in the landscape, the bush, the life that goes on there, unseen and unheard, in the "green thickness" that Walcott associates also with the European author-travelers Conrad and Marryat, not perhaps to connect Doig unambiguously with that lineage, but to say that the European observer-listener hears and sees in certain ways that are learned and that appear most forcefully in the encounter with the tropical landscape. That Doig, like other Europeans, might seek some form of escape in that landscape is perhaps suggested in the image of the "rusty hinge" that is associated with time, and the disillusionment with industrial modernity. It is not so much the heart of darkness that Doig looks for, but the heart of silence that he looks and listens for, in nature, but also in the city, and in the solitary individuals he tends to depict.

Doig is of course one of these individuals himself, and the painting that accompanies Walcott's poem, *Portrait (Under Water)*, is tellingly a self-portrait, in which the artist appears almost fully submerged in water, in the sea which is quite famously of particular significance to Walcott, as Fumagalli writes, "the sea [. . .] according to Walcott, is both where Caribbean history [. . .] and the Caribbean itself are to be found: in a 1993 interview, in fact, Walcott openly declared that 'the Caribbean is the sea'" (in Fumagalli, "Morning, Paramin" 261). In this painting, Doig seems similarly to locate himself and the Caribbean in the sea; indeed, he is surrounded by the kind of "green thickness" that Walcott associates also with the bush. Beneath the sea, Doig finds a similar greenish density, and quite tellingly his eyes are closed, which seems to place the emphasis on listening, on hearing in the sounds of the sea something of the heart of silence that he searches for. The multi-colored, horizontal lines that cut across the middle of the painting appear to enter into his head, his ears, and it is to these that he listens, his eyes shut. The white smock he wears suggests that he is at work, painting, with his eyes closed

Figure 3. *Portrait (Under Water)* (2007). Oil on canvas. 32 3/4 × 27 1/2" (83 × 70 cm). © Peter Doig. All Rights Reserved, DACS/Artimage 2023

and ears open, and quite remarkably the image looks less like himself than it does the figure evoked by Walcott, Conrad—the cheekbones, the pointed chin and beard, even the curvature of the eyes—as it appears in any number of photographs or paintings. There is clarity under water—the features are quite sharply and clearly drawn—while above the waterline, the islands appear indistinct and relatively colorless.

Indeed, even a painting such as *Milky Way* (1989–90) presents a landscape that could equally be a seascape—the trees appear like sea plants set against

Figure 4. *Milky Way* (1989–90). Oil on canvas. 152 × 204 cm. © Peter Doig. All Rights Reserved, DACS/Artimage 2023

the dark sea-sky. Darkness has a similar quality to the sea, the density of the land at night is related to that of the sea, thick, yet fluid. Doig seems to prefer darkness to daylight: he sees more clearly in the night, and also appears to hear more clearly in the dark. It is striking in this regard that it is sounds that Walcott evokes in his response to the painting:

> A tenor pan repeating its high note,
> flowers of brass cornets, maracas stars,
> an alto sax's interrupting throat,
> a burst of rain from drizzling guitars. (21)

Walcott thus reads the painting like it is a musical score; he sees notes in the stars, sounds of Trinidad, even if the painting does not represent an island scene. The night scene makes him think of music, a Trinidadian night where the sounds accompany the sight of the stars, the beauty of the night, and the improvised, musical sounds it inspires in the poet.

Walcott further emphasizes hearing in his poem, "The Tanker," which refers principally to a soundless, distant ship, and which provokes in turn reflections on the nature of sound and silence:

> Miles out and motionless in the blue heat
> the tanker lifts my heart on the horizon;
> with slow, slate-coloured wings and dangling feet
> crossing the balcony, a stupendous heron
> drops anchor from a cedar's branch, then stays
> still as the tanker; here's the perfect place
> to show you, friend, because you hallow silence,
> the distance here muffles the outboard's noise,
> even the flapping sail and the gull's screech
> in their exuberant flock around a canoe's
> wide pointed nets. Beauty without speech
> is what great painting is, so let your gift use
> the tanker, the anchored heron, the noon beach. (81)

Walcott sees the image of the tanker and the heron with something of a painter's eye, with strokes of color and a conviction that both would be good material for the painter. Both pose motionless, as if sitting to be painted. The lesson that Walcott seeks to impart, however, has less to do with seeing than hearing—the second part of the poem accentuates silence and its potential as a subject for the painter. Doig, he realizes, "hallow[s] silence," and looking out to sea has the effect of muting the sounds that he knows will be there but which are silenced by distance. It is in silence, he says, that great painting represents beauty, so that subjects as diverse and quotidian as a tanker, a heron, and a beach may become beautiful in the skilled hand of the painter.

The painting that accompanies the poem, *Untitled* (2008), bears out Walcott's remarks on beauty, sound, and painting. Doig depicts three heteroclite objects—a fishing pirogue, a steam locomotive train, and an opened "Stag" beer bottle—that perhaps evoke in turn, a form of "traditional" Caribbean living, ever-advancing industrial modernity, and a Trinidadian "lime," each one an aspect of lived experience in modern Trinidad. The advertising tagline for Stag, "A Man's Beer," seems to tie in obliquely with the theme of masculinity—the two figures on the boat appear male, and there seems to be a male driver in the train's cab, his eyes flashing red in the darkness. There is in addition an apparent connection between the funnel-shaped bottle and the engine's chimney, the two opened and letting off fumes. This connection is even more explicit in another untitled piece produced in 2008, which

Figure 5. *Untitled* (2008). Oil on linen. 18 × 27 3/4" (45.5 × 70.5 cm). © Peter Doig. All Rights Reserved, DACS/Artimage 2023

features a steam train with a beer-bottle shaped chimney (Lampert and Shiff, *Peter Doig* 321). Together, the images suggest some of the pressure built up by industrial modernity, the energy it creates, and the need to "let off steam." Referring to "The Tanker" and Doig's accompanying painting, Fumagalli makes relevant points regarding sound and representation:

> This landscape, the poem suggests, should be engaged with in silence and with a receptive mind—not overwhelmed, overdetermined, or distorted by the often disparaging or exoticizing rhetoric that has shaped, and has been shaped by, what Walcott identifies as the "wrong eye" with which the Caribbean landscape (but not only its landscape) has been traditionally approached [. . .]. In order not to accost the Caribbean with the "wrong eye," Walcott here promotes what we can call the "right ear": in other words, if one needs to learn how to look at the Caribbean with fresh eyes, one needs to create the necessary silence to be able to tune in with what his friend Seamus Heaney has called "the music of what happens" [. . .]. This "silence" is instrumental to overcoming a tradition of painting (or otherwise representing) the Caribbean that is governed by misapprehension and/or disfigurement, and countering what we can call a paradigm of *ut pictura commentatio*, which would presuppose an identity between painting and dominant discourses, often predicated on disabling "othering" practices. ("Morning, Paramin" 260–61)

Figure 6. *Moruga* (2002–08). Oil on canvas. 18 × 27 3/4" (45.5 × 70.5 cm). © Peter Doig. All Rights Reserved, DACS/Artimage 2023

The painting appears finally as a kind of postcard from modern Trinidad, its modernity in the foreground, almost eclipsing, and apparently silencing the faceless, voiceless, fishermen figures in the background.

Indeed, postcards (and other photographs), as forms of silent communication, and relics of previous visual representations of the Caribbean, are of particular importance to Doig as sources for his works. As Lampert writes, "Doig has always supplemented his memory with imagery taken from photographic sources; the images are also a practical aid to [Doig says] 'overcome my own limited drawing ability I suppose, or the ability to achieve space'" ("Peter Doig" 400). The painting, *Moruga*, for example, appears to present the arrival of Columbus to the island, but its immediate source is a newspaper clipping from 2005, in which residents of Moruga on Trinidad reenact the arrival.

Similarly, the large landscape *Music of the Future* (2002–2007), presents what appears to be a Trinidadian scene, an evening lime by the sea or a river. It is remarkable for the number of people represented—it is a social gathering,

Figure 7. *Music of the Future* (2002–07). Oil on linen. 78 3/4 × 118" (200 × 300 cm). © Peter Doig. All Rights Reserved, DACS/Artimage 2023

yet the perspective is from the distance and the figures are quite indistinct, blurred by the distance and by the heaviness of the light, the night sky that seems to hang over them like a semiopaque curtain. Remarkably, then, this most Trinidadian of Doig's paintings takes its primary visual markers not from the everyday life that surrounds the artist, but from postcards from India that depict a very similar scene. The source of the image is of course no coincidence, given that almost a half of Trinidad's population is of East Indian origin, and clearly the artist is in part representing the prominence of that culture and perhaps commenting on the ways in which it has been able to transport itself remarkably intact to another, distant part of the world. Doig is also, perhaps more pertinently, indicating the ways in which the eyes can be deceptive, or be deceived, by the visual—the "natural" representation of a place is in fact always mediated through other sources. Doig is particularly wary of painterly depictions of the islands, and appears to find in the "artless" representations of postcards and other ephemera something less mediated, more reliable and "truer" than one would find in "higher" forms, such as painting and professional photography. That the scene appears veiled and opaque reinforces the idea that Doig is suspicious of straightforward, naturalistic representation, and that the more one paints a scene, the farther one gets from the original image, be it a postcard, a memory, a photograph, or a newspaper clipping.

It is no doubt significant then, that in his response to the painting Walcott evokes almost exclusively sound, the music that Doig's title privileges over the visual effect of the scene:

> Wide over the water, but gentle, the night music
> requires the sad stars' accompaniment,
> note, true, by sparkling note, and then, a cluster,
> a single note spreads to a constellation,
> the bass breathes evenly a steady luster,
> first a few stars and then a constellation,
> first the breaker's slow clapping, and then, the ovation. (23)

The music has the rhythm of the waves breaking on the shore, the stars accompany the notes that sparkle in the night, like notes from a steel pan, perhaps, which merge into clusters and constellations, starry sounds accompanied by the lapping, then the rapturous clapping, of the waves. The images of Doig's painting thus evoke in Walcott sounds that he hears in the scene, that he knows would be present in any such gathering in Trinidad, and that are not the silences that he hears in other paintings, but the sounds of the people, their hubbub, their laughter, and finally, the "great noise" he wishes Doig to hear and to make part of his work. In this painting, perhaps more than any other in the collection, Doig does indeed tune into that noise, even if it still takes Walcott to describe it, to put it into words in the subtle and elusive play between the two artists.

In effect, Doig and Walcott play out in this book a version of a very old encounter, indeed that staged by Kei Miller in his 2014 poem "The Cartographer Tries to Map a Way to Zion," between the visually oriented European and the sound-sensitive Caribbean: to some extent, Doig looks for sounds and silences in the visual images, while Walcott listens for them. As such, Doig's relation to the island people and places recalls however obliquely and in very specific ways that of a long line of European visitors to the Caribbean and the broader Americas.[3] He seems aware and wary of the power of the master's eye, that which wielded by previous visitors considered itself omniscient, rational, and clear, even as it reproduced the most fantastic, invented, obscure notions of human difference. This recalls again Mirzoeff's writing

---

[3] Writing of a plantation slavery U.S. context, Saidiya Hartman talks of a "crisis of witnessing" (*Scenes of Subjection* 22), created ultimately there by the visual power of the whites: the enslaved are legally incapable of bearing witness against whites, so seeing embodies and actuates power, on the plantation and in present-day U.S. society. Clearly, there is in Doig's work no trace of the racism of previous representations of the Caribbean.

on modern European visual culture and the new sensorial order of things that began in the mid-seventeenth century and was produced by the needs of European expansion and encounter, "above all in the plantation colonies" (*The Right to Look* 49). Mirzoeff's notion of the counter-theater was full of noise—the voices and sounds that were never silenced and that ever challenged the regime of the eye. Indeed, it is essentially this "great noise" that Walcott refers to and into which he invites Doig. And yet, Doig remains wary, ever aware of the position into which history has cast him, and that he is one of a long line of visitors who has had the means to represent the Caribbean visually: from the early European and white travelers and chroniclers, figures such as Labat and Moreau de Saint-Méry, Descourtilz, Stedman, and countless others have considered the Caribbean in predominantly visual terms; even and especially the early surveyors and mapmakers sought to control the place and the people by visual means. Race itself is a discourse that relies primarily on vision, on apparently visible differences between groups of people. This is why Doig's work—however much it profoundly rejects notions of racial superiority—recalls in some ways and even implicitly critiques that of the European travelers discussed in previous chapters.[4] There is in his approach to his subjects, and in the careful, almost reticent way he wields the power of the visual, a quality of impermanence and provisionality that one finds also in the tourist videos of Haiti, and especially in the home videos of the expatriate family in "Time Out in Trinidad." Not being a native, he has a particular relationship to the place, and that relationship has to do with finding oneself alone with one's own silence—perhaps one of the most difficult sounds for a person to bear, and yet that silence appears also as a sort of home for Doig. Each family member in the home movies lives in their own silence, more so than they do in space, in the visual world, which is nonetheless what they try to capture, map out, explain and control through their films. Doig would have known something of that world as a small child arriving in Trinidad at much the same time as the family in "Time Out," and he seems to carry with him the places of silence that such an existence opens up, the feeling that it is to silence that he belongs most enduringly.

Indeed, for all of Walcott's references to and invitations to join with the noisy commotion of Trinidad—in this regard he echoes poets such as Césaire, Damas, Glissant, and the others analyzed in Chapter 1—Doig's silence

---

[4] At the same time, there is something in Doig's work, and indeed in his collaboration with Walcott as a whole, of what Santos calls "deep seeing," which is not only about seeing but "a meeting of seeing and being seen." Deep seeing, he says, "has more affinities with the visual perception created by artists, especially painters, a perspective of deepness built creatively to maximize either proximity or distance, ambiguity or accuracy, movement or stasis" (*The End of the Cognitive Empire* 171).

remains impenetrable, and his works are continuously drawn to and to emerge from that silence. If there is rhythm in his paintings, it is silent, felt in the body, like the soft footsteps of the man walking by Lapeyrouse Cemetery wall. Just as his visual images often draw on secondhand, indirect sources such as postcards and photos from other places, so his engagement with sound is indirect, and entered into through silence. Even in the images of speakers and other markers of Trinidad sound culture, there is a sense of soundlessness, of individuals existing in their own silences amid the noise of the place. As such, Doig again appears mindful of his own relationship to the place, its culture, its sounds—they are not his own, however much he is enthralled by and drawn to them.

The collection therefore reenacts a very old Caribbean encounter, between the visually oriented outsider and the sonically sensitive insider. One senses that neither party is completely at ease with their respective roles, and that to some extent they try to reverse their roles, but ultimately, they are compelled to play their parts. That compulsion comes from the deep history of the place, the forces that have created the society, its culture, and people. The most that the artists are able to do—and this is finally what Doig in particular does insistently—is to constantly undercut the eyes, the predominance of the visual, and to suggest that the eyes, his eyes, European eyes, cannot be trusted to deliver any kind of true representation of a world that is hypervisualized in certain ways, but which remains stubbornly unrepresentable, ever evading the eye. All that Doig is able to present visually is one element of sound, the silence that he hears and sees everywhere, and that inhabits his work like a phantom of the past and the present, such that it is the only sound he can know in any way: the silent music of the future.

Bibliography

Agamben, Giorgio. "Image and Silence." Trans. Leland De La Durantaye. *Diacritics* 40.2 (2012): 94–98. Accessed October 13, 2020. http://www.jstor.org/stable/23326472.
Altman, Rick. "Introduction: Four and a Half Film Fallacies." *Sound Theory/Sound Practice*. Ed. Rick Altman. New York: Routledge, 1992: 35–45.
Altman, Rick. "The Silence of the Silents." *The Musical Quarterly* 80.4 (Winter 1996), 648–718.
Attali, Jacques. *Noise: The Political Economy of Music*. Minneapolis: University of Minnesota Press, 1985.
Attali, Jacques. "Listening." *Hearing History: A Reader*. Ed. Mark M. Smith. Athens and London: University of Georgia Press, 2004: 10–22.
Averill, Gage. *A Day for the Hunter, A Day for the Prey: Popular Music and Power in Haiti*. Chicago: University of Chicago Press, 1997.
Bailey, Peter. "Breaking the Sound Barrier." *Hearing History: A Reader*. Ed. Mark M. Smith. Athens and London: University of Georgia Press, 2004: 23–35.
Ballantine, Christopher John. *Music and Its Social Meanings*. London: Gordon & Breach, 1984.
Baraka, Amiri. *Blues People*. New York: Harper Collins, 2002 [1963].
Barthélemy, Gérard. *Créoles-Bossales: Conflit en Haïti*. Petit-Bourg, Guadeloupe: Ibis Rouge, 2000.
Barthélemy, Gérard. "Haiti or the Confrontation between Two Creolities." *Africultures* 29 February 2004. http://africultures.com/haiti-or-the-confrontation-between-two-creolities-5718/ (Accessed 12 October 2020).
Beckles, Hilary McD. *Natural Rebels: A Social History of Enslaved Black Women in Barbados*. Brunswick, NJ: Rutgers University Press, 1989.
Benítez-Rojo, Antonio. *The Repeating Island: The Caribbean and the Postmodern Perspective*. Trans. James E. Maraniss. Durham, NC: Duke University Press, 1992.
Berrian, Brenda F. *Awakening Spaces: French Caribbean Popular Songs, Music, and Culture*. Chicago and London: University of Chicago Press, 2000.
Blackwell, Chris. *The Islander*. New York: Gallery Books, 2022.
Blanchot, Maurice. *L'Ecriture du désastre*. Paris: Gallimard, 1980.
Bleby, Henry. *Death Struggles of Slavery: Being a Narrative of Facts and Incidents Which Occurred in a British Colony, During the Two Years Immediately Preceding Negro Emancipation*. London: Hamilton, Adams and Co., 1853.
Bogues, Anthony. "C.L.R. James, Pan-Africanism and the Black Radical Tradition." *Critical Arts* 25.4 (2011), 484–499.
Borde, Pierre Gustave Louis. *The History of the Island of Trinidad under the Spanish Government*. 2 vols. 1876, 1882. Port of Spain: Paria Publishing Company, 1982.
Bradley, Lloyd. *Bass Culture: When Reggae Was King*. London: Penguin, 2001.
Brathwaite, Richard, and Trevor M. Boopsingh. "The Social Impact." *From Oil to Gas and Beyond: A Review of the Trinidad and Tobago Model and Analysis of Future Challenges*. Eds. Richard Brathwaite and Trevor M. Boopsingh. Lanham, MD: University Press of America, 2014: 283–307.
Brereton, Bridget. *Race Relations in Colonial Trinidad 1870–1900*. Cambridge: Cambridge University Press, 1979.

Brereton, Bridget. *A History of Modern Trinidad 1783-1962.* Kingston, Port of Spain, London: Heinemann, 1981.
Brereton, Bridget. "The White Elite of Trinidad, 1838-1950." *The White Minority in the Caribbean.* Eds. Howard Johnson and Karl Watson. Princeton, NJ: Wiener, 1998: 87-138.
Brereton, Bridget. "'Hé St Domingo, songé St Domingo': Haiti and the Haitian Revolution in the Political Discourse of Nineteenth-Century Trinidad." *Reinterpreting the Haitian Revolution and Its Cultural Aftershocks 1804-2004.* Eds. Martin Munro and Elizabeth Walcott-Hackshaw. Barbados, Jamaica, and Trinidad: University of the West Indies Press, 2006: 123-49.
Britton, Celia. *Édouard Glissant and Postcolonial Theory: Strategies of Language and Resistance.* Charlottesville and London: University of Virginia Press, 1999.
Bronfman, Alejandra. *Isles of Noise: Sonic Media in the Caribbean.* Chapel Hill: University of North Carolina Press, 2016.
Brown, Vincent. *The Reaper's Garden: Death and Power in the World of Atlantic Slavery.* Cambridge, MA: Harvard University Press, 2008.
Bull, Michael, and Les Back. "Introduction." *The Auditory Culture Reader.* Eds. Michael Bull and Les Back. Oxford and New York: Berg, 2003: 1-18.
Burke, Peter. *Exiles and Expatriates in the History of Knowledge, 1500-2000.* Waltham, MA: Brandeis University Press, 2017.
Camal, Jerome. *Creolized Aurality: Guadeloupean Gwoka and Postcolonial Politics.* Chicago: University of Chicago Press, 2019.
Camal, Jerome. "Touristic Rhythms: The Club Remix." *Sounds of Vacation: Political Economies of Caribbean Tourism.* Eds. Jocelyne Guilbault and Timothy Rommen. Durham, NC: Duke University Press, 2019: 77-106.
Carmichael, Mrs. A. C. *Domestic Manners and Social Condition of the White, Coloured, and Negro Population of the West Indies.* 2 vols. London, Whittaker and Co., 1833-34.
Casimir, Jean. *The Haitians: A Decolonial History.* Chapel Hill: University of North Carolina Press, 2020.
Césaire, Aimé. "Présentation." *Tropiques* (April 1941): 5-6.
Césaire, Aimé. *The Complete Poetry of Aimé Césaire: Bilingual Edition.* Trans. A. James Arnold and Clayton Eshleman. Middletown, CT: Wesleyan University Press, 2017.
Chamoiseau, Patrick. *Ecrire en pays dominé.* Paris: Gallimard, 1997.
Chang, Kevin, and Wayne Cheng. *Reggae Routes: The Story of Jamaican Music.* Kingston: Ian Randle Publishers, 1998.
Chernoff, John Miller. *African Rhythm and African Sensibility.* Chicago: University of Chicago Press, 1979.
Chude-Sokei, Louis. *The Sound of Culture: Diaspora and Black Technopoetics.* Middletown, CT: Wesleyan University Press, 2015.
Connor, Steven. "The Help of Your Good Hands: Reports on Clapping." *The Auditory Culture Reader.* Eds. Michael Bull and Les Back. Oxford and New York: Berg, 2003: 67-76.
Connor, Steven. "Sound and the Self." *Hearing History: A Reader.* Ed. Mark M. Smith. Athens and London: University of Georgia Press, 2004: 54-66.
Coombes, Sam. *Édouard Glissant: A Poetics of Resistance.* London: Bloomsbury, 2018.
Cooper, Carolyn. *Sound Clash: Jamaican Dancehall Culture at Large.* New York: Palgrave Macmillan, 2004.
Corbin, Alain. *Village Bells: Sound and Meaning in the 19th-Century French Countryside.* Trans. Martin Thom. New York: Columbia University Press, 1998.
Corbin, Alain. *Histoire du silence: De la Renaissance à nos jours.* Paris: Albin Michel, 2016.
Cowley, John. *Carnival, Canboulay, and Calypso: Traditions in the Making.* Cambridge: Cambridge University Press, 1996.
Damas, Léon Gontran. *Black-Label.* Paris: Gallimard, 1956.

Damas, Léon Gontran. *Pigments/Névralgies*. Paris: Présence Africaine, 1972.
Danielsen, Ann. "Introduction: Rhythm in the Age of Digital Reproduction." *Musical Rhythm in the Age of Digital Reproduction*. Ed. Anne Danielsen. Farnham: Ashgate, 2010: 1–16.
Danticat, Edwidge. "Foreword." *Poetry of Haitian Independence*. Eds. Doris Y. Kadish and Deborah Jenson. New Haven, CT: Yale University Press, 2015: xi–xvii.
Dash, J. Michael. *Literature and Ideology in Haiti, 1915-1961*. Totowa: Barnes and Noble, 1981.
Dash, J. Michael. *Édouard Glissant*. Cambridge: Cambridge University Press, 1995.
Dash, J. Michael. *Haiti and the United States: National Stereotypes and the Literary Imagination*. London: MacMillan, 1997.
Dash, J. Michael. *The Other America: Caribbean Literature in a New World Context*. Charlottesville and London: University Press of Virginia, 1998.
Daut, Marlene L. *Tropics of Haiti: Race and the Literary History of the Haitian Revolution in the Atlantic World, 1789-1865*. Liverpool: Liverpool University Press, 2015.
Deren, Maya. *Divine Horsemen: The Living Gods of Haiti*. London: Thames and Hudson, 1953.
Descourtilz, Michel Etienne. *Voyages d'un naturaliste: Et ses observations faites sur les trois règnes de la nature, dans plusieurs ports de mere francais, en Espagne, au continent de l'Amerique Septentrionale, a Saint-Yago de Cuba, et a St.-Domingue, ou l'auteur . . . donne les details les plus circonstancies sur l'expedition du general Leclerc*. Paris: Dufart, 1809.
Doig, Peter, Richard Shiff, and Catherine Lampert. *Peter Doig*. New York: Rizzoli Publications, 2011.
Douglas, Rachel. *Making "The Black Jacobins": C.L.R. James and the Drama of History*. Durham, NC: Duke University Press, 2019.
Dubois, Laurent. *Haiti: The Aftershocks of History*. New York: Metropolitan Books, 2013.
Dubois, Laurent, and Richard Lee Turits. *Freedom Roots: Histories from the Caribbean*. Chapel Hill: University of North Carolina Press, 2019.
Du Tertre, Jean-Baptiste. *Histoire générale des Antilles habitées par les Français*. 3 vols. Fort-de-France, Martinique: Editions des Horizons Caraïbes, 1973 [1667-71].
Elder, Jacob D. *From Congo Drum to Steelband: A Sociohistorical Account of the Emergence and Evolution of the Trinidad Steel Orchestra*. St. Augustine, Trinidad: University of the West Indies, 1969.
elhariry, yasser, ed. *Sounds Senses*. Liverpool: Liverpool University Press, 2021.
Eliot, T. S. *The Use of Poetry and The Use of Criticism: Studies in the Relation of Criticism to Poetry in England*. Cambridge, MA: Harvard University Press, 1964 [1933].
Erlmann, Veit. "But What of the Ethnographic Ear: Anthropology, Sound, and the Senses." *Hearing Cultures*. Ed. Veit Erlmann. London: Routledge, 2004: 1–20.
Falassi, Alessandro. *Time Out of Time: Essays on the Festival*. Albuquerque: University of New Mexico Press, 1987.
Fauque, P. "Lettre du P. Fauque au P. Allart." *Lettres édifiantes et curieuses concernant l'Asie, l'Afrique et l'Amérique avec quelques relations Nouvelles des missions et des note géographiques et historiques*. Ed. M. L. Aimé-Martin. Paris: Société du Panthéon Littéraire, 1851: 51–57.
Feld, Steven. "Places Sensed, Senses Placed: Toward a Sensuous Epistemology of Environments." *Empire of the Senses: The Sensual Culture Reader*. Ed. David Howes. Oxford: Berg, 2005: 179–91.
Feld, Steven. "Prologue." *Sounds of Vacation: Political Economies of Caribbean Tourism*. Eds. Jocelyne Guilbault and Timothy Rommen. Durham, NC: Duke University Press, 2019: 1–7.
Forsdick, Charles. *Victor Segalen and the Aesthetics of Diversity: Journeys between Cultures*. Oxford: Oxford University Press, 2000.
Forsdick, Charles. "Sight, Sound, and Synaesthesia: Reading the Senses in Segalen." *Sensual Reading: New Approaches to Reading in Its Relation to the Senses*. Eds. Michael Syrotinski and Ian MacLachlan. Lewisburg, PA: Bucknell University Press, 2001: 229–47.

Forsdick, Charles. "Travel and the Body: Corporeality, Speed and Technology." *The Routledge Companion to Travel Writing.* Ed. Carl Thompson. New York: Routledge, 2016: 68–77.

Francis, Gladys M., Kanor, Fabienne. *Humus.* Trans. Lynn E. Palermo. Charlottesville: University of Virginia Press, 2020 [2006]: 191–200.

Fraser, Lionel Mordaunt. *History of Trinidad (First Period) From 1781 to 1803.* 2 vols. London: Frank Cass and Company, 1971 [1891].

Fumagalli, M. C. "Morning, Paramin." *New West Indian Guide/Nieuwe West-Indische Gids* 92.3–4 (2018): 245–73. https://doi.org/10.1163/22134360-09203002.

Gallagher, Mary. *Soundings in French Caribbean Writing since 1950: The Shock of Space and Time.* Oxford: Oxford University Press, 2002.

Gallagher, Mary. "Contemporary French Caribbean Poetry: The Poetics of Reference." *Forum for Modern Language Studies* 40.4 (October 2004): 451–62.

Gaudio, Michael. *Sound, Image, Silence: Art and the Aural Imagination in the Atlantic World.* Minneapolis: University of Minnesota Press, 2019.

Genovese, Eugene D. *From Rebellion to Revolution: Afro-American Slave Revolts in the Making of the Modern World.* Baton Rouge: Louisiana State University Press, 1979.

George, Nelson. *The Death of Rhythm and Blues.* New York: Penguin, 1988.

Gilroy Paul. *There Ain't No Black in the Union Jack: The Cultural Politics of Race and Nation.* Chicago: University of Chicago Press, 1991.

Girard, Philippe. "What Language Did Toussaint Louverture Speak? The Fort de Joux Memoir and the Origins of Haitian Kreyòl." *Annales. Histoire, Sciences Sociales* 68.1 (2013): 109–32.

Girard, Philippe. *Toussaint Louverture: A Revolutionary Life.* New York: Basic Books, 2016.

Gitelman, Lisa. "Recording Sound, Race, and Property." *Hearing History: A Reader.* Ed. Mark M. Smith. Athens and London: University of Georgia Press, 2004: 279–94.

Glissant, Édouard. *L'Intention poétique.* Paris: Seuil, 1969.

Glissant, Édouard. *Le Discours antillais.* Paris: Seuil, 1981.

Glissant, Édouard. *Caribbean Discourse: Selected Essays.* Trans. J. Michael Dash. Charlottesville: University Press of Virginia, 1989.

Glissant, Édouard. *Faulkner, Mississippi.* Trans. Barbara B. Lewis and Thomas C. Spear. Chicago: University of Chicago Press, 2000.

Glissant, Édouard. *The Collected Poems of Édouard Glissant.* Trans. Jeff Humphries. Minneapolis: University of Minnesota Press, 2005.

Glissant, Édouard. *Poetic Intention.* Trans. Nathanaël. New York: Nightboat Books, 2010.

Glissant, Édouard. *Treatise on the Whole-World.* Trans. Celia Britton. Liverpool University Press, 2020.

Goodman, Steve. *Sonic Warfare: Sound, Affect, and the Ecology of Fear.* Cambridge, MA: MIT Press, 2009.

Griffith, Glyne A. *The BBC and the Development of Anglophone Caribbean Literature, 1943–1958.* London: Palgrave MacMillan, 2016.

Guerts, Kathryn. *Culture and the Senses: Bodily Ways of Knowing in an African Community.* Berkeley: University of California Press, 2003.

Guerts, Kathryn. "Consciousness as 'Feeling in the Body': A West African Theory of Embodiment, Emotion and the Making of the Mind." *Empire of the Senses: The Sensual Culture Reader.* Ed. David Howes. Oxford: Berg: 2005, 164–78.

Guilbault, Jocelyne. *Governing Sound: The Cultural Politics of Trinidad's Carnival Musics.* Chicago and London: University of Chicago Press, 2007.

Guilbault, Jocelyne. "Afterword." *Sun, Sea, and Sound: Music and Tourism in the Circum-Caribbean.* Eds. Timothy Rommen and Daniel T. Neely. Oxford University Press, 2014: 306–15.

Hamilton, Njelle W. *Phonographic Memories: Popular Music and the Contemporary Caribbean Novel.* New Brunswick, NJ: Rutgers University Press, 2019.

Harewood, Susan. "Listening for Noise: Seeking Disturbing Sounds in Tourist Spaces." *Sounds of Vacation: Political Economies of Caribbean Tourism*. Eds. Jocelyne Guilbault and Timothy Rommen. Durham, NC: Duke University Press, 2019: 107–33.

Hartman, Saidiya V. *Scenes of Subjection: Terror, Slavery, and Self-Making in Nineteenth-Century America*. Oxford: Oxford University Press, 1997.

Hartman, Saidiya V. *Wayward Lives, Beautiful Experiments: Intimate Histories of Social Upheaval*. New York and London: W.W. Norton, 2019.

Henriques, Julian. *Sonic Bodies: Reggae Sound Systems, Performance Techniques, and Ways of Knowing*. London: Continuum, 2011.

Henriques, Julian. "Dread Bodies: Doubles, Echoes, and the Skins of Sound." *Small Axe* 44 (July 2014): 190–201.

Hesmondhalgh David and Keith Negus. *Popular Music Studies*. London and New York: Arnold, 2002.

Hill, Donald R. *Calypso Calaloo: Early Carnival Music in Trinidad*. Gainesville: University Press of Florida, 1993.

Hill, Edwin C., Jr. *Black Soundscapes White Stages: The Meaning of Francophone Sound in the Black Atlantic*. Baltimore: Johns Hopkins University Press, 2013.

Hilmes, Michele. "Is There a Field Called Sound Culture Studies? And Does It Matter?" *American Quarterly* 57.1 (2005): 249–59.

Hoffmann, Léon-François. "The Climate of Haitian Poetry." *Phylon* 22.1 (1961): 59–67.

Howes, David. "Introduction: Empires of the Senses." *Empire of the Senses: The Sensual Culture Reader*. Ed. David Howes. Oxford: Berg, 2005: 1–17.

Humphries, Jeff. "Introduction." *The Collected Poems of Édouard Glissant*. Trans. Jeff Humphries. Minneapolis: University of Minnesota Press, 2005: xi–xxxiv.

Jay, Martin. *Downcast Eyes: The Denigration of Vision in Twentieth-Century French Thought*. Berkeley: University of California Press, 1993.

Jenson, Deborah. *Beyond the Slave Narrative: Politics, Sex, and Manuscripts in the Haitian Revolution*. Liverpool University Press, 2012.

Joseph, Edward Lanzer. *History of Trinidad*. London: Frank Cass and Company, 1970 [1838].

Kadish, Doris Y., and Deborah Jenson. "Introduction." *Poetry of Haitian Independence*. Eds. Doris Y. Kadish and Deborah Jenson. New Haven, CT: Yale University Press, 2015: xxi–xlii.

Kahn, Douglas. *Wireless Imagination: Sound, Radio, and the Avant-Garde*. Cambridge, MA: MIT Press, 1994.

Kanor, Fabienne. *Humus*. Trans. Lynn E. Palermo. Charlottesville: University of Virginia Press, 2020 [2006].

Kay, Sarah, and François Noudelmann. "Introduction: Soundings and Soundscapes." *Paragraph* 41.1 (2018): 1–9.

Kebede, Ashenafi. *Roots of Black Music: The Vocal Instrumental and Dance Heritage of Africa and Black America*. Englewood Cliffs, NJ: Prentice-Hall, 1982.

Labat, Jean-Baptiste. *Nouveaux voyages aux isles d'Amérique*, 8 vols. Paris: Cavelier, 1722.

Lahens, Yanick. "Afterword." *Caribbean Creolization: Reflections on the Cultural Dynamics of Language, Literature, and Identity*. Eds. Kathleen Balutansky and Marie-Agnès Sourieau. Gainesville: University Press of Florida, 1998: 155–164.

Lampert, Catherine. "Peter Doig: Dreams and the Light Imaginings of Men." *Peter Doig*. Richard Shiff, and Catherine Lampert. *Peter Doig*. New York: Rizzoli, 2016: 394–419.

Largey, Michael. *Vodou Nation: Haitian Art Music and Cultural Nationalism*. Chicago: University of Chicago Press, 2006.

Largey, Michael. "Hello New York City! Sonic Tourism in Haitian Rara." *Sun, Sea, and Sound: Music and Tourism in the Circum-Caribbean*. Eds. Timothy Rommen and Daniel T. Neely. Oxford University Press, 2014: 101–21.

Lewis, George A. *A Power Stronger Than Itself: The AACM and American Experimental Music.* Chicago: University of Chicago Press, 2008.
Madiou, Thomas. *Histoire d'Haïti.* 8 vols. Port-au-Prince: Henri Deschamps, 1989 [1847–1848].
Marly; or a Planter's Life in Jamaica. Glasgow: Richard Griffin, 1828.
Marsh, Dave. *The Heart of Rock and Soul: The 1001 Greatest Singles Ever Made.* London: Penguin, 1989.
McCusker, Maeve. "The 'Unhomely' White Women of Antillean Writing." *Paragraph* 37. 2 (2014): 273–89. Accessed October 13, 2020. https://doi.org/10.2307/26418738.
McEnaney, Tom. *Acoustic Properties: Radio, Narrative, and the New Neighborhood of the Americas.* Evanston, IL: Northwestern University Press, 2017.
Métraux, Alfred. *Le Vaudou haïtien.* Paris: Gallimard, 1958.
Mignolo, Walter D. "Foreword: Thinking Decoloniality beyond One Nation." *The Haitians: A Decolonial History.* Ed. Jean Casimir. Chapel Hill: University of North Carolina Press, 2020: vii–xvii.
Miller, Christopher L. *The French Atlantic: Literature and Culture of the Slave Trade.* Durham and London: Duke University Press, 2008.
Miller, Kei. *The Cartographer Tries to Map a Way to Zion.* Manchester, UK: Carcanet Press, 2014.
Miller, Paul B. *Elusive Origins: The Enlightenment in the Modern Caribbean Historical Imagination.* Charlottesville: University of Virginia Press, 2010.
Mills, Sean. *A Place in the Sun: Haiti, Haitians, and the Remaking of Quebec.* Montreal: McGill-Queen's University Press, 2016.
Mirzoeff, Nicholas. *The Right to Look: A Counterhistory of Visuality.* Durham, NC: Duke University Press, 2011.
Moreau de Saint-Méry, Médéric-Louis-Élie. *Description topographique, physique, civile, politique et historique de la partie française de l'isle de Saint-Domingue.* 3 vols. Paris: Société de l'histoire des colonies françaises et Librairie Larose, 1958 [1796].
Moreau de Saint-Méry, Médéric-Louis-Élie. *Loix et constitutions des colonies françoises de l'Amérique sous le vent.* 6 vols. Paris: Chez l'auteur, 1784–1790.
Morris, Michael. *Scotland and the Caribbean, c. 1740–1833: Atlantic Archipelagoes.* London: Routledge, 2015.
Moten, Fred. *In the Break: The Aesthetics of the Black Radical Tradition.* Minneapolis: University of Minnesota Press, 2003.
Munro, Martin. *Different Drummers: Rhythm and Race in the Americas.* Berkeley: University of California Press, 2010.
Munro, Martin. *Listening to the Caribbean: Sounds of Slavery, Resistance, and Race.* Liverpool University Press, 2020.
Neptune, Harvey R. *Caliban and the Yankees: Trinidad and the United States Occupation.* Chapel Hill: University of North Carolina Press, 2007.
Nicholson, Heather. "Looking beyond the Moving Moments: Adaptation, Digitization and Amateur Film Footage as Visual Histories." *The Adaptation of History: Essays on Ways of Telling the Past.* Eds. Laurence Raw and Defne Ersin Tutan. Jefferson, NC: McFarland, 2012: 196–206.
Noland, Carrie. *Voices of Negritude in Modernist Print: Aesthetic Subjectivity, Diaspora, and the Lyric Regime.* New York: Columbia University Press, 2015.
Novak, David, and Matt Sakakeeny. "Introduction." *Keywords in Sound.* Eds. David Novak and Matt Sakakeeny. Durham, NC: Duke University Press, 2015: 1–11.
Perloff, Marjorie, and Craig Dworkin. "Introduction: The Sound of Poetry/The Poetry of Sound." *The Sound of Poetry/The Poetry and Sound.* Eds. Marjorie Perloff and Craig Dworkin. Chicago: University of Chicago Press, 2009: 1–17.
Popkin, Jeremy D. *Facing Racial Revolution: Eyewitness Accounts of the Haitian Insurrection.* Chicago and London: University of Chicago Press, 2007.

Pratt, Mary Louise. *Imperial Eyes: Travel Writing and Transculturation*. New York: Routledge, 1992.
Rath, Richard Cullen. *How Early America Sounded*. Ithaca, NY: Cornell University Press, 2005.
Rath, Richard Cullen. "Acoustics and Social Order in Early America." *Hearing History: A Reader*. Ed. Mark M. Smith. Athens and London: University of Georgia Press, 2004: 207–20.
Rediker, Marcus. "Foreword." *The Common Wind: Afro-American Currents in the Age of the Haitian Revolution*. Julius S. Scott. London: Verso, 2018: ix–xiii.
Reinsel, Amy. "Poetry of Revolution: Romanticism and National Projects in Nineteenth-Century Haiti." PhD diss. University of Pittsburgh, 2008.
Robbins, Dylon Lamar. *Audible Geographies in Latin America: Sounds of Race and Place*. Cham, Switzerland: Palgrave Macmillan, 2019.
Rohlehr, Gordon. *Calypso and Society in Pre-Independence Trinidad*. Port of Spain: Gordon Rohlehr, 1990.
Rommen, Timothy. *Funky Nassau: Roots, Routes, and Representation in Bahamian Popular Music*. Berkeley: University of California Press, 2011.
Rommen, Timothy. "Introduction: Music Touristics in the Circum-Caribbean." *Sun, Sea, and Sound: Music and Tourism in the Circum-Caribbean*. Eds. Timothy Rommen and Daniel T. Neely. Oxford: Oxford University Press, 2014: 1–14.
Rommen, Timothy. "It Sounds Better in the Bahamas: Musicians, Management, and Markets in Nassau's All-Inclusive Hotels." *Sounds of Vacation: Political Economies of Caribbean Tourism*. Eds. Jocelyne Guilbault and Timothy Rommen. Durham, NC: Duke University Press, 2019: 41–76.
Rommen, Timothy, and Jocelyne Guilbault. "Introduction: The Political Economy of Music and Sound. Case Studies in the Caribbean Tourism Industry." *Sounds of Vacation: Political Economies of Caribbean Tourism*. Eds. Jocelyne Guilbault and Timothy Rommen. Durham, NC: Duke University Press, 2019: 9–39.
Rose, Cynthia. *Living in America: The Soul Saga of James Brown*. London: Serpent's Tail, 1990.
Rosello, Mireille. *Littérature et Identité Aux Antilles*. Paris: Karthala, 1992.
Rosemain, Jacqueline. *La Musique dans la société antillaise*. Paris: L'Harmattan, 1986.
Rosemain, Jacqueline. *La Danse aux Antilles, des rythmes sacrés au zouk*. Paris: L'Harmattan, 1990.
Salewicz, Chris. *Redemption Song: The Ballad of Joe Strummer*. New York: Faber and Faber, 2007.
Samuels, David W., Louise Meintjes, Ana Maria Ochoa, and Thomas Porcello. "Soundscapes: Toward a Sounded Anthropology." *Annual Review of Anthropology* 39 (2010): 329–45.
Santos, Boaventura De Sousa. *The End of the Cognitive Empire: The Coming of Age of Epistemologies of the South*. Durham NC: Duke University Press, 2018.
Schafer, R. Murray. *The Tuning of the World: Toward a Theory of Soundscape Design*. Philadelphia: University of Pennsylvania Press, 1980.
Schafer, R. Murray. "Open Ears." *The Auditory Culture Reader*. Eds. Michael Bull and Les Back. Oxford and New York: Berg, 2003: 25–39.
Schafer, R. Murray. "Soundscapes and Earwitnesses." *Hearing History: A Reader*. Ed. Mark M. Smith. Athens and London: University of Georgia Press, 2004: 3–9.
Schmidt, Leigh Eric. *Hearing Things: Religion, Illusion, and the American Enlightenment*. Cambridge, MA: Harvard University Press, 2000.
Schmidt, Leigh Eric. "Hearing Loss." *The Auditory Culture Reader*. Eds. Michael Bull and Les Back. Oxford and New York: Berg, 2003: 41–59.
Schmidt, Leigh Eric. "Sound Christians and Religious Hearing." *Hearing History: A Reader*. Ed. Mark M. Smith. Athens and London: University of Georgia Press, 2004: 221–46.
Scott, David. *Conscripts of Modernity: The Tragedy of Colonial Enlightenment*. Durham, NC: Duke University Press, 2004.
Scott, David. *Omens of Adversity: Tragedy, Time, Memory, Justice*. Durham, NC: Duke University Press, 2014.

196 Bibliography

Scott, Julius S. *The Common Wind: Afro-American Currents in the Age of the Haitian Revolution*. London: Verso, 2018.

Serres, Michel. *Le Parasite*. Paris: Grasset, 1980.

Shapiro, Peter. *Turn the Beat Around: The Secret History of Disco*. Basingstoke: Macmillan, 2006.

Sheller, Mimi. *Citizenship from Below: Erotic Agency and Caribbean Freedom*. Durham, NC: Duke University Press, 2012.

Shriff, Peter. "Drift." *Peter Doig*. Peter Doig, Richard Shiff, and Catherine Lampert. New York: Rizzoli, 2016: 340–93.

Sieger, Jacqueline. "Entretien avec Aimé Césaire." *Afrique* (October 1962): 64–66.

Stieber, Chelsea. *Haiti's Paper War: Post-Independence Writing, Civil War, and the Making of the Republic, 1804–1954*. New York: New York University Press, 2020.

Smile Orange. Dir. Trevor D. Rhone. Knuts Films, 1976.

Smith, Bruce R. "How Sound Is Sound History?" *Hearing History: A Reader*. Ed. Mark M. Smith. Athens and London: University of Georgia Press, 2004: 389–94.

Smith, Mark M. "Time, Slavery, and Plantation Capitalism in the Ante-Bellum American South." *Past and Present* 150 (February 1996): 142–68.

Smith, Mark M. *Mastered by the Clock: Time, Slavery, and Freedom in the American South*. Chapel Hill: University of North Carolina Press, 1997.

Smith, Mark M. "Listening to the Heard Worlds of Antebellum America." *The Auditory Culture Reader*. Eds. Michael Bull and Les Back. Oxford and New York: Berg, 2003: 137–63.

Smith, Mark M. "Making Sense of Social History." *Journal of Social History* 37 (September 2003): 165–86.

Smith, Mark M., ed. *Hearing History: A Reader*. Athens and London: University of Georgia Press, 2004.

Smith, Mark M. "Introduction. Onward to Audible Pasts." *Hearing History: A Reader*. Ed. Mark M. Smith. Athens and London: University of Georgia Press, 2004: ix–xxii.

Smith, Mark M. "Listening to the Heard Worlds of Antebellum America." *Hearing History: A Reader*. Ed. Mark M. Smith. Athens and London: University of Georgia Press, 2004: 365–84.

Smith, Mark M. *How Race Is Made: Slavery Segregation, and the Senses*. Chapel Hill: University of North Carolina Press, 2006.

Smith, Matthew J. *Red and Black in Haiti: Radicalism, Conflict, and Political Change, 1934–1957*. Chapel Hill: University of North Carolina Press, 2009.

Smith, Matthew J. "Wanderers of Love: Touring and Tourism in the Jamaica-Haiti Musical Circuit of the 1950s." *Sun, Sea, and Sound: Music and Tourism in the Circum-Caribbean*. Eds. Timothy Rommen and Daniel T. Neely. Oxford University Press, 2014: 125–50.

Solheim, Jennifer. *The Performance of Listening in Postcolonial Francophone Culture*. Liverpool University Press, 2018.

Steingo, Gavin, and Jim Sykes. "Introduction: Remapping Sound Studies in the Global South." *Remapping Sound Studies*. Eds. Gavin Steingo and Jim Sykes. Durham, NC: Duke University Press, 2019: 1–36.

Sterne, Jonathan. *The Audible Past: Cultural Origins of Sound Reproduction*. Durham, NC: Duke University Press, 2003.

Sterne, Jonathan. "Sonic Imaginations." *The Sound Studies Reader*. Ed. Jonathan Sterne. London: Routledge, 2012: 1–17.

Stoever, Jennifer Lynn. *The Sonic Color Line: Race and the Cultural Politics of Listening*. New York: New York University Press, 2016.

Stolzoff, Norman. *Wake the Town and Tell the People: Dancehall Culture in Jamaica*. Durham, NC: Duke University Press, 2000.

Synnott, Anthony. "Puzzling Over the Senses: From Plato to Marx." *The Varieties of Sensory Experience: A Sourcebook in the Anthropology of the Senses*. Ed. David Howes. University of Toronto Press, 1991: 61–76.

Taillemite, Etienne. "Moreau de Saint-Méry." Introduction to Médéric-Louis-Élie Moreau de Saint-Méry, *Description topographique, physique, civile, politique et historique de la partie française de l'isle de Saint-Domingue*, 3 vols. Paris: Société de l'histoire des colonies françaises et Librairie Larose, 1958 [1796], 1: vii–xxxvi.

Tamby, Jean-Luc. "The Sorcerer and the *Quimboiseur*: Poetic Intention in the Works of Miles Davis and Edouard Glissant." *American Creoles: The Francophone Caribbean and the American South*. Eds. Martin Munro and Celia Britton. Liverpool: University of Liverpool Press, 2012: 147–164.

Thompson, Krista A. *An Eye for the Tropics: Tourism, Photography, and Framing the Caribbean Picturesque*. Durham, NC: Duke University Press, 2007.

Toop, David. *Sinister Resonance: The Mediumship of the Listener*. London: Continuum, 2010.

Vayo, Lloyd I. "Turning Rebellion into Money: The Roots of The Clash." *The Clash Takes on the World: Transnational Perspectives on the Only Band That Matters*. Eds. Samuel Cohen and James Peacock. New York: Bloomsbury, 2017: 65–80.

Walcott, Derek, and Peter Doig. *Morning, Paramin*. London: Faber & Faber, 2016.

Wartofsky, Alona. "Dancehall Don." *South Florida Sun Sentinel*, April 3, 2004. Accessed November 16, 2020. https://www.sun-sentinel.com/news/fl-xpm-2004-04-03-0404020119-story.html.

Weheliye, Alexander G. *Phonographies: Grooves in Sonic Afro-Modernity*. Durham, NC: Duke University Press, 2005.

Weheliye, Alexander G. "Engendering Phonographies: Sonic Technologies of Blackness." *Small Axe* 44 (July 2014): 180–90.

Werner, Craig. *A Change Is Gonna Come: Music, Race, and the Soul of America*. Revised and updated. Ann Arbor: University of Michigan Press, 2006. (Orig. pub. 1998.)

White, Shane, and Graham White. "Listening to Southern Slavery." *Hearing History: A Reader*. Ed. Mark M. Smith. Athens and London: University of Georgia Press, 2004: 247–66.

White, Shane, and Graham White. *The Sounds of Slavery: Discovering African American History through Songs, Sermons, and Speech*. Boston, MA: Beacon Press, 2005.

White, Sophie. *Voices of the Enslaved: Love, Labor, and Longing in French Louisiana*. Chapel Hill: University of North Carolina Press, 2019.

Yelvington, Kevin, Jean Casimir, Jean-Pierre Sainton, and Michel Hector. "Caribbean Social Structure in the Nineteenth Century." *General History of the Caribbean*, vol. 4. Ed. K. O. Laurence and Jorge Ibarra Cuesta. Paris: UNESCO Publishing, 1997: 25–56.

Zimmerman, Patricia R. "The Home Movie Movement: Excavations, Artifacts, Minings." *Mining the Home Movie: Excavations in Histories and Memories*. Eds. Karen L. Ishizuka and Patricia R. Zimmermann. Berkeley: University of California Press, 2008: 1–28.

Zoellner, Tom. *Island on Fire: The Revolt That Ended Slavery in the British Empire*. Cambridge, MA: Harvard University Press, 2020.

Index

For the benefit of digital users, indexed terms that span two pages (e.g., 52–53) may, on occasion, appear on only one of those pages.

abolition, 15, 160
"Abstraction" (Walcott), 177–78
aesthetic elements, 16, 52, 63–64, 71–72, 73, 146–47, 148–49, 167–70
African heritage, 1
Agamben, Giorgio, 76–79
amateur movies in Trinidad
   Carnival 1957, 87–88
   Chinese Laundry Burn Down!, 85–86
   colonialism and, 69, 73–76, 80–82, 86–87, 90, 92–94, 98–101, 104–6, 108–9
   Drilling operations at Fyzabad, Pitch Lake, Forest Reserve turntable, Point Fortin, and Pointe a Pierre, 91–93
   Drive from Siparia to Port of Spain, 89–90
   expatriates and, 73–75, 76–82, 85, 91, 101, 108–11
   Farewell to Trinidad, 24 October 1958, 108–10
   Gaudio, Michael and, 18, 69–72
   introduction to, 18, 69–73
   Life and Schooldays at the T&TEC Power Station Compound 1955-58, 93–94
   Loading Cane. Erin Dairy. Rural Trinidad, 104–6
   The Longstaffs at Apex Oilfields 1956, 94–95
   Los Iros, Morne Diablo, Mayaro, 82–84
   Maracas Bay and North Coast Road, 95–97
   memory and, 72–73, 79–81, 84, 94–95, 104–6
   Mount St. Benedict, 97
   Navy Base, Stauble's, and Kingfisher to St. Mary's Bay, 84–85
   noise/noisemaking, 76–77, 87–88
   Opening Day, Penal Power Plant, 103–4
   Princess Margaret's Visit to Trinidad 1958, 90–91
   Produce of Trinidad, Fresh Fish at Mosquito Creek, Shrimp at North Beach, Rice Paddies, 106–7
   Ram Lila in Penal 1958, 88–89
   San Fernando Hill, PoS Docks and USAF at Piarco, 107–8
   Shell Camp Club, Point Fortin, 101–2
   Shell Penal, Penal Market, Shopping at Allum's Grocery, Forest Reserve, 102–3
   silence and, 69–70, 73, 76–80, 82, 102–3, 111
   singing/songs and, 76–77, 95–96, 104
   Sunday Afternoon around the Savannah, 97–100
   Time out in Trinidad, 81–82
   tourism and, 71, 73–74, 87–88, 90, 96–97, 107–8
   Union Park Turf Club and San Fernando, 86–87
   whiteness and, 73–76, 80–82, 84–101, 103–6, 109–11
   Yacht Club, Goodwood Park, Blue Basin Waterfall, 100–1
Amour, colère, folie (Chauvet), 165
anticolonialism, 18–19, 26–27, 57–58, 144–45, 151, 165, 168–69, 170–72
anti-rhythmic crusade, 144
Ardouin, Coriolan, 40–42
audentia, 71–72
auditory culture studies, 12–13
auditory imagination, 32–33

Banton, Buju, 2–3
Barthélémy, Gérard, 148–49
Benítez-Rojo, Antonio, 151
black culture, 149–50, 151, 152, 153–55
Black Power movement, 151, 165–66, 169
Black Soundscapes, White Stages (Hill), 9–10
Blackwell, Chris, 124–26
Boyer, Jean-Pierre, 36–37
Bronfman, Alejandra, 9–10
Brown, James, 152–53
Burke, Peter, 73–74
Burru rhythms, 164–65
Butler, T. U. B., 75

Camal, Jérôme, 124
Canadian National Film Board, 129
Carnival 1957 amateur movie, 87–88
"The Cartographer Tries to Map a Way to Zion" (Miller), 1–5, 69
Casimir, Jean, 29–30
Césaire, Aimé, 17–18, 43–51, 151
Chanlatte, Juste, 36, 37
Chauvet, Marie, 165
Chinese Laundry Burn Down! amateur movie, 85–86
Christophe, Henri, 35–36
civil rights movement, 144, 168–69
The Clash, 5
Code Noir, 11–13, 24–25, 160
collective memory, 3–4, 26–27, 43
colonialism
    amateur movies in Trinidad and, 69, 73–76, 80–82, 86–87, 90, 92–94, 98–101, 104–6, 108–9
    poetry and, 17–18
    postslavery Francophone Caribbean poetry and, 29–34, 37–38, 42, 49–53, 56–59, 62
    rhythm and race in digital age, 144, 152–53, 155, 160, 161–62, 165, 168–69, 170–72
    sonic tourism and, 121–26, 128–29, 132–33, 142–43
Columbia Phonograph Company, 123
"Come to Haiti" film, 130–43
commemorative verse, 32
The Common Wind (Scott), 23
computer-based rhythmic music, 146–47
Creole language, 24–25, 26

Damas, Léon Gontran, 17–18, 51–57
Danielsen, Anne, 146–47
Danticat, Edwidge, 28–29
Dash, Michael, 137–38
decolonialism, 11, 29, 30n.4
deracialization of rhythm, 18–19, 144–45, 151–52, 168–69
Deren, Maya, 137–38
Doig, Peter, 19, 173–87
Drilling operations at Fyzabad, Pitch Lake, Forest Reserve turntable, Point Fortin, and Pointe a Pierre amateur movie, 91–93
Drive from Siparia to Port of Spain amateur movie, 89–90

drums/drumming
    amateur movies in Trinidad, 89
    postslavery Francophone Caribbean, 23–26, 40–41, 61–63, 66–67
    rhythm and race in digital age, 144–46, 147–49, 152–53, 159, 161, 162–63, 167–68
    sonic tourism and, 115, 116–18, 124–26, 132, 136–37, 139–41
Duchamp, Marcel, 71–72
Dumesle, Hérard, 37–38

Eliot, T. S., 32–33
Enlightenment, 15–16
Ensoniment, 15–16
expatriates, 73–75, 76–82, 85, 91, 101, 108–11

Farewell to Trinidad, 24 October 1958 amateur movie, 108–10
Feld, Steven, 124
films, 69, 70–71, 78–80, 127–43. *See also* amateur movies in Trinidad
Francophone Caribbean. *See* postslavery Francophone Caribbean
Fumagalli, Maria Cristina, 177

Gallagher, Mary, 44–45
Gaudio, Michael, 18, 69–72
George, Nelson, 145–46
Glissant, Edouard, 17–18, 24–27, 44–45, 57–68, 71–72, 169–70
Gong, Junior, 2–3
groove-directed popular music, 146–47, 153–54, 167–68
Guerts, Kathryn Linn, 12–13

Haitian Indigenism, 144, 151, 169
Haitian Poetry, 28–51
The Haitians: A Decolonial History (Casimir), 29–30
Harewood, Susan, 124
Hayward, Lance, 124–26
Henriques, Julian, 154–55
Hill, Edwin C., Jr., 9–10, 51–52
home movies. *See* amateur movies in Trinidad
House of Flowers (See You There) (Doig), 174–75
Humus (Kanor), 17–18, 20–26

imperial gaze, 1–5, 10–11
industrialization, 50–51, 54, 60–61
insurrectionary song, 118–19

Jenson, Deborah, 17–18
Jones, Mick, 4–9
Jost, Ekkehard, 169–70

Kadish, Doris, 17–18
Kanor, Fabienne, 17–18, 20–26
King Tubby, 166
Kumina rhythms, 154–55, 164–65

language of poetry, 57–68
Lapeyrouse Wall (Doig), 175–77
Life and Schooldays at the T&TEC Power Station Compound 1955-58 amateur movie, 93–94
listening to poetry, 28–30, 32–35, 44–46, 51–57, 59–60, 62, 67–68
Loading Cane. Erin Dairy. Rural Trinidad amateur movie, 104–6
The Longstaffs at Apex Oilfields 1956 amateur movie, 94–95
Los Iros, Morne Diablo, Mayaro amateur movie, 82–84
Louverture, Toussaint, 40
Lovey's Band, 123
Luciano, 2–3

Magnan, Jean-Charles, 138
Maracas Bay and North Coast Road amateur movie, 95–97
Marley, Bob, 2–3
Marsh, Dave, 152–53
memory
    amateur movies in Trinidad, 72–73, 79–81, 84, 94–95, 104–6
    collective memory, 3–4, 26–27, 43
    imagery and, 183–84
    in postslavery Francophone Caribbean, 20–24, 27, 32–35, 37–38, 39–40, 43–44, 46–51, 54–57, 59–61, 64–67
    rhythm and race in digital age, 148–49, 163–64
    sonic tourism and, 128–29, 135, 139
Milky Way (Doig), 179–80
Miller, Kei, 1–5, 8–10, 69
Mintz, Sidney, 137–38
Mirzoeff, Nicholas, 4, 121–23
modern visual culture, 4, 121–23, 160

Morgan, Delroy, 2–3
Morisseau-Leroy, Félix, 119–28, 140–41
Moruga (Doig), 183
Mount St. Benedict amateur movie, 97
Murvin, Junior, 5
Music of the Future (Doig), 183–85
music touristics, 124, 128–29. *See also* sonic tourism
Muslims, 23–24, 86–87

Naipaul, V. S., 76–77
National Film Board, 138
National Organization Group of Guadeloupe (GONG), 165
Navy Base, Stauble's, and Kingfisher to St. Mary's Bay amateur movie, 84–85
Negritude movement, 51–52, 63–64, 144, 151–52, 155, 168–69
Neptune, Harvey, 75–76
Nicholson, Heather, 72–73
noise/noisemaking
    amateur movies in Trinidad, 76–77, 87–88
    in poetry and painting, 174–77, 185–87
    in postslavery Francophone Caribbean, 22–26, 34–35, 44–46, 47–48, 50, 56–58, 63, 64, 67
    rhythm and race in digital age, 156–57, 160, 162
    sonic tourism and, 113–14, 116, 123–24
Noland, Carrie, 51–52
nyabinghi beat, 2–3

Opening Day, Penal Power Plant amateur movie, 103–4
oral traditions, 27–28

painting and poetry, 173–87
"Peter, I'm Glad You Asked Me Along" (Walcott), 173–87
Pétion, Alexandre, 35–36
Phonographies: Grooves in Sonic Afro-Modernity (Weheliye), 153–54
poetry. *See also* postslavery Francophone Caribbean poetry
    Haitian Poetry, 28–51
    introduction to, 17–18
    language of, 57–68
    listening to, 28–30, 32–35, 44–46, 51–57, 59–60, 62, 67–68
    rhythm and race in digital age, 144–45, 150–51, 168–70

poetry (*cont.*)
 sonic tourism and, 119–28
 as structuring of sound, 32–33
 verbal and visual collaborations, 173–87
 voice in, 119–28
Poetry of Haitian Independence (Kadish, Jenson), 17–18
Portrait (Under Water) (Walcott), 178–79
postslavery Francophone Caribbean poetry
 Césaire, Aimé and, 43–51
 colonialism and, 29–34, 37–38, 42, 49–53, 56–59, 62
 Damas, Léon Gontran and, 51–57
 drums/drumming and, 23–26, 40–41, 61–63, 66–67
 Glissant, Édouard and, 17–18, 24–27, 44–45, 57–68
 Haitian Poetry, 28–51
 industrialization and, 50–51, 54, 60–61
 introduction to, 20–28
 listening to poetry, 28–30, 32–35, 44–46, 51–57, 59–60, 62, 67–68
 memory in, 20–24, 27, 32–35, 37–38, 39–40, 43–44, 46–51, 54–57, 59–61, 64–67
 noise/noisemaking in, 22–26, 34–35, 44–46, 47–48, 50, 56–58, 63, 64, 67
 resistance to slavery, 23–25, 30, 42, 44, 54, 56–57
 silence and, 33–34, 36–37, 38–39, 40–42, 43–51, 54–55, 60–67
 songs and, 32–35, 38–40, 41–43, 47, 54–57, 62
 un-becoming a slave, 28–30
Pratt, Mary Louise, 10–11
Princess Margaret's Visit to Trinidad 1958 amateur movie, 90–91
Produce of Trinidad, Fresh Fish at Mosquito Creek, Shrimp at North Beach, Rice Paddies amateur movie, 106–7
psychobiological systems, 12–13
punk rockers, 4–5, 7–8, 7n.2, 9

radical politics, 168–72
Ram Lila in Penal 1958 amateur movie, 88–89
Ranglin, Ernst, 124–26
Rastafarian
 introduction to, 1–5
 rhythm in, 2–3
 slavery and, 2–3
R&B (rhythm and blues), 145–46

Rediker, Marcus, 26
reggae music, 5, 7n.2, 164–65, 167–68
rhythm. *See also* drums/drumming
 Burru rhythms, 164–65
 in Caribbean music, 11–12
 Kumina rhythms, 154–55, 164–65
 in Rastafarian music, 2–3
 sonic tourism and, 112–13, 114, 123–24, 127–28, 136–37, 140–41
rhythm and race in digital age
 anti-rhythmic crusade, 144
 black culture and, 149–50, 151, 152, 153–55
 Black Power movement and, 151, 165–66, 169
 colonialism and, 144, 152–53, 155, 160, 161–62, 165, 168–69, 170–72
 deracialization of rhythm, 18–19, 144–45, 151–52, 168–69
 drums/drumming, 144–46, 147–49, 152–53, 159, 161, 162–63, 167–68
 introduction to, 18–19, 144–47
 memory, 148–49, 163–64
 noise/noisemaking, 156–57, 160, 162
 poetry and, 144–45, 150–51, 168–70
 radical politics and, 168–72
 silence and, 160, 164–65
 singing/songs and, 144, 147–50, 162–63
 slavery and, 147–50, 154–55, 156–57, 160, 167–68
 whiteness and, 144, 147–53, 155, 156–57, 169–70
Romane, Jean-Baptiste, 38–39
Rommen, Timothy, 126
Rosello, Mireille, 44–45

"Safe European Home" (The Clash), 5–7
Sam Sharpe Rebellion (1831), 14–15
San Fernando Hill, PoS Docks and USAF at Piarco amateur movie, 107–8
Sang rivé (Glissant), 57–63
Scott, David, 18–19, 144–45, 170–72
Scott, Julius, 23
Shell Camp Club, Point Fortin amateur movie, 101–2
Shell Penal, Penal Market, Shopping at Allum's Grocery, Forest Reserve amateur movie, 102–3
silence
 amateur movies in Trinidad, 69–70, 73, 76–80, 82, 102–3, 111

Index 203

in poetry and painting, 174–79, 181–83, 185–87
postslavery Francophone Caribbean, 33–34, 36–37, 38–39, 40–42, 43–51, 54–55, 60–67
rhythm and race in digital age, 160, 164–65
sonic tourism and, 121, 124, 127–29
silent films/movies, 69, 70–71, 78–80
Simonon, Paul, 5
singing/songs
　amateur movies in Trinidad, 76–77, 95–96, 104
　postslavery Francophone Caribbean, 32–35, 38–40, 41–43, 47, 54–57, 62
　rhythm and race in digital age, 144, 147–50, 162–63
　sonic tourism and, 112–13, 115–19, 123, 126–28, 136–40, 142
singsong tones, 19, 174
slavery. *See also* postslavery Francophone Caribbean poetry
　auditory dimensions of enslaved, 13
　Rastafarianism and, 2–3
　resistance to, 1–2, 4, 13–14, 23–25, 30, 42, 44, 54, 56–57, 87, 112–13, 115–16, 144–45, 147–48, 160, 168–70
　revolts against, 13–14, 26
　rhythm and race in digital age, 147–50, 154–55, 156–57, 160, 167–68
　sonic tourism and, 112–19
　writing slavery, 17–18
Smith, Matthew J., 126
Smith, Wayne, 145–68
Sonic Bodies (Henriques), 154–55
sonic tourism
　colonialism and, 121–26, 128–29, 132–33, 142–43
　"Come to Haiti" film, 130–43
　films and, 127–43
　in Haiti, 128–43
　insurrectionary song, 118–19
　introduction to, 112–19
　memory and, 128–29, 135, 139
　music touristics, 124, 128–29
　noise/noisemaking and, 113–14, 116, 123–24
　poetry and, 119–28
　rhythm and, 112–13, 114, 123–24, 127–28, 136–37, 140–41
　silence and, 121, 124, 127–29

　singing/songs and, 112–13, 115–19, 123, 126–28, 136–40, 142
　whiteness and, 112–18, 119–20, 128–29, 136–37
sonic transformation, 20
Sound, Image, Silence: Art and the Aural Imagination in the Atlantic World (Gaudio), 69–72
soundings, 45, 69–70
sound-studies approach, 9–12
sound-vision relation, 3–4, 16–17, 69
St. Louis Exposition, 15
Strummer, Joe, 4–9
Sunday Afternoon around the Savannah amateur movie, 97–100

"The Tanker" (Walcott), 181–82
Télémaque, C. César, 34–35
Thompson, Krista, 121–24
Time out in Trinidad amateur movie, 81–82
Toop, David, 18, 71–73
Torres Straits expedition, 15
tourism, 71, 73–74, 87–88, 90, 96–97, 107–8. *See also* sonic tourism
"Tourist" (Morisseau-Leroy), 119–28
Travel Film Archive, 129
travel narratives, 11, 80–81
travel writing, 9, 11–12, 16–17, 32
Trinidadian amateur movies. *See* amateur movies in Trinidad
Trinidad Theatre Workshop, 76–77

un-becoming a slave, 28–30
Un champ d'îles (Glissant), 63–68
Union Park Turf Club and San Fernando amateur movie, 86–87
Untitled (Doig), 181–83
U-Roy (DJ), 166

Victor Talking Company, 123
visualism, 1–3, 9, 11, 160
Vodou religion, 31, 37–38, 40–41, 135–38, 140–41, 142–43, 149–50
voice in poetry, 119–28

Walcott, Derek, 19, 76–77, 173–87
Walcott, Roderick, 76–77
Weheliye, Alexander G., 153–54
West African people, 11–13, 24–25, 147–48, 163–64

whiteness
 amateur movies in Trinidad and, 73–76, 80–82, 84–101, 103–6, 109–11
 Creole name for, 24–25
 rhythm and race in digital age, 144, 147–53, 155, 156–57, 169–70
 sonic tourism and, 112–18, 119–20, 128–29, 136–37

Wingless Angels, 2–3
writing slavery, 17–18

Yacht Club, Goodwood Park, Blue Basin Waterfall amateur movie, 100–1

Zimmerman, Patricia R., 72–73